Critical Theory

TRADITIONS IN SOCIAL THEORY

Series Editor: Ian Craib

This series offers a selection of concise introductions to particular traditions in sociological thought. It aims to deepen the reader's knowledge of particular theoretical
approaches and at the same time to enhance their wider understanding of sociological
theorising. Each book will offer: a history of the chosen approach and the debates that
have driven it forward; a discussion of the current state of the debates within the
approach (or debates with other approaches); and an argument for the distinctive contribution of the approach and its likely future value.

Published

PHILOSOPHY OF SOCIAL SCIENCE: THE PHILOSOPHICAL
FOUNDATIONS OF SOCIAL THOUGHT
Ted Benton and Ian Craib

CRITICAL THEORY
Alan How

Forthcoming

FEMINIST SOCIAL THEORY
Sam Ashenden

STRUCTURALISM, POST-STRUCTURALISM AND POST-MODERNISM
David Howarth

MARXISM AND SOCIAL THEORY
Jonathan Joseph

MICRO SOCIAL THEORY
Brian Roberts

STRUCTURATION THEORY
Rob Stones

DURKHEIM AND THE DURKHEIMIANS
Willie Watts Miller and Susan Stedman Jones

Further titles in preparation

Critical Theory

Alan How PhD Senior Lecturer at University College Worcester

First published 2003 by
PALGRAVE MACMILLAN
Houndmills, Basingstoke, Hampshire RG21 6XS and
175 Fifth Avenue, New York, N.Y. 10010
Companies and representatives throughout the world

PALGRAVE MACMILLAN is the global academic imprint of the Palgrave
Macmillan division of St. Martin's Press, LLC and of Palgrave Macmillan Ltd.
Macmillan® is a registered trademark in the United States, United Kingdom
and other countries, Palgrave is a registered trademark in the European
Union and other countries.

ISBN 0–333–75151–5 hardback
ISBN 0–333–75152–3 paperback

This book is printed on paper suitable for recycling and made from fully
managed and sustained forest sources.

A catalogue record for this book is available from the British Library

Library of Congress Cataloging-in-Publication Data
How, Alan.
    Critical theory / Alan How.
        p.   cm. – (Traditions in social theory)
    Includes bibliographical references and index.
        ISBN 0–333–75151–5 (cloth) – ISBN 0–333–75152–3 (pbk.) ISBN 978-0-333-75152-7
        1. Critical theory.   2. Habermas, Jèrgen.   I. Title.   II. Series.

    HM585.H69   2003
    301'.01 – dc21   2003050950

10   9   8   7   6   5   4   3   2   1
12 11 10 09 08 07 06 05 04 03
Transferred to Digital Printing 2009

For Ian Craib, 1945–2003

During the final stages of writing this book, Ian Craib, the Series Editor died. He was very much a genuine thinker in his own right, as well as being someone who gave his time freely and amiably to me when I needed it.

Contents

Part Four
Conclusion

Preface

The tradition of Critical Theory stretches back now more than seventy-five years to its nominal inception at the Institute for Social Research in Frankfurt, Germany, in 1923 – hence the more familiar name, Frankfurt School. It is a tradition of thought that continues to leave a considerable mark on the intellectual landscape of western Europe and North America and has the happy knack of spluttering back into life just when it would seem to have run its natural course. The vigour of its critical challenge to some of the most influential intellectual trends of the twentieth century, such as existentialism, positivism, and more recently postmodernism, has regularly reminded the academic world of the richness and relevance of its ideas. Even its relation to Marxism, the outlook to which it originally adhered, has been one of challenge if not complete denial. It has tried to peel back those elements in Marx's ideas it found problematic, while holding to those it felt enhanced our understanding of the world.

In writing the book, the aim has been to revivify the spirit of the tradition for the contemporary reader, while adhering to the principle of fidelity to its texts. One cannot simply declare the 'relevance' of texts written in the 1930s and expect the reader to see the truth of it; I have therefore illustrated my account with contemporary examples. These, I hope will serve to bring alive material that might otherwise seem to belong to another era. While all texts show the marks of their originating context, if they are distinguished enough they will, in some degree, exceed that context. My hope is that I have been able to show that the 'excess' of meaning I find in Critical Theory still speaks to us today; a topic I pursue more thoroughly in Chapter 9.

Inevitably, in a book that covers such a long and variegated tradition, some things have been left out. I am conscious that its critiques of positivism and of existentialism have not been dwelt on in a sustained way, when both could warrant chapters in their own right. However, given the decline in siginficance of both these outlooks, I have not pursued the matter. Instead, in Chapter 8, I have compared the contemporary postmodernist outlook with the diagnoses of the times offered by first and second generation Critical Theory.

While the book is driven by the desire to illuminate the works of Critical Theory now, it is structured in a broadly chronological way. Chapters 2 to 4 provide an overview of the main theoretical shifts in the tradition from first to second generation. Even though this can be read as Habermas and Honneth improving, by reconstructing, the ideas of the first generation, Horkheimer, Marcuse and Adorno, the reader should beware of assuming that what comes later is automatically superior to what went before. In order to make clear the continuing value of Horkheimer et al., I explore in more detail their work in Chapters 5 and 6.

In Chapters 7 and 8, I examine some of Habermas's contributions to Critical Theory. Again, I am conscious that this has meant excluding things; excluding other important aspects of his intellectual work in areas such as moral philosophy and legal theory. Nevertheless, in Chapter 6, I consider his absorption with, and partial adoption of, two apparently disparate outlooks: hermeneutics and sociological systems theory, illustrating this development by reference to some contemporary examples. In Chapter 8, the postmodernist view of contemporary life is contrasted with that of Critical Theory, perhaps unsurprisingly I find in favour of the latter.

Chapters 1 and 9 represent two 'end-pieces', where I express my first, hesitant encounters with some of the seminal ideas of the tradition, and why I still find them of rich and enduring value. There is a 'further reading' section at the end of each chapter that offers advice to those who might wish to expand further their understanding of Critical Theory.

Alan How
Worcester, February 2003

Acknowledgements

I would like to thank a number of people who commented on drafts of chapters in this book or helped in other ways; their assistance is now invisible but has been invaluable. I am grateful to Bob Carter, Ian Craib, Kate MacDonald, Niki Griffiths, Caroline New, Mike Webb, Catherine Neale, Andy Cooper, Lesley Spiers, Derek Padget, Lee Marshall, Antonella Coe and Lynne How. Often underestimated in writing academic books is the role students play in the process. Students, both past and present, have listened patiently as I have tried to unravel the complexity of Frankfurt School Critical Theory. The questions they asked have forced me to clarify my ideas and search for expressions that would illuminate matters while maintaining fidelity to the material. To the extent that I have succeeded in this, the book is also a tribute to them.

Note to the Reader

I have adopted the term, Critical Theory, using capital letters at the beginning of the words to distinguish it from, 'critical theory', which is now a synonym in literary studies for theories which identify the literary work as part of a wider cultural field, rather than as primarily an autonomous work of art. I have also used the term in preference to, Frankfurt School, though the reader will find both in general use. Neither term is fully apt but Frankfurt School was a latter day invention and only really geographically accurate for a few years; nor was it invented by those involved.

1

Introduction

First Encounters

I first came across Critical Theory in the late 1960s when I bought a copy of Herbert Marcuse's *One Dimensional Man*. It was bought rather ambivalently for while I was aware of its radical cachet, something that appealed to me, I also knew it was a bestseller, something that for me subtly reduced its status. I thought if it was popular it probably was not very good. In fact someone told me not only was it popular, it was *populist*; then as now this was the ultimate intellectual slight. It took me a while to realise it is better to read books before accepting the judgements of others.

Even after I had bought it I wasn't sure if my money had been well spent. The bright red cover on my Routledge and Kegan Paul paperback declared how many copies had been sold worldwide and to make matters worse the prose inside was impregnable; I could hardly understand a word of it – how could this be populist? Only the intuition that the opening lines of Chapter 1 captured something important about contemporary life kept it alive for me till later:

> A comfortable, smooth, reasonable, democratic unfreedom prevails in advanced industrial civilisation, a token of technical progress. Indeed what could be more reasonable than the suppression of individuality in the mechanization of socially necessary but painful performances; the concentration of individual enterprises in more effective, more productive corporations; the regulation of free competition among unequally equipped economic subjects; the curtailment of prerogatives and national sovereignties which impede the international organisation of resources. (Marcuse 1994 [1964]: 1)

The sharp irony I heard in his declaration that nothing could be more reasonable than the suppression of individuality in contemporary society struck a true, if discomfiting note. Likewise when he used that peculiar neologism, *un*freedom, rather than constraint or oppression, it alerted me to the insight that the opposite of freedom might now prevail without having announced itself.

1

It was only a few years later in the early 1970s, as part of a first-year undergraduate sociology course called Industrial Society that I really started to understand what Marcuse was up to in *One Dimensional Man*. In fact it took the patience of a lecturer prepared to give a 'reading class' for those interested, outside normal hours, to unravel its mysteries.

The style of language was the plainest obstacle. Marcuse mostly did not write in short easily absorbable sentences, but in long, roving, muscular phrases where a sentence could last a whole paragraph and where the subject and object of the sentence seemed only distant cousins. In fact, in some sentences, qualifying clauses themselves became a kind of collective subject–object. In dialectical fashion each clause reciprocally (re)defined the one that went before while simultaneously adding meaning to the one that came after. The effect was to produce a shimmering fresco of ideas, which allowed the author to explore complex ideas complexly. It forced the reader to hold a variety of interrelated ideas together and allowed them to co-mingle and influence each other. It did not foreshorten this process by resolving the sentence with a straightforward conclusion. I should add that only gradually did I find such writing the almost palpable trigger to thought it can be and, whatever difficulties I experienced reading Marcuse, they were small beer compared to those I would face with his colleague, Adorno.

Critical Theory, Speculation and the Facts

I, like any other youngster growing up in the UK, had been subtly influenced by the assumptions of an Anglo-American tradition of thought where empirical facts were always the privileged entity. The speculative thread that runs throughout Critical Theory was certainly regarded by some of my teachers with suspicion as being a heady mixture of ideology and unjustified assertion. Perhaps the times were ripe for change, but I found myself increasingly and happily vulnerable to Critical Theory's anti-empiricist bias and the importance it placed on relations between the facts. I learnt, what is now a cliché in sociology, that facts do not speak for themselves, but that it is the network of relations in which facts are embedded that produces explanatory significance and that this is something different to statistical significance.

I also learnt from Critical Theory that speculation should not be thought a pejorative term. In everyday English usage, the word 'speculation' suggests something vague and probably unjustified, the kind of thing journalists mischievously use to amplify a story when they are short on facts. Certainly, it is the kind of thing that positivist minded social scientists warned me against. But because Critical Theory always sought to bring the social sciences into conjunction with philosophy I discovered the role of speculation could be seen in a quite different light. The importance of Hegel's work to first generation of Critical Theorists should not be underestimated. Marcuse (1973 [1941]) in particular explicitly drew out Hegel's ideas on the intrinsically speculative nature of reason to form the basis of Critical Theory's critique of empiricism. Marcuse argued that in the wake of natural science's success modern forms of thought had come to deify facts. Facts had come to be seen as the pure vessel in which truth was to be found. The effect of this was to trivialise speculation as something dubiously un-factual. For Marcuse though, as for Hegel, what was dubious was the foreshortening of reason in favour of facts, indeed Marcuse calls this an 'abdication of reason' (1973: 20).

For Critical Theory, 'speculation' was a vital element of reason; it is related to the word 'speculum' or mirror that reflects something else. When we understand something we reflect or mirror its image. This reflection has no being of its own but is what appears to us at that point. The speculative person is one who does not dogmatically accept this or that appearance as being all there is, but recognises that appearances mirror a particular historical relation between subject and object. I learnt that when Critical Theorists wrote in their to-and-fro dialectical style, shifting back and forth between subject and object, they were only echoing what they saw as the properly speculative element in reason itself.

Dialectical Reason and Politics

However, whilst dialectical thought is a methodological principle for Critical Theory, I also learnt it was emphatically a political one too. For Marcuse the positivist-empiricist (I use the words to mean virtually the same thing) emphasis on the givenness of facts entails a distinctly conservative acceptance of things as they are. By 'givenness', I mean the idea that for the empiricist social scientist what appears as factual evidence is taken as the basis for the truth of the situation, such that only contrary facts could change it. If a particular society believes certain things to be true about its system of justice for example, the empiricist must accept that justice can only mean what can be observed as justice in that situation. Its conservatism lies in its indifference to, and acceptance of, empirical appearances, of what is 'given' to the observer at a particular point. Marcuse is not making a direct link between empiricism and political conservatism, though he is sometimes accused of it, but that the relation between empiricism and any social condition while not one of advocacy is one of detached compliance (see Katz 1982: 98).

Critical Theory by contrast always had a concern with how things had come to be the way they are and what they might be in the future, a concern with the wider truth or validity of what is currently the case. As Marcuse put it, 'the real field of knowledge is not the given facts about things as they are, but the critical evaluation of them as a prelude to passing beyond their given form' (1973: 145). For Marcuse, the distinction Hegel made between essence and existence was a crucial one. Where existence referred to what actually exists, essence referred to what might yet come into being, a potentiality. For human justice to exist, to be justice at all, it must suggest the potentiality for fairness, rightness, equity, and so forth. The form justice actually takes at a particular time can, and should, be critically measured against the potential inherent in the concept for higher levels of fairness, rightness and equity. If a society frustrates its potential for realising the higher states it should be prone to critique from within its own walls. Therein lies the potential for something more thoroughly rational to emerge. Such critique, I discovered, was termed 'immanent critique', and Critical Theory's task, at least at this stage in the 1930s and early 1940s, was to articulate immanent critique.

Critical Theory, then, aimed to be dialectical, not just because such an outlook echoed the speculative nature of reason, but also politically because reason and reality were intimately tied in with each other. Critical Theory claimed the back and forth quality of dialectical reasoning reflected its immanent relation to social reality, which was a dialectical process too. In a dialectical relationship one element in the process is presupposed by, and contains an opposing element as part of its own identity. The two are a unity of opposites. In our modern world, Critical Theory argued, various forces are set in opposition to, but interlinked with, each other: science and technology as emancipatory or destructive; culture as stimulating or tranquillising, art as progressive or regressive, and so forth. The task for Critical Theory was to interrogate these dialectically related opposites and discern the outlines of what could become a more rational state of affairs.

Justifying Critique

The linking of these Hegelian ideas with a Marxian emphasis on the material nature of existence is what originally put the 'critical' in Critical Theory. Critical Theorists used the word 'critical' to refer to the idea of critique, rather than just criticism. 'Critique' appears in the title of many of Marx's writings and was part of an effort to distinguish his approach from that of other radicals. Mere criticism, he argued, involves imposing norms onto facts, as it were, from the outside. The (mere) critic objects to particular things for his or her own reasons, and criticises them on this basis. This approach privileges the critic's position but doesn't justify it. It involves a kind of dogmatism in that it *assumes* the critic's position is valid prior to applying it, and exempts the position from having to meet its own critical criteria. In making its own position invisible (mere) criticism is self-defeating as it is prone to infinite regression. One (mere) critic's views can be criticised by another (mere) critic's views, and so on, ad infinitum, without one view ever being found more valid than any other (see Benhabib 1986: 32ff).

By contrast, critique that is immanent or indwelling presupposes the criteria that are present in the situation, criteria by which the situation judges itself, and asks whether it meets its own raison d'être. On this account critique seeks to pull reality towards what it ought to be, what is immanent to it and what, if all other things were equal, it would become. It is often claimed, for example, that in the same way that a free market is best at meeting the economic needs of individuals, so capitalism's political organisation, based on 'possessive individualism' is best at meeting the individual's need for justice and freedom: there is a corollary between the two. The term 'possessive individualism' was coined by C. B. MacPherson (1962) to capture the idea that our western sense of the importance of a right to own things, especially ourselves, and to be, as it were, the proprietors of our own lives, runs deeper than first appears. However, if one confronts, or as Critical Theory puts it, 'negates' these claims with the fact that the free market is dominated by multinational corporations and is indifferent to the interests of individuals, then a different critical picture emerges. Critical Theory's critique of industrial capitalism in the late 1930s and 1940s located itself at the disjunction between ostensible claims and what actually happens, which is where the potential for new more rational forms of thought and action might appear.

Although amongst the post-1960s' generation of Critical Theorists, notably Jürgen Habermas, there has been a clear shift away from the Hegelian and Marxian motifs articulated by the first generation Marcuse, Horkheimer and Adorno, the underlying concern to *ground* or justify critique has persisted. In sociology, in the last twenty years, there has been a rejection of positivist assumptions, notably of the idea of the value-free, disinterested observer and with it a corresponding marked increase in what might be called morally involved critique, something which at times has veered towards mere moralism. Although such changes seem to echo the spirit of Critical Theory's anti-positivism, they are in certain respects at odds with it. As a tradition, Critical Theory has always sought to ground or base its critique in something more substantial than high dudgeon. It has always believed that critique must be justified, not by reference to some contingent source of ire, but to something that relates in a more ultimate sense to the human condition. Only then will critique be able to make claims of a kind that have a universal reach, claims that ask to be thought the harbinger of a more rational future.

Critical Theory and Reason

Even in my early, faltering efforts to understand Critical Theory via *One Dimensional Man* and *Reason and Revolution* (1973 [1941]), I learnt that a central characteristic of the tradition was the importance it attributed to Reason, and reason sometimes spelt with a capital 'R'. It was never easy to work out exactly what reason meant to Critical Theorists, nor why they were sometimes inclined to capitalise the first letter. However, I gradually came to see that for them Reason proper was an altogether bigger and more significant concept than *mere* reason. Part of their aim was to challenge what currently passed for reason, and extend it into something more comprehensive. Again, it was Marcuse who opened the door.

He pointed out that Hegel had made reason the defining characteristic of being human (Marcuse 1973: 5–11). Where a stone, for example, is always a stone, and is altered only by the effects of other things working on it, a plant exists more thoroughly in a state of 'becoming'. 'It unfolds and develops itself . . . it is not now a bud, then a blossom, but is rather the whole movement from bud through blossom to decay' (1973: 11–12). It comes close to being a 'subject' in a distinctively human sense in that its development is not simply imposed on it from the outside. However the plant does not 'comprehend' what it is doing, it just does it, weather and soil permitting. Only with the human subject can we talk of a self-conscious awareness of doing things, of a measure of deliberation being involved. As Marcuse (1973: 9) put it:

> Man *(sic)* alone has the power of self-realisation, the power to be a self-determining subject in all processes of becoming, for he alone has an understanding of potentialities and knowledge of 'notions'. His very existence is the process of actualising his potentialities, of moulding his life according to the notions of reason.

On this account the human world was not co-extensive with nature and made up of flat, empirical objects as positivism would have it, but something that had to some degree risen out of nature, and eluded nature's causal processes.

Reason enabled humans to have the potentiality for self-determination. Unsurprisingly then, reason was also intimately tied in with that other key Critical Theory concept – freedom or emancipation. In fact, freedom and reason were to be seen as dialectically related (Marcuse 1973: 9). Reason presupposes freedom because to reason involves being able to orientate oneself towards determining one's own life. On the other hand freedom presupposes reason, because only through reasoning could we decide what a better, more emancipated life would be like.

For Marcuse, not only was freedom to be found closely related to reason, but also they were both to be thought close cousin to the idea of the self-conscious human subject, and of 'geist' or mind-spirit. The human subject only comes into its own, only really becomes fully fledged slowly, through an historical process of self-formation. Only human subjects possessed of mind could come to recognise themselves, not just as a part of nature, but in some degree, apart from nature. Reason with a capital 'R', for Critical Theory I found, was at the centre of this web of possibilities.

In *Reason and Revolution* Marcuse had argued that empiricism threatened to kill off Reason in the larger sense by denying the possibility of 'universals'. The idea that there might be generally (universally) valid truths presupposed by the human condition, of which the current facts are but one moment in their development, and that the status quo should be challenged on this basis, was ruled out of court by empiricism. For empiricism, either something could be observed as factually universal, or it could not. If not, and of course nothing finally could be, then claims about Reason and freedom being 'universal goods' related to the human condition, were pie in the sky. They were merely the product of local 'custom or habit' or a 'psychological mechanism' (1973: 18, 20). In empiricist terms, if there was to be criticism of the status quo, it could not spring from any inherent lack or contradiction in reality, but only from someone imposing their 'subjective' values in a critical manner onto an objective, factual, situation.

Originally I found it confusing that Marcuse's rejection of the empiricist version of reason and his bullish advocacy of an Hegelian alternative in 1941, was at odds with the gloomy mood of his *One Dimensional Man* in 1964. However, I learned that Critical Theory responds to historical changes and that the two outlooks were not unconnected[1]. While *Reason and Revolution* was concerned with Hegel's critique of empiricism, in the latter stages it was also concerned with a general critique of philosophical positivism and its conservative 'political' assumptions. In *One Dimensional Man*, Marcuse drew out these moral and political implications, showing how much, by 1964, they had gained ground and that this heralded the closing down of the political and social world.

Reason had become, he argued, a pale and rather malevolent shadow of its real self. Reason under the aegis of empiricist assumptions had turned away from larger, universal questions of what freedom and justice might look like, and become concerned only with what it could do with what already exists: the facts. Anyone who spoke of these larger matters could have their ideas dismissed as ideological or metaphysical, or just plain subjective. The task reason had now set itself was to become an instrument for manipulating facts, a facility for measuring only what was technically feasible. I could see this form of reason bore more than a passing resemblance to Max Weber's account of the process of 'rationalisation' (Zweckrationalität), where the best means for achieving a given end hold sway over concerns with the validity of the end. Marcuse identified it in political terms as the correlate of a subtle form of social control. The application of this technical, one-dimensional reason enabled industrial-capitalist societies to produce and consume goods at ever higher levels, though the price to be paid was in correspondingly ever higher levels of conformity, assimilation and unfreedom. The latter being the opposite of what such societies claimed to be about.

Marcuse's critique of positivism did not go unchallenged. The English radical, Sidney Hook, criticised it on the grounds that for science, facts were not 'given' but were things to be discovered, and the relation they bore to our ideals and principles would reveal how intelligently we had chosen the latter. It should be noted though that Marcuse never denied the relevance of facts as such, indeed he believed that empiricism with its focus on fact had originally been radical and effective in challenging superstitious pre-modern ideas. Problems arose when the facts of a particular situation restricted thought, as though those facts were all that we could conceive as existing (see Kellner 1984: ch. 5 and relevant footnotes).

Marcuse's argument in *One Dimensional Man* was Hegelian and Marxist (and much else besides). I had expected this would entail him giving priority to collective entities such as social classes, but what was, and still is, striking, is the vehemence of his defence of the individual, and the way he rails against the loss of authentic individualism in societies that proclaim it most loudly. Though I did not know it at the time, Critical Theory is a highly variegated tradition and such surprises should be expected. It has always been intellectually loose-limbed, comprising a wide variety of authors subject to diverse influences and with distinct intellectual styles, personalities and interests of their own. It may never have quite become the transdisciplinary theory its founders hoped for, but its capacity to cover an extraordinarily wide range of topics revealing the interplay of the personal, social, economic, political and cultural dimensions of life from a more or less common point of view, is remarkable.

A cursory glance at four Critical Theory readers, namely Arato and Gebhardt (1978), Bronner and Kellner (1989), Ingram and Simon-Ingram (1992), and Rasmussen (1996) reveal the range of its ideas. They extend from 'lyric poetry' to 'state capitalism', from 'the fetish character of music' to the idea of a 'legitimation crisis', from 'the social implications of technology' to 'surrealism', from 'critical theory and the public sphere' to 'critical theory and postmodernism'. Indeed, an ever present danger in recounting the tradition is the unwitting habit one has of rounding up loose ends the better to render the whole thing more coherent for the reader; something certainly out of tune with the spirit of Critical Theory.

Appearance and Reality

Nevertheless there are common threads, which exist in part because authors sometimes collaborated with each other, or because theoretical development took place on the basis of mutual critique; but even beyond this there are surprising elements of common purpose. For example, Marcuse attacked the predominant empiricist-positivist paradigm of the time with what he believed was its inability to see anything beyond appearances. Some forty years on and a lot of theoretical change later, Jürgen Habermas, the most famous of the second generation, in a similar way challenged what he saw as the neo-conservatism of postmodernist thought and its commitment to appearances.

This is not to suggest that Habermas's work continues Marcuse's; he made clear in the late 1960s that he has a more receptive to attitude towards positivism, science and the 'facts', than did Marcuse (Habermas 1971a: ch. 6). Yet Habermas's critique of poststructuralism and more broadly postmodernism is similarly based on the idea that appearances, in this case 'cultural' appearances, are not all there is to society. He argues that postmodernism has mistaken cultural appearances for being the whole of the story, and lost track of the fact that postmodern culture is the outcome of wider societal processes. Like Marcuse he still holds to the idea that the task of Critical Theory is to broaden our conception of reason and bring it to fruition in a more rational society. For both, reason and modernity are unfinished projects, things not yet fully formed, and thus not to be rejected prematurely (Habermas 1996).

Summary

In this chapter I have introduced some of Critical Theory's basic themes via my own first encounters with its train of thought. At first I found its authors' style of writing confusing and difficult, but gradually learnt that the way they wrote was tied in with how they saw the world. Their approach was dialectical in that it tacked back and forth between ideas, gradually elucidating one in terms of another and in doing this was naturally speculative. In contrast to empiricism, Critical Theorists regarded speculation in a positive light rather than as the poor relation to thought based only on facts. It reversed the usual priority empiricism accorded to the facts, arguing that facts had to be understood, not as 'given', but in terms of the circumstances that produced them. Empiricism's failure lies in the way it foreshortens the full implications of reason by limiting its emphasis to the manipulation of facts to achieve given ends. Critical Theory, by contrast, has always believed that Reason in a wider sense should also be concerned with the nature of ends, something that entails a critical-evaluative focus on human potential for emancipation.

While in recent years a variety of different streams of thought have challenged the pre-eminence of empiricism in the social sciences, what makes Critical Theory unique is its need to ground or justify its critique of the status quo. For Critical Theory, critique needs to be more than criticism. It must be immanent to, or grounded in, particular historical circumstances and the potential they have to generate a better life.

My early engagement with Critical Theory was focused on Marcuse's work, but as such it provided me with access to themes and ideas that surface and resurface throughout the tradition. I discovered later that his concern with the gap between appearance and reality, with the withering of the individual in individualistic societies, with the idea of grounding critique and of extending the concept of reason, all figure as general themes throughout the tradition.

However, before looking at these and other themes in more detail, I want to put the material in context by presenting a broad overview of the tradition as it developed from the 1920s onwards, with particular reference to the shift from the first to the second generation.

Part 1

Historical Contours

2

Early Days, Early Doubts:
From Optimism to Ambiguity

In this chapter I want to explore some of the early ideas developed at The Institute for Social Research in Frankfurt, which became the basis for first generation Critical Theory. Although I shall briefly situate these ideas in an historical context my aim is theoretical. I want to provide the reader with some insight into the intellectual milieu from which these ideas emerged.

Max Horkheimer became the Institute's Director in 1930 and under his tutelage Critical Theory was formed. I want to use his inaugural lecture as a vehicle to highlight issues that became central to the tradition. I shall also indicate the effect the ideas of the Hungarian Marxist, Georg Lukacs, had on Critical Theory, both in terms of its early optimism and the latent ambiguity present in Lukacs's account of the theory-practice relationship. In an excursus and using the ideas of Jürgen Habermas, I shall highlight Critical Theory's growing need for a conception of practice that assumes a more active notion of the human subject.

The Institute for Social Research

The Institute for Social Research was set up under the directorship of an Austrian Professor of political economy, the Marxist Carl Grunberg. The period immediately after the First World War had been one of widespread social unrest with the Russian revolution and subsequently-formed Soviet Union acting as a focal point for left-wing ambitions in western Europe generally. By 1923 though, internecine party battles within the left and powerful right-wing responses had made the possibility of a working-class revolution in Germany recede. Indeed, Marcuse declared that as early as 1921 if not before, with the murders of left-wing leaders Karl Liebknecht and Rosa Luxemburg in 1919, he was aware that the Left was being defeated (Marcuse 1978/9: 125, Kellner 1984: 14–18). The Institute for Social Research was therefore set up in a particular context as a kind of intellectual bulwark against the elimination of left-wing ideas. It was affiliated to Frankfurt University but gained independent funding through the efforts of Felix Weil, the son of a rich grain merchant.

The Institute had a peculiar status; it was neither a department of Frankfurt University nor a political organ for furthering working-class interests. Depending on how you look at it, its 'independent' status was either the origin of its failure to be properly Marxist (Anderson 1976, Slater 1977, Bottomore 1984), or for others, myself included, the source of the tradition's real intellectual vitality (Held 1980: ch. 13, Kellner 1989, Jay 1996: ch. 2). Institute members had no reason to please interested parties, refused to prescribe what the working-class should do next, felt no need to follow the intellectual trends of University life and were therefore able to absorb and develop the disparate influences *they* found productive.

The criticisms of Anderson, Slater, and Bottomore that Critical Theory failed to provide a theory to unite and forward the interests of the industrial working class rather misses the point. Central to Critical Theory became the belief that conditions had changed so much that the working class was being incorporated into the system. Indeed, some authors (Piccone 1978) take precisely the opposite view, that first generation Critical Theory's failure was in remaining *too* wedded to Marxist assumptions, a view partly shared by the more recent developments within the tradition at the hands of Habermas and Honneth.

However, deciding whether Critical Theorists were insufficiently or excessively Marxist is not the issue here. It is too easy to decide with cool hindsight what they should or should not have done. I think it is more fruitful to consider their work in terms of the insights it generated albeit within the context of its formation. While we should not try to read off ideas as mere products of context, it should be remembered that first generation Critical Theorists lived much of their productive life in a state of 'permanent exile' (Jay 1985), not just literal geographical exile, but intellectual, cultural, political and emotional exile. It was the manner in which they came to terms with, though were never reconciled to, this condition that is at the heart of their keen if sometimes one-eyed critical acumen.

If the relative independence of the Institute seems like a luxury today, the temper of the times was anything but luxurious. To be, as most Institute members were, both Jewish and left-wing in Germany in the 1920s and 1930s, was a recipe for disaster. Nevertheless, under Grunberg's directorship from 1923–29 the Institute pursued an optimistic, fairly orthodox Marxism, based on gathering a wide variety of data on all aspects of working-class life. It would take pride in providing the first intellectual home for Marxism. The data collected from across Europe was to be articulated within the historical materialist assumption that history was inevitably moving towards socialism, and that the times were still very much ripe for this transition. In his inaugural lecture in 1924, Grunberg argued that the Institute could not prescribe what a future socialist society would look like. The task was rather to examine 'every expression of the life of society [as] a reflection of the current form of economic life' which anyway was tending towards socialism (Jay 1973: Wiggerhaus 1994: 26).

The problem was that the self-understanding of the western working class did not reflect a tendency towards socialism for in Germany, particularly, it turned not 'left' but sharply 'right'. The history of the Frankfurt Institute from Max Horkheimer's assumption of the Directorship in 1930 onwards expresses the dilemma of a Marxist social theory having to come to terms, in the most direct of ways, with the recalcitrant nature of human subjectivity. Critical Theory proper, in its first phase during the 1930s, was born out of the need to generate concepts that acknowledged agency as something considerably more than a reflex of supposedly objective economic conditions.

A New Beginning: Horkheimer's Directorship, 1930

The shift in outlook however was not a simple one-off affair but a gradual development. Horkheimer retained many of his predecessor's Marxist assumptions but with subtle changes woven into them. In his inaugural address (1993 [1931]), unlike Grunberg's, he did not affirm 'every single expression of society' as a reflection of the state of economic life, but briefly and pointedly reversed the claim, calling such a view *bad* Marxism, though without mentioning Grunberg in this respect[2]. It is just as mistaken to believe, he declared, that 'ideas or "spiritual" contents break into history and determine the action of human beings' as it is to believe that the economy 'is the only true reality'. To argue that 'the psyche of human beings, personality, as well as law, art and philosophy, are to be completely derived from the economy . . . [is to] . . . abstractly and thus badly understand Marx' (1993: 12). To privilege one at the expense of the other, he maintained, is dogmatic in the sense that it immunises itself from 'critical', or as he calls it, 'experimental' control. By this he seems to mean what in contemporary sociological terms we would refer to as the structure–agency relation. As structures limit what agents can do, agents expose and transform the limits of structures. Each side of the equation acts as a critical or experimental control on the other: knowledge emerges when we grasp what happens at the intersection between the two.

Horkheimer sets out his approach as a dialectical one, and away from the more inductive outlook of his predecessor. The inductive (positivist) approach works on the basis of accumulating more and more evidence that confirms the truth of a proposition – exemplified in Grunberg's claim that every societal expression has to be seen as a reflection of its economic life. It entails gathering evidence, the meaning of which would always be known ahead of time as an expression of economic life. It thus uncritically assumes that societal expressions, ideas, artifacts, laws and forms of family life, correspond directly to economic ones.

It should be noted though that while Horkheimer is here setting out for the first time what was to become a long-standing theme of Critical Theory, its opposition to positivism, he also briefly puts down a marker against another broad form of social thought current at the time, *Lebensphilosophie* (life philosophy), or more colloquially, existentialism. This is an outlook that rejects the idea of superimposing positivist assumptions, or any other intellectual formula onto life. It searches instead for life's essential meaning in life itself, whether this is conceived on an individual basis (Heidegger) or supra-individually (Scheler, Hartmann). The connection between the assumptions of this kind of outlook and the development of interpretive sociology, social psychology and grounded theory, will not be lost on a social science audience.

Horkheimer notes that contemporary social philosophy in its various forms has opposed the dehumanising (positivist) trend towards seeing human life solely in scientific terms and tried to rescue the individual from experiencing life as a mere 'medley of arbitrariness'. It has tried to make sense of the contradictoriness of individualism with its promise of unbroken progress towards individual happiness and the actual reality of suffering, but mistakenly has turned *inwards*. Social philosophy in its various existentialist forms has sought to make life seem meaningful by bracketing off the actual conditions under which it is lived, examining the inner nature of the human being as if it were an autonomous entity.

Horkheimer's objections to this existentialist outlook are plain though muted compared with the later and more caustic views expressed by Marcuse in his essays, 'The Struggle Against Liberalism in the Totalitarian View of the State' (1968 [1934]), 'Sartre's Existentialism' (1972 [1948]), and Adorno's book, *The Jargon of Authenticity* (1973a: [1964]). In the latter, existentialist thinkers such as Karl Jaspers and Martin Heidegger are taken to task for using language to describe human existence which sounds meaningful and authentic, but actually mystifies and conceals the wider social and economic conditions of alienation. Such appeals, Adorno (1973a: 29–30) believed, have all the pathos of a well-constructed TV commercial, and about as much authenticity. Nevertheless, Horkheimer's point no less than Marcuse's and Adorno's, is that existentialist philosophy, by ignoring the alienating conditions of life, blindly expresses them, and in so doing becomes an ideology.

By contrast, Critical Theory's proposed dialectical approach sought to link the partial insights of economic reductionism and existentialism. Critical Theory, Horkheimer, argues, opens up the possibility of real research. Real research, he claims, only comes into view when one examines the interconnections between specific economic forces and the ideas and psychic structures of the people that created them. Interestingly, he defines this dialectical approach, not just as undogmatic, but as more scientific, and though Critical Theory has a reputation for being in some degree anti-science, Horkheimer's views are not unusual in expressing the idea that science, in a wide sense, shares common ground with Critical Theory; both have a concern with the relation between knowledge and emancipation.

As one might expect, given that Horkheimer was a professor of social philosophy, not political economy, the orientation of the Institute changed and the change in name of the Institute's journal is symptomatic of this; from Grunberg's avowedly Marxist *Archiv für die Geschichte des Sozialismus und der Arbeiter* (Archive for the History of Socialism and the Workers Movement), to the more neutral *Zeitschrift für Sozial Forschung* (Journal for Social Research) of Horkheimer's era. But even beyond Horkheimer's concern to inhibit economic reductionism there were some distinctly novel areas of research set out in his programme that characterized Critical Theory up to the mid 1960s. He declares the Institute to be interested not only in the relationship between the economic life of society and the psychical development of individuals, itself unusual given the normal Marxian priority of social classes, but also

> changes in the realm of culture . . . not only the so called intellectual elements, such as science, art, and religion, but also law, customs, fashion, public opinion, sports, leisure activities, lifestyle etc. . . . The project of investigating these three processes is nothing but a reformulation . . . of the old question concerning the connection of particular existence and universal Reason, of reality and Idea of life and Spirit. (1993: 11–12)

It is noteworthy here that Horkheimer is extending the Institute's concerns to include areas of everyday life, sport, fashion, and so forth; things which might now seem commonplace fields of study, but were not so then.

Horkheimer wants to analyse the relationships between economic, psychological and cultural phenomena, but unlike much analysis today he is also intent on locating the meaning of these things within a wider, more ultimate concern for the relation between a particular instance of something and universal Reason, of reality and Idea, of life and Spirit'. The terms, 'Reason', 'Spirit' and 'Idea' each in different ways refers to a potentiality for something more complete. For Horkheimer and subsequent Critical Theory, cultural artifacts are not just things that happen to exist, empirical entities which are relevant only because they exist and get consumed a lot, but are phenomena which warrant critical attention in terms of how well they realise Reason, Spirit or Idea[3], or more usually, how much they distort them.

In his inaugural lecture Horkheimer indicates that the main task of Critical Theory is to link social philosophy with empirically oriented social science. Social philosophy since Hegel, he argues, has been tinged with the idealist assumption that it can discern life's meaning independent of empirical evidence. Equally, Horkheimer remarks, social science has grown up at odds with the concerns of social philosophy, carrying out 'its long, boring, individual studies that split up into a thousand partial questions, culminating in a chaos of countless enclaves of specialists'. The solution to this mutual enfeeblement is to engender mutual influence. The philosophical concern with the 'general' and the 'essential' should provide the impulse that animates particular studies, while it must remain 'open enough to let itself be influenced and changed by these concrete studies' (p. 9). Thus, his plan is for a more interdisciplinary approach to social analysis, one which entails not just battening empirical evidence on to Marxist political economy, but of bringing different outlooks into conjunction, of what Kellner (1989: ch. 2) more accurately describes as developing a *supra*disciplinary Critical Theory. Kellner, rightly I think, uses the term, 'supradisciplinary', rather than 'interdisciplinary', as Horkheimer's aim was to acknowledge the differences between disciplines rather than meld them together. Certainly the authors he gathered around him were no mere spear-carriers in an already written play, but talented thinkers set to become notable academics in their own right. Amongst the most well known, besides Horkheimer, were Theodor Adorno, Erich Fromm, Herbert Marcuse, Franz Neumann and Otto Kircheimer, all of whom worked within the Institute. Others such as Sigfried Kracauer and Walter Benjamin were more loosely associated with it, the latter receiving a small stipend from it[4]. Leo Lowenthal and Friedrick Pollock continued their membership from the 1920s.

Both in his concern to link diverse social phenomena to wider concepts and in his desire for a supradisciplinary approach to things, Horkheimer is indirectly expressing the influence of the Hungarian Marxist, Georg Lukacs. In *History and Class Consciousness* (1971 [1922]), especially in the essay 'The Marxism of Rosa Luxemburg', Lukacs argued that the concept of totality signals Marxism's superiority to all bourgeois theory. Whether he is accurate in making such a claim (Jay 1984), or indeed whether Horkheimer and his colleagues were really enamoured of Lukacs's ideas, is doubtful[5]. Nevertheless the latent significance of this concept is plain. At its simplest, the concept of totality refers to the need for knowledge to move beyond the appearance of things, beyond the facts as it were, towards a more total view – something obviously present in Marcuse's recounting of Hegel's radicalism. The aim is to grasp how the facts appear as they do by exploring the way they are affected, or mediated by other elements, and then move to ever greater levels of generality (totality) in pursuit of the most fundamentally determining factors (see Craib 1998: ch. 2).

For Horkheimer, the impulse towards recognising the interrelatedness and ultimate unity of things is not only a methodological precept but a practical one too. To settle for the disconnected and fragmented (bourgeois) approach to social phenomena, involves a naive acceptance of the status quo. Lukacs had argued that the free market produces a society of ever greater fragmentation and dissociation amongst its members, and those atomised individuals carry on their lives 'producing without rhyme or reason' (p. 27). This kind of societal blindness produces a similarly fragmented intellectual outlook both in terms of the artificiality of the boundaries that separate academic disciplines, and the way those disciplines isolate phenomena from the whole for their own purposes. Horkheimer's supradisciplinary plans for the Institute as well as the widening of its interests can thus be seen as both an intellectual and practical challenge to a status quo described by Lukacs nearly ten years earlier.

However, Horkheimer's view was different from Lukacs' in one crucial respect. Horkheimer's did not want to demean so-called bourgeois disciplines in the name of a totality only Marxism could grasp. Critical Theory did not seek to dissolve discipline boundaries in the name of an all-knowing Marxism. When Critical Theory in the 1930s embraced Freud's work via Fromm and Marcuse, it did so because it needed it, and needed it full-blown, not as a watered-down adjunct to some other more important enterprise. Critical Theory from Horkheimer to Habermas always refused the term 'bourgeois' to disparage non-Marxist academic disciplines, instead it has embraced them as generators of the real knowledge they provide.

Whether Horkheimer was, or could have been, entirely successful in his aim of establishing a supradisciplinary Critical Theory is another matter. Indeed ironically, Eric Fromm's acrimonious split from the Institute in 1938 followed from his dispute with Marcuse over the latter's reduction of Freud's work to fit Critical Theory's still overly Marxian categories. Certainly, for the second generation, Axel Honneth (1987, 1993: 9ff) has argued that though Horkheimer et al. envisaged something radically new, their overall frame of reference was still Marxist and functionalist in character. As a result, only one kind of action could be envisaged, action that was a function of capitalist imperatives. However dialectical the account, action would be conceived as 'labour' in the Marxist sense and as something that was only derivable from the capitalist system. The effect would be to close down any wider sense of the creativity of action and blunt Critical Theory's dialectical hopes.

Oddly perhaps, one of the effects of the blocking of a more creative way of conceiving action was the growth of an alternative kind of impulse within Critical Theory. By the 1940s, alongside, and partly replacing its concern with the interconnectedness and dialectical unity of things within the totality, was a contrary impulse towards disunity; a recalcitrant refusal to accept too much harmony, a witheringly critical if pessimistic defence of the individual in the face of 'bad' totalities. Theoretically these totalities were 'bad' because they achieved a spurious unity in reconciling the individual too readily and destructively with society. They were critically described under the headings of 'instrumental reason', 'reification', and later, 'one-dimensionality'. Though Critical Theorist's critiques of totality were mostly directed against the manipulative world of mass culture, particularly in the USA, still louring in the background were the spurious harmonies and quite literally destructive totalities of Nazi Germany and Stalinist Russia. They had their own ways of 'accommodating' individuals who did not or could not conform.

A Growing Ambiguity: Critical Theory and the Work of Georg Lukacs

If Horkheimer's inaugural address in 1931 expresses a fairly optimistic and unproblematic belief in joining dialectical methodological principles with

Marxian political aims, fifteen or so years on the tone of the Institute's output is rather different. Horkheimer's *Eclipse of Reason* (1947), Adorno's *Minima Moralia: Reflections from a Damaged Life* (1951), and their combined *Dialectic of Enlightenment* (1947), all illustrate a shift towards a much darker mood. Such a mood developed in part because of their tacit acceptance of Lukacs's too instrumental a view of the theory–practice relationship.

In *History and Class Consciousness* (1922) Lukacs had described the proletariat (the industrial working class) as both the subject and the object of history. By this he meant that the proletariat was the 'subject' of history, the main mover in the process of bringing human history to fruition; but they were also its 'object', the end state or purpose of that process. This is quite a difficult idea to grasp as it melds together Marxian and Hegelian ideas about social classes, the nature of reason and the purpose of history. Lukacs had argued that the proletariat was the historical force that would unify the highly fragmented and exploitative world of modern capitalism. It was the proletariat's historical destiny to do so because it was most alienated and exploited by capitalism; upon it capitalism rested. The proletariat's struggle for existence represented the deepest challenge to the capitalist status quo and would be the source of its supercession by communism (Marx). In terms of our knowledge of the world, the distinction between the knowing subject and the world of objects, which had been turned into a key methodological principle by positivism, would be superseded in the same process. Humanity would come into a state of true self-knowledge where for the first time its understanding of the world would correspond to the way the world was, and the world would correspond to humanity's understanding of it. The subject–object relation, unclouded by historical distortions would truly come into its own (Hegel). When the proletariat finally sank capitalism, Lukacs argued, subject and object would be united, and humanity could begin its real (communist) history.

It was not that Critical Theorists were simply opposed to Lukacs's work, indeed in his inaugural lecture Horkheimer had expressed his desire to develop a theory that would overcome the deficiencies of a fragmented intellectual world, and thus in some measure herald a more unified totality. He did though express it without any of the grandiose language or metaphysical claims found in *History and Class Consciousness*. Like Lukacs, Critical Theorists were concerned with the theory–practice (praxis) relationship, but towards this also there was a certain coolness.

In modern usage the word, practice, has an instrumental ring to it. When something is practical it means we know it can be done. Someone who is practical gets things done. We identify a practical problem as something for which there is a technical solution, and theory (science) will describe in formal-abstract terms, independent of particular situations, how these technical solutions can be achieved. However, for Critical Theorists we misunderstand the social-historical world if we apply the same assumptions to it. Practice, (or praxis to use the Aristotelian term) is conceived by them in a different way, in that solutions to human problems are always situated and dependent not on being technically correct, but on what is to count as desirable in terms of justice, happiness and freedom. Theory cannot prescribe what must happen in practice to achieve a given end but must wait for a kind of verification from the realm of praxis.

Excursus: Habermas on Theory and Practice

Habermas, a generation later sought to clarify the theory–practice relationship by drawing an analogy between Critical Theory and psychoanalysis (1988 [1971]). The psychoanalyst certainly applies theoretical assumptions to the life-problems the patient (or analysand) brings, but cannot expect them to be solved in an automatic, technical way. The analysand must truly accept or 'verify' the analyst's explanation as appropriate to his or her life before it can be regarded as true. If the analysand does not accept the truth of the analyst's account, then some aspects of the interpretation, even some theoretical precepts may have to be revised. In short, the relation between theory and practice is a two-way dialectical process.

At one level this seems straightforward in that it acknowledges the separate but interrelated nature of two different aspects of reality, theorising and doing things. The trouble was, as Habermas pointed out, neither Marx nor Lukacs really gave praxis its due, both saw it as flowing fairly unproblematically from theory – and if it didn't it was wrong. In *Knowledge and Human Interests* (1971b: ch. 3), Habermas re-examined the relationship between Marx and Hegel noting the effect Marx's materialist assumptions had on the framework he took over from Hegel. For Marx, the historical process of the human subject coming to self-realisation was conceived in instrumental terms as the progressive capacity of human beings to 'externalise' themselves through controlling the world of nature. Once this materialist lens is in place in Marx's ideas, there is no turning back. Human nature is put on a par with physical nature with the result that 'knowledge that makes possible the control of natural processes turns into knowledge that makes possible the control of the social life process' (p. 47). The real (inter)active characteristic of praxis, which should involve a necessary reciprocity with theory is lost because like the processes of nature it is conceived in a deterministic way as the inevitable effect of nature-like causes. Marxist theory oriented in this fashion takes on the positivistic hue of a natural science. It decides in a purely technical way, what is correct or incorrect praxis.

In another discussion of the same topic, 'Labor and Interaction: Remarks on Hegel's Jena Philosophy of Mind' in *Theory and Practice* (1974), Habermas showed in more detail how Hegel's account of the self-formation of the subject was a more differentiated process than Marx allowed. Where Marx always focused on the importance of labour and the way a society must primarily meet its material needs for physical survival, Hegel recognised that the moral world of interaction was a different but equally important medium of self-formation, and both were mediated through a third: language.

For Marx though, morality and interaction were always read through the categorical framework of the production process. In mastering nature and sustaining itself materially, a society develops its forces of production, (its raw materials, tools and machines) to certain levels of technical sophistication. Changes in this area that are triggered by the apparently natural capacity to innovate technically, effectively create the conditions to provoke revolutionary change at the level of social organisation. However, while Marx did make an important distinction between the forces and relations of production (social classes) and recognised the latter as the catalyst of historical change, for Habermas, his efforts to relate the two elements dialectically still fails to grasp their irreducibility; the fact that they are distinctly separate areas with distinctly separate characteristics. Marx always sees the revolutionary class as 'caused' into action by ongoing pressure from the quasi-natural forces of production In this he is blind to the inherently interactive, communicative, characteristics of praxis and his work is thus prone to the criticism that it presents a mechanistic and inaccurate account of historical change.

Apart from its inaccuracy there are other implications that flow from Marx's work. For example, Lukacs in his 1922 essay, 'Towards a Methodology of the Problem of Organisation' (1971: 295–342), dubiously reproduces Marx's assumptions in terms of the Communist Party's relation to the proletariat, filtering the idea of both theory and praxis through the same instrumentalist lens. Because central to Lukacs is the idea that the proletariat are the subject–object of history, when he conceives Marxist theory in instrumental terms he insists that it must only concern itself with what is strategically useful to achieving the historical goal. Any theoretical hypotheses that deviate from this trajectory Lukacs rules out of court (1971: 300–1). The idea that a theory might be tested for validity in some other way than as a tool for Communist Party was anathema to Lukacs, just as Lukacs' intellectual philistinism was anathema to Critical Theory.

A similar implication emerges on the side of praxis when it is conceived instrumentally. Any form of proletarian consciousness which does not match up with correct revolutionary theory must be deemed wrong as actual (empirical) working-class consciousness, unlike that of the Communist Party, is still ensnared in the ideological thought processes of capitalism. Because the Party is in possession of Marxist theory it can 'impute' naturalistically a correct class-consciousness to the proletariat that corresponds to its objective revolutionary situation. If the proletariat fail to grasp its revolutionary role in all this, it must be disabused of its mistake and told what to think by the Party that represents it and embodies correct theory. Praxis is thus reduced to being an instrumental reflex of theory. As Habermas (1974: 34–6) bluntly put it, for Lukacs, proletarian enlightenment consisted in being subordinated to the

Party, and the theory, which sought to enhance the self-formation of the subject, finishes up denying it has any need for confirmation through praxis.

The dictatorial implications of Lukacs's ideas in terms of the Leninism and Stalinism that so influenced the history of the Soviet Union are well known, but the wider problem of the theory–praxis relationship, of how social science might serve human emancipation, still persists. In contemporary feminism for example, standpoint theory is subject to the same uncertainty. Dorothy Smith (1987) has made an important contribution to our understanding of the way women's experience is often rendered invisible in everyday life and to the way sociology has tended to reproduce this invisibility. The task, she argues, is to show how the process of concealment takes place and thereby to recover women's authentic voice. Though she acknowledges the importance of the wider economic and political order in maintaining these relationships, phenomenological primacy is attributed to the woman's standpoint. Sandra Harding (1987: 185), though, in pointing to the Lukacsian origins, not of *women's* but of *feminist* standpoint theory, notes that the very understanding of women's experiences has to be 'informed' by feminist *theory*. The implication being that where women's actual (empirical) consciousness lags behind what theory thinks it should be, it has the right to impute correct consciousness. To be fair feminist theory has to some extent recognised the problem and continues to wrestle with it (Stanley and Wise 1993).

Habermas's carefully considered criticism of Marx and Lukacs certainly echoes themes developed by the first generation, notably their growing dislike of the instrumental outlook that increasingly pervaded modern life, but was written in the more equable times of the early 1960s. For Critical Theorists in the 1930s the problems of theory and praxis conceived in this instrumental way were all too palpable. They looked with increasing disbelief at the theory of the proletariat as the subject–object of history, and its praxis the vehicle for bringing a metaphysical process of emancipation to fruition. Plainly in Germany, 'metaphysics' had gone badly wrong; in fact under a tide of Nazi-inspired popular anti-Semitism the Institute for Social Research was forced to flee the country, first to Geneva in 1933, and then New York in 1934, where Columbia University provided the accommodation. In the 1940s, Horkheimer, Adorno and Pollock quit New York for California, while Marcuse and others worked in various capacities for the American government for the duration of the Second World War. After the war Horkheimer and Adorno returned from exile in the USA to some acclaim in Germany, while others including Lowenthal, Fromm, Neumann and Marcuse, remained in the USA, the latter becoming an influential catalyst for the 'New Left' and the counter cultural movements of the 1960s.

However one should not conclude that the darkening mood of Critical Theory was merely the result of the personal response to the political events that befell its protagonists, nor should the cooling of their attitude to Marx and Lukacs be read as a rejection of the broad materialist framework they inherited from these two authors. It was the substantive analyses of the Institute members themselves in the late 1930s, '40s and '50s undertaken *within* the orbit of Marx and Lukacs that generated the gloomy social prognosis for which they are famous, and for which Habermas later sought a more positive alternative.

Summary and Conclusion

In this chapter I have outlined the early efforts of Horkheimer to establish a dialectical theory in contrast to the (inductive) positivist outlook of his predecessor, Grunberg. The target of Critical Theory's dialectical outlook however was not only positivist Marxism, but also the equally one-sided existentialism of the time. In line with these principles and in the light of the proletariat's refusal to take the socialist path, Horkheimer stressed the explanatory importance of culture as a sphere of influence worthy of analysis in its own right, albeit one dialectically related to economic change.

One stumbling block to the optimistic programme presented by Horkheimer was the instrumental implications of the theory–practice relationship as received from Marx and Lukacs. I have used Habermas's ideas to clarify why Critical Theory felt less than enthusiastic over this aspect of Marxism. I now want to examine in more detail the work of Horkheimer et al. during this period, particularly in relation to their growing pessimism over the issue of social practice.

Further Reading

Chapters 1 and 2

There are now a number of commentaries on Critical Theory, each coming from a different angle. Martin Jay's *The Dialectical Imagination* (1973) was the first in the field and highlights the diversity of influences on first generation Critical Theorists. It is essentially a history of ideas and tends to play down the political element in their writings. David Held's *Introduction to Critical Theory* (1980) is more theoretical in outlook, examining in some detail the claims made in different analytical areas. I particularly like his Chapter 6 on 'The Culture Industry', which he illustrates with useful examples. Rolf Wiggerhaus's *The Frankfurt School* (1994) is the most comprehensive history of Critical Theory, both in terms of ideas and the empirical events that overtook its writers. It is though, like Jay's book, a 'history' and does not deal in a substantive way with the ideas. It is also a mighty tome, (787 pages) and may be something into which a new reader might dip. Douglas Kellner's *Critical Theory, Marxism and Modernity* (1989) is very readable and well informed, it also captures the political edge of Critical Theory in a way that Jay's book does not. David Ingram's *Critical Theory and Philosophy* (1990) is out of print, but is an excellent and genuinely accessible introduction to some of the main themes of Critical Theory, including those produced by Habermas, which tend to get less of an airing in the other commentaries.

There is no substitute for the real thing and Marcuse's *One Dimensional Man* (1994 [1964]) remains a good starting point. It is polemical and pessimistic and arguably not his best book (see Habermas's essay 'The Differing Rhythms of Philosophy and Politics: Marcuse at 100' in Habermas (2001)). Nevertheless the brio with which Marcuse critiques life in modern industrial society is still quite stirring and it doesn't take much imagination to mentally bring it up to date. Kellner's (1984) study of Marcuse is comprehensive and the best supplement for a Marcuse enthusiast.

Adorno's *Minima Moralia: Reflections From Damaged Life* (1974), is even more acerbic and consists of short, terse fragments, which make it fairly accessible. Adorno's *The Culture Industry* (1991) is also a good starting point, and has an informative introduction by Jay Bernstein that compares Adorno's view of mass culture with that of postmodernists, finding in favour of the former.

Reading Habermas can be a formidable task until the main parameters of his ideas become apparent, even then he is rarely easy. The appendix to *Knowledge and Human Interests* (1971b) offers an early philosophically-oriented summary of his ideas, which are given a more of a sociological illustration in Chapter 6 of *Towards a Rational Society* (1971a); Pusey (1987) sets Habermas' work in a sociological context.

3

Disillusion and the Emergence of a Nietzschean Streak

In the previous chapter I set out the basic ambitions of early Critical Theory as revealed in Max Horkheimer's inaugural address. His hope was to develop a dialectical theory that moved back and forth between the wider demands of capitalist development and the development of different forms of action at the level of social agency or praxis. I drew attention to an ambiguity in Critical Theory's (inherited) account of praxis, which had the aim of recognising the importance of social action, but still tended to see it as something passive and derived from the demands of capitalism.

In Chapter 3 I want to explore how this ambiguity fed into Critical Theory's changing view of the world. The main shift was from an early optimism in the 1930s about how the world might move towards socialism, to a thoroughgoing pessimism over its unchanging, controlling and 'wholly administered' nature, by the 1960s. The change in outlook was not solely the result of a theoretical flaw, indeed this 'flaw' enabled its authors to produce some of their most remarkable insights into the nature of social control in apparently democratic countries; also crucial in effecting the change was the rise of totalitarianism in Nazi Germany and the Soviet Union, of state capitalism and mass culture in democratic countries, all of which fuelled a fear that real human progress was grinding to a halt. It should also be remembered that the change of view was gradual and contested even within the ranks of Critical Theory. I want to bring out some of the counter-tendencies that make the work of Critical Theorists more nuanced than critics would sometimes have it.

In his inaugural lecture Horkheimer drew up a research programme for Critical Theory built around the relations between three areas, which I deal with in turn:

(a) the political-economic organisation of society,
(b) the psychology that underpins social integration, and
(c) mass-culture phenomena, leisure, lifestyle, and so on, which work towards particular kinds of social reproduction.

In line with growing disillusionment there emerged a broader suspicion, what I have called a Nietzschean streak, in their writing, a bleakly critical view, not just of what was happening in particular areas of life, but of the whole tradition of western reason. Critical theorists increasingly believed reason, in a wide sense, had been reduced to its instrumental function. Instrumental reasoning involves an outlook where the world is made up of *mere* objects, and reason's task is only to show subjects how best to manipulate these objects, be they natural or human objects. The success of natural science in its use of such instrumental assumptions fuelled Critical Theory's critique of positivism.

Political Economy and the Rise of Instrumental Reason

With regard to political economy it was the work of Frederick Pollock that seems to have held sway at least with two core members, Horkheimer and Adorno, (though not Marcuse). In an article entitled, 'State Capitalism: Its Possibilities and Limitations' (1941), Pollock set out what he sees as the main features of a new emerging form of societal state organisation: state capitalism. The gist of his argument is that in modern societies, following the economic dislocation of the 1920s and 1930s, the state had increasingly taken over the role of the market in regulating capitalist economic relations. It did this to maintain the social fabric and general stability of society. The nineteenth-century liberal-competitive form of capitalism has been replaced by a more interventionist outlook appropriate to managing the effects of an economy based on large concentrations of corporate capital, that is monopoly capitalism.

The emergence of discussions around Keynesian economics, and ultimately the welfare state in Britain, of the New Deal in Roosevelt's America, and of the role of the Nazi Party in Germany all serve as examples of the perceived need to control the exigencies of a free market that could lumber out of control. Pollock does note that there is a significant difference between totalitarian and democratic forms of state capitalism, but in both cases there had been a shift from the primacy of the economic to the primacy of the political.

In and of itself Pollock's essay seems unprovocative. It is written in a brisk matter-of-fact style and with plenty of qualification. He does, for example, recognise that his account is not essentially new, but a summary of ideas that were scattered about at the time in various places. He also points out that his 'model' may not actually exist, but rather refers to a long-standing tendency. His model should be seen, he says, as an ideal type, in Max Weber's sense. Nevertheless this essay can be seen as opening up a wider sense of pessimism in Critical Theory as it suggests that political-administrative forces could now 'manage' the contradictions of capitalism and the only issue, according to Pollock, was whether democratic forces would be sufficient to 'control the controllers'. The significance of exploitation, and other features of capitalist class relations have receded on Pollock's account, in the face of what Adorno was later to call the 'wholly administered world'.

Up to this point Critical Theorists had fairly much taken for granted Marx's idea that capitalism was inherently self destructive, in that it could not maintain the economic growth a competitive market called forth as well as full employment. The Marxist claim that a 'falling rate of profit' and the increasing 'emiseration' of the working class would make the system break down had not previously been brought into question. However, the tricky implication of Pollock's essay was that these changes heralded an apparently classless society, or at least one where the significance of class had been massaged out of sight by careful administration. Whether accurate or not, for Critical Theorists to hold such a view would signal a partial but significant departure from the ideas of Marx or Lukacs, and a clear dampening for their emancipatory hopes.

Pollock's views on political-economic change were not the only ones produced by Institute members. Franz Neumann in his book, *Behemoth: The Structure and Practice of National Socialism* (1963 [1944]) took issue with Pollock on the grounds that even in Nazi Germany where the political seemed to be overwhelmingly important, normal capitalist economic relations had continued. It is still not exactly clear today the extent to which Pollock's pessimistic view was accepted by Horkheimer et al. Conventional wisdom has it that it was, (Dubiel 1985, Honneth 1987, 1993: ch. 1), but Deborah Cook (1996:10–13, 1998) drawing on a variety of textual evidence has shown that particularly for Adorno, nominally the most pessimistic of Critical Theorists, there was an ambivalence towards Pollock's thesis. Adorno's dialectical instincts were never at ease with a flat description of a new political universe that was capable of managing an antagonistic capitalist economy.

Nevertheless, a sense of foreboding that the political, and with it the moral universe, was closing down is apparent in two of Horkheimer's early 1940s essays, 'The Authoritarian State' and 'The End of Reason' (Arato and Gebhardt 1978). In 'The Authoritarian State', Horkheimer dwells on the disenchantment that is only implicit in Pollock's essay pointing to the increasingly enclosed, authoritarian form that state organisation is taking. He often refers to Germany but his remarks are clearly meant to have a broad application. He sets the tone at the outset by noting that under monopoly capitalism both proletariat and bourgeoisie are somewhat superfluous to the running of the system. At the level of persons both classes have become functionaries of the *organisation*, be it the state, the corporation, or the financial trust. He does acknowledge that the organisational grip exerted by this form of society should be a passing historical phase, but the essay mostly points in another direction. For example, trade unions, in order to function effectively in this kind of set up, *have* to develop their own bureaucratic apparatuses which necessarily requires a level of integration into the system with which they are nominally at odds. Integration, he says 'is the price which individuals and groups have to pay in order to flourish under capitalism'. He sees no alternative to this situation but is disquieted by its apparent inevitability.

In 'The End of Reason' he takes issue with the way reason has been limited to its instrumental function in so many areas of life. This essay marks a covert break with Marx in that it identifies an ideology (instrumental reason) built into modern life, and yet unperceived (or unperceivable) by Marx himself. In a quite complex (perhaps just difficult) argument, Horkheimer claims that for philosophy 'reason' has always been prone to self-doubt or scepticism, to the belief that 'reason' is not what it seems to be, the highest and most definitive expression of being human. In its modern positivist form though, it has become peculiarly enfeebled, rendering meaningless all larger questions about 'freedom, truth or human dignity'. Instead:

> Its features can be summarised as the optimum adaptation of means to ends, think-ing as an energy conserving operation. It is a pragmatic instrument oriented to expe-diency, cold and sober. The belief in cleverness rests on motives much more cogent than metaphysical propositions. When even the dictators of today appeal to reason, they mean that they possess the most tanks. They were rational enough to build them; others should be rational enough to yield to them.

I quote Horkheimer (Arato and Gebhardt 1978: 28) because his words capture one of the key concepts of first generation Critical Theory – instrumental reason. The point he is making is that reason, in sloughing off all concern with wider issues and reducing itself to mere cleverness, has left human subjects acting reasonably only if they act manipulatively; and more worryingly, being reasonable only if they *yield* to manipulation.

Important though this idea is to Critical Theory, Horkheimer's case is more involved. He believes that reason is something that should enable us to par-tially transcend existing conditions, but also that it is not purely transcenden-tal, not a supra-historical entity, rather very much something of this world too. But his fear is that reason's 'this worldliness', its embedment in society's current concerns has become all that it is.

He couches his concerns in a discussion of the growth of the individualism that accompanied capitalism. As competitive capitalism's free market liberated people from the fetters of the feudal world it allowed the 'free' individual to emerge, albeit within the limits set by capitalist economic relations. Even though the bourgeois nuclear family was an expression of the society it rep-resented, it also provided a genuine psychic bulwark against the destructive effects of life in a market economy. It allowed individuals to sense their own individuality and right to freedom and happiness, often in contrast to what the capitalist order dealt them. Individualism was thus a resource for an immanent critique of the status quo. However, with the emergence of a more organised, monopoly capitalism, and using Freud's ideas about the importance of the instinct for self-preservation, Horkheimer points out that currently, in order to preserve themselves, individuals *have* to become more and more integrated into the system. They have to buy into their own exploitation at a deeper level as a necessary condition for their survival. They must learn to become flexible and accommodate themselves to reality. The logical accompaniment to this decline in individuality is the reduction of reason to its instrumental function, because the new 'selfless' individual in learning to adapt must apply instrumental reason to himself. He must make himself amenable, be rational enough to yield, and not concern himself with issues that might require wider reflection.

Social Psychology

From the angle of social psychology it was the work of Eric Fromm upon which Critical Theory initially relied. Fromm had become a psychoanalyst in 1926, started his own practice in 1928 and became a full member of the Institute for Social Research in 1930. The basic idea he brought was straightforward, that a necessary complementarity exists between the (Freudian) psychoanalytic outlook and that of Marxism, or at least Critical Theory's version of it. The attempt to link Freud and Marx seems unremarkable today but at the time was quite radical in that neither side had much sympathy for the other. Indeed another Freudian thinker and associate of the Institute, Wilhelm Reich, managed to get himself thrown out of both the International Psychoanalytic Association and the Communist Party for holding to both outlooks at the same time.

Though Fromm was keen to link the psychological and the sociological realms he also sought to avoid reducing the explanatory power of one to the other. In this, his ideas resemble contemporary 'critical realism', which argues that reality is ontologically stratified, that different areas of social reality are fundamentally different from each other and thus require different methodological principles to explain them[6]. For his part, Fromm warned against trying to give psychoanalytic answers to societal questions where perfectly adequate sociological explanations existed. Equally, he warned against trying to read off human motivation from broad, abstract conceptions of society (1989a [1929]). It was the thinness of the Marxist account of motivation that prompted Fromm and Horkheimer to seek greater purchase on the psychic structure of the individual, via Freud's work.

Standardly, Marxists had tended to regard Freud's work as something typically bourgeois and self-indulgent in its concern for inner mental life, when all around an exploitative capitalism romped on apace. However, the Marxist habit of reading off action as though it was solely motivated by the desire for economic advantage, was clearly deficient for Critical Theory. It assumed people were no more than the cognitive calculators of their economic interests and would act accordingly, something the 1930s' German proletariat demonstrated to be quite untrue. It said nothing about people's deeper identity, their affective commitments, their fears, wishes, loves and hates, as mediated through family or community. Freud, it was felt, provided an altogether more elaborate and adequate way into the 'subjective' dimension, and became the touchstone for much of first generation Critical Theory's pioneering work on authority, the family and culture.

In the early 1930s, Fromm argued that in spite of their apparent differences both psychoanalysis and historical materialism shared certain aspects. They both had what contemporary theory calls a de-centred view of the subject. Instead of looking upon the consciousness of the subject as the source of thought and action, 'both theories depose consciousness from the throne from which it appeared to direct the actions of people and represent their emotions' (1989b: 214–15 [1931]). In short, both theories from the outset were suspicious of the everyday perceptions of the subject, arguing instead that there were either psychic or economic forces that determined the contents of consciousness before the subject could become aware of them.

Freud's work is almost synonymous with his discovery of the unconscious, a mental realm that lies beneath the conscious world of everyday life. Baldly speaking, Freud argued that the unconscious is made up of psychic forces centred on two quasi-biological instincts, the instinct for self-preservation and the sex instinct. The latter is particularly influential in shaping human behaviour behind the scenes. The unconscious realm of instinctual drives is a dynamic one and its contents seek gratification in the conscious world. However, the conscious world is also the world of everyday life and necessarily prohibits or represses the blatant expression of such drives as anti-social. As the child grows to adulthood one of the key emergent properties of his or her psyche is an *ego* capable of securing a reasonable fit between these important but awkward anti-social drives and the constraints of the equally important moral norms of society.

Critical Theorists are well known for their critiques of ideology but from the beginning they sought to ground critique in something more than notions of economic exploitation. Ideology was not so much a matter of false consciousness, of people holding to mistaken ideas about their class interests; ideology went all the way down, structuring how events in the everyday world were perceived. It reached into the very fabric of the individual psyche and would thus not be prone to any simple challenge over issues of exploitation or inequality. It is an odd fact that societies in which large numbers of people suffer extreme poverty and blatant injustice often show no signs of any wish for revolutionary change. Indeed the reverse may be the case: the French Revolution (1789), for example, came at a time when in a material sense things for the mass of French people were actually improving. Critical Theory's interest in Freud sprang from its desire to explain the deep attachment workers felt for a system that at an overt level exploited them.

What interested Fromm initially was the interface between the world of the psyche and the world of everyday life in capitalist society. In 'The Method and Function of an Analytic Social Psychology' (1978 [1932]) Fromm set about describing why the two theories should be seen as complementing one another. He notes that the sex instinct, unlike the instinct for self-preservation, is flexible and capable of adaptation to 'reality'; it can be sublimated and oriented in ways that are congruent with 'what is socially available and desirable from the standpoint of the ruling classes' (p. 480). The structure of drives is not completely malleable but is certainly affected by the structure of the mode of production that exists at a particular time. More narrowly, different social classes will find their drives bearing a different stamp according to the way they are shaped by the relations they have to the means of production. In turn the instinctual apparatus that generates needs and wishes that seek gratification at the level of ideology will affect socio-economic conditions. Thus, for example, because capitalism places particular value on the acquisition of wealth it is unsurprising that the 'acquisitive drive' becomes peculiarly amplified in such a society, generating 'a narcissistic need or wish to win recognition from oneself and others' (p. 488).

For Freud 'narcissism' is a normal stage through which infants pass as they gradually come to terms with the fact they are not the centre of everything, but one separate ego amongst others. Adult narcissism on the other hand refers to the desire to aggrandize oneself in the eyes of others, to make oneself the centre of attention by evoking admiration through the manipulation of appearances. In its adult form it is abnormal even pathological, yet it is interesting to note that nearly fifty years after Fromm's paper, Christopher Lasch in his *The Culture of Narcissism* (1979) pointed up just how culturally normal such abnormal tendencies had become.

For Critical Theory, the family was the crucial social institution as it was there that instinctual drives met wider society. The family provided the forum in which the instinctual drives of children were conditioned and mediated by their emotional relationships to adults; at the same time the lives of adults were shaped by the conditions determined by the economy. Critical Theory's hope was that the tension between instinct and economy would become the source of progressive change. Fromm (1978: 495) put it like this:

> With the growth of objective contradictions and conflicts within the society, and the acceleration of the disintegrative process, certain changes in society's libidinal structure also take place. We see the disappearance of the traditional ties that maintained the stability of the society; there is a change in traditional emotional attitudes. Libidinal energies are freed for new uses, and thus change their social function. They no longer serve the preservation of society, but contribute to the development of new social formations. They cease to be cement and turn into dynamite.

The problem was that in this kind of explanation lay the source of the same disillusion that characterised Horkheimer and Pollock's account of the closing down of the political universe. The space between instinctual (libidinous) structures and modes of production was no space at all. It was certainly no space where *action* could take place. Social action became trapped, inert, between two irresistible materialist forces: instincts and economic production. There could be no guarantee that when cement turned into dynamite a more rational world would come into being. For, in the strict sense, no rational action was possible as anything that happened, happened because the relative fit between the two irresistible forces triggered it. How *conscious* agents might be involved was not at all clear. When Horkheimer et al. accepted Fromm's meshing of psychoanalysis and historical materialism they accepted an outlook that produced a vision of a seamless world of determined behaviour. Beyond certain core elements instinctual drives were relatively malleable but such malleability was straightaway met by the determining effects of economic relations, any creative action was thus lost from view somewhere between, as it were, a rock and a hard place.

There was more than one irony involved here. Critical Theory had sought out Freud's work to give it a greater understanding of the heart and mind of the proletariat and thus develop a less deterministic, more dialectical account of history (Horkheimer 1993 [1932]: 111–28). What they finished up with was an explanation of society's capacity to stay the same by producing ideologies that would meld the malleable aspects of the unconscious with the needs of the economy. Ironic too was the fact that it was Fromm, the only trained psychoanalyst amongst the Institute's key members, that by the late 1930s came to distance himself from Freud's work, or at least from idea of the primacy of instinctual drives as a closed system. He emphasised instead that interpersonal relations were as much if not more determining of human character than instinctual drives (Fromm 1942: 247–51, 1956: 44–6). To Marcuse and Adorno this smacked of an unhealthy 'revisionism', which would only weaken the Freudian input to a truly *critical* theory. Certainly if one looks at a later (collective) Institute essay, 'The Family', dating from 1956 (in Horkheimer and Adorno 1973), the case presented bears the pessimistic implications of Fromm's early ideas. Changing economic conditions are seen to undermine the authority of the patriarchal, nuclear family, but not thereby to liberate its members; they only acquire new character traits (for example, ego, weakness) that make them more amenable to the requirements of the 'administered' life.

Culture

One might have expected that in the area of culture, Critical Theory would have retained its early optimism. Culture is not an obviously fixed, 'material' phenomenon in the way that economic relations and the unconscious are. One might have expected signs of emancipatory potential to appear in the realm of culture, and in fact Horkheimer, in the mid 1930s, felt able to write that culture was 'caught up in the dynamism of history', and its various spheres 'dynamic influences on the maintenance or breakdown of a particular form of society' (1972: 54). Yet the bleak nature of its culture critique has become almost a byword for Critical Theory itself.

Certainly by the mid 1940s, culture was being seen as both an expression of, and a causal element in, society's stasis. For Critical Theorists, culture was notable for being distinctly *un*dynamic, in fact Adorno coined the disparaging term, 'culture industry' to capture the extent to which it had been overtaken by industrial forces. His work is sometimes seen as an attack on popular or mass culture generally, but this is wide of the mark. The term, mass culture, was insufficient for him because it implied that modern culture was in some sense the product of the masses, when in fact it was an industrial product sold to the masses as a commodity (Adorno 1991: 85–7). It was only the strange juxtaposing of 'culture' and 'industry' that did justice to the dispiriting fact that culture should now be thought less a vital human expression of social integration, more the manipulative product of interlocking commercial interests.

Much of Adorno's culture critique is pitched at the American entertainment industry, but the process of industrialising culture had emerged both in the USA and Europe in the 1920s and 1930s and was seen by Critical Theory as a logical complement to the shift from competitive to monopoly capitalism. In Marxist terms it meant that where competitive capitalism extolled the virtues of a rugged, Robinson Crusoe-like individualism, monopoly capitalism required individuals to have altogether more pliable egos. Workers should be prepared to commit themselves to their company and buy their own a sense of individuality through commodities.

For Critical Theorists, culture represented the third corner of an emergent triangle of increasing domination. The changes in political economy, (for instance, the growth of monopoly capitalism and the state-administrative apparatus that went with it), along with the changes in social psychology, were now serviced by a third process: seduction by the culture industry. Films, radio, television, popular music and newspapers all fell under the withering gaze of Adorno in particular, as all, in their way, blithely fostered the illusion that the 'good life' was to be found in the commodity.

If the good life had something to do with happiness, with sensuousness, and of finding meaning in life, the products of the culture industries did not lead the subject towards their realisation, but diverted it from them. Culture had once been a storehouse of elements such as truth and beauty, and even though these carried the stamp of class relations they nevertheless lit up a potential for human fulfillment. By contrast, culture now served only as a diversion from reality. Adorno and Horkheimer, writing in 1947 about film in *Dialectic of Enlightenment* (1972: 126–7), describe its effects as stimulated sedation.

The sound film, far surpassing the theater of illusion, leaves no room for imagination or reflection on the part of the audience, who is unable to respond within the structure of the film, yet deviate from its precise detail without losing the thread of the story; hence the film forces its victims to equate it directly with reality. . . . They (films) are so designed that quickness, powers of observation and experience are needed to apprehend them at all; yet sustained thought is out of the question if the spectator is not to miss the relentless rush of facts. Even though the effort required for his response is semi-automatic, no scope is left for the imagination.

Apart from the speed and fierceness of the images, the reason audience response is semi-automatic is because the structure and content of films are so predictable; 'as soon as the film begins it is clear how it will end, and who will be rewarded, punished or forgotten' (p. 125). The whole thing is constructed of interchangeable, ready-made clichés. The culture industry on this account provides a key mechanism for smoothly adjusting individuals into the behavioural requirements of monopoly capitalism. It simultaneously provides a sense of excitement while at the same time being soporific. It truncates and reifies the fullness of the aesthetic experience in a way entirely in line with the decline of the individual.

Although Adorno's work should not be thought unpolitical it was Marcuse's *One Dimensional Man* that made the political implications of cultural closure, at a societal level, explicit. In arguing that modern capitalist societies had successfully incorporated not only the working class, but also all oppositional forces into the system, Marcuse claimed that alternatives to the status quo had been virtually stifled, and life had become one-dimensional.

The un-Marxist implications of this 'pacification' thesis were controversial on the left, but Marcuse actually utilised Marxian categories to produce his analysis. He argued that the forces of production, particularly technology, had developed so successfully that they had rendered the relations of production (class relations) superfluous. The sharpness of class antagonism that Marx had anticipated was largely absent from advanced capitalist societies, because such factors as increasing mechanisation in the work place had had a subduing effect on workers, while generating higher levels of affluence. The higher the levels of affluence the more effectively exploitation and inequality could be concealed. When everyone has access to a variety of commodities, inequalities between people appear to spring only from consumer choice. Marcuse recognised in a way that Marx could not have that the consumption of commodities now played a significant role in the social integration of individuals into the wider system. As he put it, 'people recognise themselves in their commodities; they find their soul in their automobile, hi-fi set, split level home, kitchen equipment' (Marcuse 1994: 9 [1964]). The kind of work done also increasingly entailed involvement in large-scale automated work-systems, where individuals would recognise themselves as *needing to fit in*, and where professional autonomy was irrelevant. It was the kind of thing Harry Braverman (1974) would later describe in detail as the process of 'deskilling' the workforce. People thus learnt that individualism was not something to be practised, but purchased.

The embroiling of the individual into the system both at the point of production and consumption was at the heart of *One Dimensional Man* (Marcuse 1994 12 [1964]):

> The productive apparatus and the goods and services it produces 'sell' or impose the social system as a whole. The means of mass transportation and communication, the commodities of lodging, food and clothing, the irresistible output of the entertainment and information industry carry with them prescribed attitudes and habits, certain intellectual and emotional reactions which bind the consumers more or less pleasantly to the producers and, through the latter to the whole.

It is the closed nature of this situation, where social integration and system integration appear fused together as a seamless whole, that Marcuse finds so dispiriting. Critics of first generation Critical Theory, including Habermas and Honneth, have argued that its essential failing was in representing the world in an *overly* one-dimensional way, ignoring the possibility of emergent alternatives. Yet, as in the other areas of its work, there were always undercurrents running counter to this judgment. For example, Kellner points out that Marcuse rarely uses the term, 'one-dimensionality', in a totalising way, as a noun that flatly designates what the whole of society is like. Rather, he uses it as an adjective to describe the main tendency of an historical era, and in contrast to a situation where a second dimension exists, one that in a rational society would be critical of the status quo (Marcuse 1994: xxvi).

Marcuse also makes clear at the beginning of *One Dimensional Man* (pp. 5–6) that his task is to show that what factually *is* the case, namely, that people are increasingly well integrated into society, is something that normatively *ought* not to be so. To do this he needs to draw attention to the reality of the human subject as something more than a socialised appendage of the system, and does so by making a distinction between true and false needs. He recognises that beyond the biological, all those things we regard as needs, are to a significant degree the product of what society designates to be a need. However, we can and should distinguish a false need, as something superimposed on the individual from the outside, by forces that have an interest in repressing him or her. The individual may experience gratification in satisfying these false needs, even a kind of euphoria, but no matter how much he or she identifies with them as his or her own, they remain 'what they were from the beginning – products of a society whose dominant interest demands repression'.

Other Critical Theorists echo Marcuse's defence of the reality of the subject in the face of forces that would subvert it. In two essays, one on Thorstein Veblen the other on Aldous Huxley, dating from the 1940s, Adorno (1981) defended the idea of the individual's potential for authentic happiness. Veblen, a not unimportant early American sociologist introduced the concept of conspicuous consumption in his book, *The Theory of the Leisure Class* (1994 [1899]). Conspicuous consumption referred to the idea that some forms of consumption are not driven by any obvious use the goods have, but by the consumer's desire to display their status and wealth. Adorno shares Veblen's critical view that culture's civilised appearance is to a large degree an ostentatious way of justifying greed and arrogance. He approves, for example, of Veblen's recognition that women, particularly amongst the leisure classes, are often little more than the social ornaments of men's lives, and that this leads to the general denigration of women. The association of women with consumerism in the form of shopping only reflects their social position as close cousin to the commodity itself.

However, Adorno notes that Veblen's criticism is based on the supposed simple virtues of work as the source of the 'fullness of life'. Such a vague term, Adorno claims, is inadequate for dealing with the reality of human happiness, the more so when it is to be measured only in terms of finding fulfillment through work. He believes there is a puritanical streak in Veblen's privileging of work as 'the supreme anthropological category'. For Adorno, Veblen has something about him of 'the bourgeois who takes the admonition to be thrifty with grim seriousness' (p. 87). The effect of this kind of analysis is to treat culture (consumption) as worthless, even though it is dialectically related to production (work). Veblen sees in cultural products only worthless luxuries that reinforce the system. Yet for Adorno there is another side to luxury. Luxury is an idea that speaks of happiness as something worthwhile in its own right, and not as something dependent on work. If the instrumental principles of work are always to be the measure of value, then the reality of happiness to the human subject is diminished.

Even in the modern world where culture functions as an industry, Adorno believes a kind of ghost of real happiness exists in the consumption of its most cynically produced commodities. The kitsch products that are used to achieve it may laughably distort happiness, but in life happiness cannot be separated from the conditions in which subjects find themselves. Adorno (1981: 87) cites a rather odd, but quite telling example of how even the erotic may be as much tied in with showing off as with sex itself:

> Walter Benjamin once wrote that it is as erotically important to the man for his beloved to appear in his company as for her to give herself to him. Veblen would have joined in the bourgeois jeering at this remark and would have talked about conspicuous consumption. But the happiness man finds cannot be separated from conspicuous consumption. There is no happiness that does not promise to satisfy a socially constituted desire, but there is also none that does not promise something qualitatively different in this fulfillment.

The last sentence of the quotation is striking as it challenges the idea that Critical Theorists saw modern culture as nought but deception and manipulation, and people as mere dupes of the system. Adorno is claiming that though people's happiness is conditioned by society, and in ours bound up with conspicuous consumption, the latter nevertheless always carries the promise of something quite different, the promise, if not the fulfillment, of genuine happiness.

Adorno expresses similar sentiments about Aldous Huxley's novel, *Brave New World*. He shares Huxley's uncompromisingly chilling view of what a 'rational', wholly administered society would be like. It is a world where individuals are born into different homogenised groups, where behaviours are standardised and no deviation in thought or action tolerated. In effect it is an ideal typical consumer society built on the principles of niche marketing. Sex and narcotic drugs are instantly available in prescribed forms, serving to gratify and pacify people, functioning as forms of social control. However, while Adorno admires the way Huxley has not compromised his vision with sentimental ideas about progress, and things always turning out all right in the end, he nevertheless finds the denunciation of sexual gratification too thoroughgoing. Huxley, as it were, throws the baby out with the bathwater, 'he fails to distinguish between the liberation of sexuality and its debasement . . . his anger at false happiness sacrifices the idea of true happiness (p. 103). For Adorno, Huxley like Veblen, has a puritanical streak that blunts his capacity to see the ultimate relevance of gratification, including sexual gratification, for individual happiness.

Whilst Critical Theorists were never advocates of a simple individualism, they equally refused to eliminate the individual from their concerns. Emancipation, they argued, would entail sensuousness and personal gratification, something that stood in contrast to the asceticism characteristic of revolutionary zeal, no less than the hedonism of mass culture. One should not overstate the undercurrents that run counter to the more familiar Critical Theory judgment that culture is one-dimensional, but they do exist, and should not be ignored.

Another important distinction made by Critical Theorists was between the products of the culture industry and 'autonomous' or 'authentic' art. By 1941, Max Horkheimer (1972: 273ff) was signaling a shift in his attitude towards culture generally from the broadly optimistic outlook he expressed in his original programme, to a more qualified one in 'Art and Mass Culture', (NB this essay was written before he and Adorno adopted the more disparaging term – culture industry – in *Dialectic of Enlightenment* 1947)[7]. In this rather digressive essay he argued that art as we know it came into its own in the era of modern individualism, and that individuals are able to recognise themselves as such, in art, at least to the extent that they have not succumbed to a general levelling of experience and their responses are not the automatic, mechanical ones required by the culture industries. Authentic art, he declared, is art that 'has withstood the plastic surgery of the prevailing economic system which carves all men to one pattern' (p. 273). The validity of authentic art lies in its capacity to have some autonomy from the status quo, and for the individual to find him or herself in this (metaphorical) space. Unlike mass culture, which directly expresses the commodified world of capitalism, autonomous art has an element of resistance inherent in it; it represents a challenge to the status quo even though it is mediated by it. The kind of artworks Adorno had in mind, as able to resist assimilation by the culture industries, were the very dissonant music of composers such as Schoenberg, and the equally dissonant plays of Samuel Beckett.

However, while the distinction between autonomous art and the products of the culture industry was pretty much shared by all the Critical Theorists, there were counter currents here too. Walter Benjamin, a personal friend of Adorno, and an associate of the Institute had a rather different attitude towards mass culture. He felt that mass culture had a certain liberatory potential because it was accessible both intellectually and financially to large numbers of people, and broke with the reverential, class attitudes that surrounded the autonomous artworks of high culture (Benjamin 1973: ch. 9). I shall deal with the debate between Benjamin and Adorno on this issue later in the book, but it serves here to reinforce the idea that in the area of culture, as in the areas of political economy and psychology, Critical Theory's pessimism was not as blunt and undifferentiated as sometimes claimed.

The Nietzschean Streak

Whilst it is important to be aware that the picture of Critical Theory's development is a nuanced one, it is still the case that there was a shift from a broadly optimistic view of things in the early 1930s, to a more sardonic tone through the 1940s, 50s and early 60s. Increasingly, the idea that history had some purpose to it, that it was, in effect, going somewhere, diminished. Where once Critical Theory had thought that forces existed in society which could herald a more rational future, they came to feel that progress now meant, not change, but only more of the same: more commodities, more affluence, more manipulation of the psyche, more administrative control. The suspicion was that history had, in effect, come to a standstill. In philosophical terms, it entailed something of a shift away from Hegel, Marx and Lukacs towards the more obstinate, anti-progressivist views of Friedrich Nietzsche. It was not a wholesale shift, more of a change in tone; indeed they drew the concepts of reification and commodity fetishism that Lukacs had used into this loosely Nietzschean frame of reference.

It seems odd at first sight that one should even associate Critical Theory with the ideas of Friedrich Nietzsche as he is often described as an originator of existentialist thought, something for which Horkheimer et al. expressed no sympathy. Yet, as Putz (1981) points out, they had a sneaking admiration for him even if they did not refer directly to his work much[8]. Nietzsche is a philosopher famous for the saying, 'God is dead', by which he meant that our deepest sense that life is underpinned by some metaphysical purpose, that there is some reason for our being, has gone. The modern western world's claim to have had *the* Enlightenment, to value reason and objectivity, are misplaced pretensions, and really expressions of a 'will to power', a way of rationalising an unjustified claim to superiority and of enforcing its view of things. All the values we take to be naturally true, right and good, he argued, were really the result of our imposing them on an essentially meaninglessness world, and any claims we make that they spring from another source, were illusions. In recent times, Michel Foucault's (1979) genealogical approach to tracing the emergence of the human subject can be seen to reflect the influence of one of Nietzsche's most famous books, *The Genealogy of Morals*[9]. Genealogy is a way of explaining things in terms of a system of descent, like a family tree. Morality, Nietzsche argued, did not refer to what is inherently good or evil, something God-given, but is the description of a family tree of moral claims. In modern parlance, morality is a social construction and has a history that clearly shows the imprint of the dominant social forces that produced it.

It was Nietzsche's unrelenting iconoclasm that touched a crucial nerve in Critical Theorists, for they too found themselves disenchanted with the western world's implicit pretensions to progress. They too had come to feel that the process of rationalisation, to which Max Weber had drawn attention, realised not reason, but a distortion of it. In each of the areas of research Horkheimer had seen as holding out the possibility for social progress, he and his colleagues now sensed a deep malaise. Such was the level of their disquiet, that at times it cast doubt on the very nature of western reason as being reason at all, and led them to challenge its validity, both substantively and stylistically.

If the Lukacsian impulse in Critical Theory was towards dialectical unity, the identity of subject and object and the proletariat as the universal class that would bring this into being, then the Nietzschean impulse ran fiercely in the opposite direction. This counter tendency emphasised that the totality was to be conceived as fragmented and beyond any redemptive effort we might make to conceive it as a whole with a progressive purpose written into it. History was going nowhere, except to the bad. As Adorno sarcastically remarked, human progress does indeed have a history, it is one that has moved 'from the slingshot to the megaton bomb!'

For Adorno, particularly, the totality was to be conceived as a fragmented and disharmonious force field, something reflected in his terse, aphoristic style of writing. Anything too systematic or smooth was to be regarded with suspicion, as reflecting the false harmonies emanating from society. Indeed, Adorno finally came up with the curt *anti*-Lukacsian adage that 'the whole is the untrue'. By this he meant that the forces of 'administration' and 'commodification' were embracing society as a whole, not for the purpose of opening up its real progressive potential, but for the manipulative purpose of controlling and diverting that potential into a reinforcement of the status quo. Thus Critical Theory, to be rational, would now have to bracket off the totality and dwell not on the general, but on the particular and the contingent. It would have to speak up for the individual in an age of rampant, but quite spurious individualism and it would have to speak, in some degree, with an anti-rationalist voice.

There was no ultimate identity between subject and object and, for Adorno, *non*identity became the watchword. Dialectical method for him became 'negative dialectics', with an emphasis on the separateness of subject and object. Critical Theory's earlier more affirmative notion of critique involved the idea of dialectically comparing what is actually the case (for example, justice), with what the concept of justice suggests, and thereby indicating how praxis might render the world more rational by bringing concept and object closer together. For Adorno, by the early 1940s, the very idea of unifying social objects with concepts had a totalitarian ring to it. In practical terms it could (and sometimes did) mean that the powerful could subsume social objects under the concepts they chose, they could make people obedient to the way they conceived the world. Adorno certainly did not renounce dialectics but became ever more astringent in the way he used it. Subject and object may presuppose one another, but had to be kept naggingly at odds if reason was to have the ghost of a chance.

Like Nietzsche, Critical Theorists had become sceptical of reason itself, or at least of reason in the western tradition. Everywhere it seemed to them reason only showed its instrumental face, producing a manic desire to control nature, especially human nature. Indeed, the central theme of Adorno and Horkheimer's *Dialectic of Enlightenment* is that every iota of human progress, by virtue of its instrumental orientation, amounts to no more than an iota of repression, entailing ever increasing levels of manipulation, both of others and oneself.

In its latter stages, then, first generation Critical Theory pitched its intellectual forces against the growing 'false totality', stressing negative, critical thought wherever it might be found. This outlook persisted through the 1950s. However, from the mid 1960s onwards a new generation emerged, largely influenced by the work of Jürgen Habermas. Though originally Habermas was Adorno's student, his work diverged quite sharply in character from that of the older generation. The task Habermas set himself was to break out of the theoretical cul-de-sac that, as he saw it, had stifled his predecessors' efforts to such an extent that in the end they could perceive no positive virtues in modernity at all.

Summary and Conclusion

For first generation Critical Theorists there was a gradual shift from a relatively optimistic start to a thoroughgoing pessimism by the 1960s. The pessimism sprang from a belief that the naturally unstable nature of capitalism had been overcome by the development of a one-dimensional society and the increasing impossibility of emancipation. This one-dimensionality was expressed in the three areas of research Horkheimer originally earmarked for analysis: political and economic organisation, social psychology and culture.

In the area of political economy, Frederick Pollock argued that not only had government intervention stabilised capitalist markets, but that large organisations, including trade unions, now cultivated a new style of pliable personality, one that we could call the 'organisation man', one that was amenable to the emergence of a wholly administered society. In terms of psychology, Eric Fromm tried to link a dialectical view of political economy with a Freudian view of the unconscious to show how the subject developed a deep attachment to modern society in spite of its exploitative nature. However, far from showing a way out of this impasse his emphasis on the implacability of both material forces and instinctive forces similarly fuelled Critical Theory's pessimism. In the area of culture Adorno's analyses echoed the same theme, seeing the products of the 'culture industry' as a tool to stupefy the masses, a source of spurious excitement that served only to pacify people.

It should not be overlooked that in each of the areas there were important counter currents that suggested a less pessimistic scenario, nevertheless the general tendency was towards a bleak view of the future. The disenchantment felt by Critical Theorists was expressed in, what I have called a Nietzschean streak, in their writing, which gradually revealed their disillusionment, not just with the specifics of modern society, but with whole idea of western reason. Although I believe there is still much to be learnt from first generation Critical Theory, it was against this train of thought that Habermas from the mid 1960s sought to reconstruct the tradition, something to which I turn in the next chapter.

Further Reading

Arato's and Gebhardt's *The Essential Frankfurt School Reader* (1978) and Bronner's and Kellner's *Critical Theory and Society: A Reader* (1989) contain most of the essays referred to in this chapter by Pollock, Horkheimer, Neumann, Fromm and Adorno. None of the essays make easy reading, but Arato and Gebhardt provide useful introductions to the various contributions. A more detailed account of the Pollock-Neumann debate can be found in David Held's *Introduction to Critical Theory: Horkheimer to Habermas* (1980). An interesting defence of Veblen, contra-Critical Theory, can be found in Tilman (1999). For a good text-based defence of the idea that Adorno was not flatly pessimistic in his critique of mass culture see Cook D., *The Culture Industry Revisited: Theodor Adorno on Mass Culture* (1996), especially Chapter 6.

4

The Reconstruction of Critical Theory: From Ideology Critique to Communicative Reason

In this chapter I want to explore the way in which Jürgen Habermas, since the mid 1960s, has sought to reconstruct Critical Theory along lines that overcome the pessimism and contradictoriness of his predecessors' work. After the Second World War, in 1950, Horkheimer revived the Institute for Social Research fairly successfully though ties were broken with Neumann and Kircheimer, and Fromm, and Marcuse settled in America. However, the broader dilemmas underpinning its existence were not resolved, but came more sharply into focus. The contradiction between its early Marxist optimism and its later 'Nietzschean' pessimism remained, and its relation to wider German society also became rather odd. Increasingly, the Institute found itself seeking funds from any quarter it could, and identified itself as part of the renewal of German capitalism. Whether one takes the early Marxist version, or the later 'Nietzschean' one to be the real Critical Theory, neither model lends itself, in an obvious way, to being a vehicle for commercial or state sponsorship. Yet this was the official direction in which Horkheimer, perhaps inevitably, led the Institute. Wiggerhaus (1994: ch. 6), rather unkindly I think, describes the Institute's position in the early 1950s as the 'Critical Ornament of a Restoration Society'.

In intellectual terms in the early 1960s, the most successful work was, arguably, Adorno's, in the areas of philosophy and aesthetic theory, but this was not concerned with the empirical condition of German society (Adorno 1973b, 1984). It was the drift apart between the wider potential of the Critical Theory tradition and the personal needs of its main protagonists to pursue their own intellectual pathways that left a vacuum into which Jürgen Habermas pitched his ideas. Although Habermas had been Adorno's assistant and *Habilitation*[10] student, his work was gradually seen to diverge in significant ways from that of his teacher and the rest of the older generation, even to the point where it was doubted whether the term 'Critical Theory' should apply to both.

Habermas has certainly carved out an intellectual terrain all of his own. His work is extraordinarily extensive, and the sub-literature that surrounds it almost an academic industry in its own right. Nevertheless, his desire to establish a supra-disciplinary theory of society, his effort to discern the nature of reason as a context for more rational forms of praxis, and his effort to justify critique, all bear the hallmarks of Critical Theory, even if the pathway he has chosen is quite different from that of his predecessors. Plainly, Habermas is a rationalist, he believes that the world can be made a better place by bringing out the 'reason' in it.

A major part of his task has been to discover the different forms reason takes, and to see how aptly these forms relate to different areas of life. A primary claim of first generation Critical Theory had been that the contours of a more rational society could, with dialectical effort, be discerned in the interstices of existing society. However, latterly their substantive writings denied this possibility, confirming ever more gloomily that reason was a flickering flame soon to be doused in a cloud of irrationality. Society, as it were, was closing down, becoming one-dimensional, such that by the late 1930s there seemed to be no immanent forces working *for* reason. Yet Horkheimer's Critical Theory was harnessed to the very possibility that Reason *would* come to fruition in society. At the heart of Habermas's critique of his predecessors, then, was awareness that these two contradictory principles were at work in the same theory and a radical reconstruction was needed.

Habermas and the 'Performative Contradiction': A Short Excursus

Habermas's emphasis on the self-contradictions of a theory illustrates one of the major argumentative strategies he uses to tease out the limits of any theory. His concern is often with what he calls a 'performative contradiction', which is somewhat similar to what is usually meant by the term 'logical contradiction', but is oriented in a rather different way. A 'logical contradiction' refers to two propositions that mean the opposite of each other, such that both cannot be true at the same time; it is a conflictive relation between two ideas. A 'performative contradiction', on the other hand, refers to a conflict between the ostensive claim made in a statement and the *way* in which the claim is made. A performative contradiction runs counter to the communicative intent of the claim. At an individual level it bears a certain resemblance to something R. D. Laing, in his psychiatric work, referred to as a 'double-bind'. Laing cites the example of a small boy who is invited by his mother to kiss her good-bye, but when he does she quickly turns away showing no physical affection in return. Thus, the (communicative) intent of the mother's claim is undermined by the insincere way she performs it.

A recent academic example of 'performative contradiction' can be found in Habermas's critique of Michel Foucault. In *Discipline and Punish* (1979), Foucault describes two historical regimes of power epitomised by different styles of punishment. One is exemplified by the exercise of physical retribution, hanging, drawing and quartering: the other, later form, by imprisonment. Foucault's point is that these two regimes exist self-sufficiently in their own right, and we should not assume that the latter regime is more humane and civilised than the former, as there are no supra-historical ways of judging this; both are an expression of the context in which they are found. For Habermas, Foucault's account entails a performative contradiction, as all communication entails evaluation too. Foucault denies there are any supra-historical ways of judging one regime to be better or worse than another, but at the same time clearly wants to burst his reader's normative bubble, a bubble that is likely to assume that imprisonment is a more humane form of justice than bloody retribution. The claim that these regimes cannot be judged as better or worse, but must be accepted only as different, is undermined by Foucault's desire to expose the myth that in the modern world we are more civilised than our forebears. Foucault is (inevitably) evaluating things but trying to conceal his evaluative intentions. For Habermas, communicative reason requires Foucault to justify his evaluative judgments. It is this notion of performative contradiction that Habermas applies to earlier Critical Theory.

Making the Break

Although Habermas, in his inaugural lecture at Frankfurt University in 1966 (1971b: appendix), made reference to Horkheimer, signaling that his project was going to be different, it was only later that the meaning of these differences became clear. Indeed, Habermas in interview has declared that when he arrived as an associate with the Institute in 1955, 'there was no Critical Theory, no coherent doctrine'. In fact, Horkheimer deliberately kept the pre-war editions of the Institute's journal locked in the cellar, and it was 'only when some clever people in the late 1960s discovered Critical Theory' that it became clear 'a theory of society should be systematic' (Dews 1986: 97, Wiggerhaus 1994: 544)[11]. Thus, there was no simple overcoming of earlier problems, it was only in retrospect that Habermas recognised these problems *as* problems, for which his work might provide solutions. The idea of a performative contradiction in fact depends on his theory of communicative rationality that was only developed during the 1970s, and came to fruition in the early 1980s with the appearance of the two volumes of *The Theory of Communicative Action* (Habermas 1984, 1987a). In a section at the end of the second volume, Habermas sets out 'The Tasks of a Critical Theory', where he formally marks off his project from that of Horkheimer, Adorno and Marcuse, not just as different, but as a theoretical advance that overcomes their limitations (1987a: 378ff).

Habermas's Critique

Habermas's critique of first generation Critical Theory takes different forms and is found in different places (Habermas 1984: ch. IV, section 2, 1987a: ch. VIII, section 3, 1987b: ch. V). In some respects, the whole of his work can be seen as a response to, and reconstruction of, the tradition, so I shall draw from it in ways that aim at clarification, rather than slavishly following the references above. I shall also draw on Axel Honneth's work (1987, 1993) for, although he can be thought of as part of a possible third generation, his critique of the first largely follows and amplifies Habermas's own.

There are three elements to Habermas's critique: (a) 'normative foundations', (b) the 'concept of truth and its relation to science', and (c) 'the undervaluation of democracy and the constitutional state' (Habermas in Dews 1986: 97).

Normative Foundations

The idea of normative foundations refers to the grounds or underlying justification for early Critical Theory's view of things. Habermas, of course, shares with the first generation the recognition that critique needs to be justified; it must be more than mere criticism if it is to be thought reasonable. The flaw in the earlier position, as he sees it, is that its normative foundations are too firmly embedded in Hegel and Marx. Despite the desire to reverse Marxism away from dogmatic economic-determinism and reorientate it along dialectical, and interdisciplinary lines, first generation Critical Theorists were unable to extricate themselves from the implications of Marx's philosophy of history. Their Marxism always worked on the basis that history was an unfolding process, through which the industrial proletariat would be the social class that finally brought into being a truly rational society. Once this assumption becomes problematic, then the whole raison d'être for their critique becomes doubtful.

However, for Habermas and Honneth, the fact that the Western working class had turned its back on Marxism, was only the tip of a more radically misconceived iceberg. Marx had conceived the social development of the human species along the same instrumental lines as the development of its capacity to control nature. Human reason, for Marx, was essentially the same whether it was directed towards physical survival or social relations. It involved subjects coming to grasp objects in an ever more thoroughgoing way. The priority of the subject–object relation is a characteristic of what Habermas calls the modern 'philosophy of consciousness', or 'philosophy of the subject'; an outlook which sees the world as fundamentally made up of subjects facing a world of external objects. Once this (ontological) assumption is made, then invariably the (epistemological) relation between subject and object becomes an instrumental one. Because, as it were, we are up against the world, we see it as external to us, and our knowledge of it becomes geared to learning how best we can manipulate it to our advantage.

The huge success of the natural sciences in modern times is based on a capacity to distil the subject–object relationship, and purify it of extraneous values, so that the scientist can see the 'object' in a disinterested, purely observational way – the better to manipulate it. For the social sciences this is problematic. In sociology, Max Weber is well known for the tortuous efforts he put into reconceiving the subject–object relation, so as to acknowledge that there is also a relationship *between subjects*, a distinctive area of 'meaning', which had to be incorporated into sociological explanation. But, more broadly, Weber recognised that beyond the practice of science, western reason itself was being reduced to its instrumental core. The very process of modern rationalization, Weber claimed, entailed sloughing off value-rational residues in the name of the manipulative virtues of purposive-rational, or technical reason (Zweckrationalität). Reason had become just a matter of finding the most technically effective means of achieving a given end. The reasonableness of ends in themselves fell outside what reason could judge; it became a matter of arbitrary choice.

Horkheimer's and Adorno's concept of instrumental reason is, in effect, a revision of Weber's concept of purposive-rational action, but for them it is a concept imbued with the bitter sense that we are being led, not towards a more rational world, but back to an irrational one. It is their commitment to this idea, bolstered by Marx's philosophy of history that places first generation Critical Theory in an impasse: to go forwards with (instrumental) reason means to go backwards with human emancipation. They want to make the world a more rational place through critique, but reason, the normative tool they would employ, has become an instrument of repression. To escape the predicament, Habermas knows he has to take a step back and reconstruct the normative foundations of Critical Theory from the ground up.

Horkheimer certainly recognised *some* difference between the instrumental logic of labour and the critical activity necessary for social change, but could not see the radical distinctions that characterise the two areas. He did not possess the concepts that would have enabled him to grasp the real differences between the instrumental logic of technical progress, and the emancipatory logic of social progress. He, along with Adorno and Marcuse, came to assume that the instrumental version of reason was the whole of reason, at least in the modern world. They were not happy about this state of affairs, and much of their work is riven through with a bitter critique of it. Adorno and Marcuse still found in Art the remains of another, non-instrumental sensibility, but they were under no illusions about its wider significance or influence, nor its vulnerability to the pervasive effects of instrumental reason (Marcuse 1979, 1994: 228ff, Adorno 1989). Horkheimer too recognised the impasse of modern reason, but felt unable to follow Adorno or Marcuse down their alternative route of seeking some redemptive quality in Art, something which Habermas (1993a: 61–77) believes accounts for the decline in the volume and creativity of his writing in the 1950s and 1960s.

Horkheimer's original programme for Critical Theory with its emphasis on transdisciplinarity, dialectical processes, and so forth, certainly challenged the reductionism of much contemporary Marxism, but never broke sufficiently with it to explore the 'critical activity' that might underpin emancipation. Reason was always implicitly conceived in instrumental terms, and social action, wherever it happened in society, was correspondingly the result of a nexus of causal connections. For all the abrasiveness they expressed towards the growing instrumentality of modern life, Horkheimer, Adorno and Marcuse failed to open up the wider interpretive reality of everyday life. As Honneth (1993: 17) remarks:

> Despite his epistemological definition of critical theory, he does not seriously treat the dimension of action present in social struggle as an autonomous sphere of social reproduction. But, for that reason, Horkheimer gives up the possibility of considering sufficiently the interpretive organisation of social reality.

What in essence Horkheimer et al. lack, are the sociological concepts of 'action' and 'interaction' that originate with authors such as George Herbert Mead and Max Weber, for these concepts would have enabled them to see more clearly what was going on in the sphere of everyday life. The creative accomplishments of actors were effectively squeezed out of sight, and in the end viewed only as a function of the closed circuits of a pervasive system of domination. Action, for the first generation, Honneth argues, became merely 'functional' behaviour, something derivable from first principles of a Marxian philosophy of history. There were countercurrents, in the sphere of culture analysis. Walter Benjamin challenged Adorno's view that mass culture was nought but manipulation, arguing instead that it had the potential to innovate new collective perceptions (see ch. 5). In the sphere of social psychology, Eric Fromm's (later) work pointed to the importance of conscious interaction, as much as to the force of instinct, as a determinant of social life. But these more open textured countercurrents did not hold centre stage, and they did not convince Horkheimer, Adorno and Marcuse.

When Habermas first met Adorno in the mid 1950s, he was impressed by the way he applied Marx and Freud so directly and effectively to modern society, without reference to the countless revisions their work had undergone; it was as though Marx and Freud were speaking now. But he also noted that there was little sense that other traditions of thought had developed and might provide the conceptual resources to lead Critical Theory out of its theoretical cul-de-sac. Almost directly in response to this, Habermas has voraciously pursued ideas from whatever source seems most productive. The language philosophy of Wittgenstein, Gadamer's hermeneutics, Talcott Parsons's systems theory, the cognitive and moral psychology of Piaget and Kohlberg have all provided grist for his intellectual mill. At one stage he described his approach as a 'hermeneutically informed functionalism', something that would certainly not have been countenanced by first generation Critical Theory.

Habermas's work is voluminous, stretching fresco-like across a range of areas. However, central to his project is the desire to make up the 'intersubjective deficit' of his predecessors. Where they saw everyday life (unhappily) through the instrumental lens of subject-object rationality, with all the deleterious effects this has on human progress, he claims that this is only part of the story. Another significant side to reason is its communicative, intersubjective quality. Of course, Habermas was never simply going to convert to 'interactionism', it was the *theoretical rationale* inherent in everyday communication that interested him. For Habermas, *communicative* action stands in contrast to *instrumental* action as something that is oriented towards reaching mutual agreement, rather than instrumental intervention in the social or physical world. As such, the rationale for communicative action provides a means of challenging the predominance of the instrumental form that so undermined the hopes of Horkheimer, Adorno and Marcuse.

Communicative action is not something we do occasionally, but something tied in to the human condition. Human beings always find themselves communicatively united with others through the language they use. Language provides the communicative scaffolding that underpins the common features of our 'world', enabling us to actively reach agreement with others. In fact, it is the telos or purpose of language to reach agreement, because when we use it we are always implicitly asking others to see the world as we do, something they may or may not do. Language gives us a distance from things, it allows a hearer to take up either a 'yes' or a 'no' attitude to what a speaker says. As a result, if the hearer disagrees, the speaker must provide further 'evidence' to convince them that their view is right. The reciprocal nature of these requirements means that the potential for human consensus is built into communicative action.

Much of Habermas's work from the mid 1970s onwards has been concerned with describing the wider structures of communicative action and the nature of communicative rationality in general, and these have become the normative foundations for his reconstructed Critical Theory. He characterises these structures as 'necessary presuppositions' or sometimes 'idealisations', the factors that we always presuppose in every actual communication, even if they are not fully realised in any communication. In his early work, for example, he used the term, 'ideal speech situation', to refer to the idea that the reciprocal quality of linguistic communication, in principle, presupposes that all parties have equal opportunity to engage in the dialogue, without restriction or ideological pressure from the outside and that only the force of the better argument should hold sway. He extends and elaborates these kinds of pre-supposition in his later work to show how the same dialogic principles at the heart of communicative action also provide the ground to justify democracy and ethics.

The consensual, intersubjective nature of communicative rationality thus not only serves as a bulwark against the destructiveness of instrumental reason, but also as a normative benchmark for his new version of Critical Theory. The task of Critical Theory for Habermas becomes one of reconstructing models of various human competencies, including communicative competence, and comparing the ideal-type with what actually happens in society. Rather baldly stated, the closer what actually happens in society is to the ideal, the more rational a society can claim to be. It is the act of comparing and evaluating what is, with what in an ideal situation it would be, that keeps the 'critical' in Critical Theory alive and kicking.

Interestingly, the business of comparing what is, with what it would be in an ideal situation echoes the early dialectical ambitions of Horkheimer's project, but with one important difference. Habermas describes the structures of our communicative capacities as 'species-wide competences', as something *all* ordinary language users possess. Thus, on his account of Critical Theory one does not have to search for elusive, (even metaphysical), historical forces, such as the proletariat, to bring a more rational society into being, because, in a sense, (communicative) reason is always in being. Of course, whether the structural presuppositions of communication are as universal as Habermas contends, is difficult to assess. It can be argued that the characteristics of communication that Habermas dwells on, reciprocity, equality of communicative opportunity, and so forth, are most highly developed in western societies, where for historical reasons such things have been put centre-stage (Benhabib 1992: 26–38, Cook, M. 1994: ch. 2). However, Habermas's claim is that all social relations presuppose some level of communicative agreement, and anyway, in western societies, such agreement still only exists in an undeveloped form, distorted by external factors. If this all seems rather abstract, and Habermas is often accused of being too abstract, he is unrepentant, believing that one has to become *more* abstract to find what is universal to the social world.

While communicative rationality provided Habermas with a new normative foundation for Critical Theory, the implications of breaking with the Hegel-Marx legacy of the first generation were felt elsewhere too, notably in the area of the relation between science and philosophical truth.

'Truth and its Relation to Science'

Where Adorno, Horkheimer and Marcuse in different degrees took the Hegelian view that Reason was essentially a 'total' dialectical process that revealed itself through history, Habermas has not accepted that view. He uses dialectical elements in his arguments and, while endeavouring to grasp the nature of reason as a whole, echoes more the philosophical legacy of Kant, with its emphasis on the distinctiveness of different categories of knowledge, and how they relate to different regions of life.

The pessimism of the first generation came to seem total because, for them, Reason had in effect become Unreason. Habermas was never happy with this diagnosis, feeling that part of the problem lay in the fact that they used an undifferentiated concept of reason, such that when part of reason became unreasonable, the whole lot went with it.

He felt there was something awkward in the way his predecessors' Hegelian way of thinking, implicitly rejected scientific truth. Certainly, he shared their doubts about the negative effects of instrumental reason, and the way it has come to predominate in modern life, but was keen to distinguish the ideological form it took (positivism), from the legitimate claims of science. In the essay, 'Technology and Science as "Ideology"' (1971a: ch. 6), he mapped out a critique of the way Marcuse used Weber's concept of 'rationalization' to reveal it as a process of 'unacknowledged political domination'. Marcuse, following the logic of his own case, is forced to argue that science and technology, being the epitome of 'rationalised' thinking, are also intrinsically manipulative, their telos is not emancipation, but domination; domination of nature and people. Thus, Marcuse, in order to even conceive of an emancipated world, has in a sense to 'deny' science, and anticipate the possibility of a different, 'new' science, one that seeks a more fraternal, less manipulative relationship with nature that will serve the goal of emancipation.

In contrast, Habermas believes that the achievements of science and technology are now indispensable and cannot be substituted by a relationship with an 'awakened nature'. Even if we can imagine human beings having a more intimate partnership with nature, and even if we regard science and technology as a particular kind of historical project, one that emerged in the capitalist West, it will not undo the fact that science and technology *have* grown up in certain way and modern societies depend upon technical control in a way that cannot be unraveled. In short, our relationship to nature is now inevitably instrumental. However, for Habermas this should not be read 'pessimistically', for if we understand reason in a more differentiated ways we can see that an interest in control represents only one part of it.

In the appendix to *Knowledge and Human Interests* (1971b) he set out the idea that different kinds of knowledge have different kinds of cognitive interest built into them. By 'interest' he does not mean that knowledge serves the interests of particular individuals or groups, but that knowledge, how we 'cognize' or know things, itself is oriented in certain ways to produce certain kinds of truth. What lay behind this idea was a challenge to the (then) predominant positivist claim that true knowledge could only be of one kind, *disinterested*, scientific knowledge. Habermas argued that there were three interrelated, but separate 'knowledge-constitutive interests'. (Habermas 1971b: 308–15).

(1) Empirical-analytic knowledge, characteristic of natural science, is not disinterested, but has an interest in the control of nature, and when employed by the social sciences, of the social world too. Even if the intention of the natural scientist is only one of discovery and the work has no obvious application, its framework is still geared towards explaining things in terms of invariant causes and effects, which implies the possibility of control. Theory, in this area, requires that key propositions have to be chosen on the basis that they can be tested in a hypothetico-deductive way to see how well they express a law-like relationship. The truth of theory, here, is measured in terms of the technical effectiveness of the operations the scientist brings to bear. Habermas did not denigrate this form of knowledge, but recognised that it permits certain things while excluding others. A quite different, but equally important form of knowledge is that produced by the historical-hermeneutic sciences[12].

(2) Historical-hermeneutic knowledge, characteristic of humanities disciplines, is concerned with interpretation, especially of texts. Unlike empirical-analytic knowledge, it regards facts, not as observational data, but as sources of meaning. Its theories are 'not constructed deductively, and experience is not organised with regard to the success of operations'. Theory is located at the intersection between the horizons of the 'text' and interpreter. The outlook is governed by an interest in 'the preservation and expansion of the intersubjectivity of possible action-orienting mutual understanding' (p. 310). Habermas calls this a practical interest. He means that these disciplines have an interest in clarifying and enriching the meaning-horizon in which action, or life-practice, takes place. Horizons of meaning are to be understood as deriving from historical tradition. However, the *practical* interest, like the interest in *technical control*, excludes important elements. In fact it excludes the very things that the empirical-analytic outlook grasps, which is the way causal factors impact on things. Thus, Habermas proposes a third knowledge-constitutive interest, an *emancipatory* interest.

(3) In effect, the emancipatory interest compensates for the deficiencies of the other two and represents Habermas's first attempt to deal with the same deep-seated connection his predecessors felt existed between reason and freedom. He intends this cognitive interest to become the basis of his version of Critical Theory. The cognitive interest in technical control may be capable of low level prediction in the social world, (for example, behaviourism), but this is more or less fortuitous in that the wider horizon in which the meaning of action is embedded, is absent. As it were, only half the picture is present. Similarly, the practical interest is limited because it fails to recognize the way external conditions impress themselves upon the meaning of actors' life-practice (praxis), perhaps as ideology. To deal adequately with this, the prac-

tical interest must be supplemented with a more causal kind of explanation, which is precisely what the cognitive interest in control is best at providing. In effect, the emancipatory interest that will guide Critical Theory seeks to dialectically combine in a more *reflective* way the complementary virtues of the two other interests.

There was, and I think still is, a certain ambiguity in the status Habermas attributed to these interests. Clearly what he is criticising is the *un*reflective nature of positivism, whose failure is to imagine that it is disinterestedly perceiving reality directly, when in fact its cognitive interest organises reality according to the principle of technical control. What Habermas emphasises is that knowledge is a 'synthetic' accomplishment; it presupposes the intervention of our concepts in the process of eliciting it. However, equally he is not claiming that these knowledge-constitutive interests are accidental, or merely the product of historical conditions that may change. They are, 'anthropologically deep-seated', or 'quasi-transcendental'. In other words they are not ephemeral conditions, but seem almost to be given with our perception of reality. Certainly, Outhwaite (1987: 79–91) draws Habermas towards the 'realist' camp in social philosophy, which similarly acknowledges the intervention of concepts in the constitution of knowledge, but equally refuses to accept that knowledge is merely relative to them. It should also be noted that while Habermas, unlike the realists, has always refused to consider issues of social ontology as such (that is, what the fundamental nature of social being is like), preferring to see the human world more as an unfolding process, he still shares with them a commitment to the idea that the social world is made up of two (ontologically) distinct but related levels: system and lifeworld.

From the early 1970s, Habermas's epistemological concerns with truth and its relation to science shifted towards social theory, from a concern with how we know things to a concern with how society works, or with the nature of social action. However, one of the remaining effects of the debates he had at the time was to reconsider the status of the emancipatory interest, from which developed his theory of *communication*, and the broad methodological outlook that currently underpins his Critical Theory as a *reconstructive* science.

He had originally tended to assume that emancipation was a fairly unproblematic category, and that at least in theory it flowed from bringing the technical and the practical interest together under the one roof of Critical Theory. However, the *reflective* qualities he attributed to the emancipatory interest were found to be more complex than he first thought. In *Knowledge and Human Interests* (1971b) he had identified Freud's psychoanalytic method as a model of an emancipatory science. The analyst has to embrace the hermeneutic horizon of the patient in a spirit of reciprocal understanding and avoid the blind, impositional habits of mind of the technical interest in control. At the same time, the analyst brings elements of Freud's theory into the picture as explanatory devices that go beyond the existing self-understanding of the patient. The emancipatory interest is realised to the extent that the patient can, with reflective effort, recognise themselves in the account that has been reciprocally produced, and be able to dissolve the oppressive character of their psychological situation.

Problems arose with this model when Habermas suggested that it would serve as a template for his Critical Theory, which would become a sort of 'socioanalysis'. It is one thing for an analyst and a willing patient to have a mutual interest in resolving problems, quite another when one tries to apply the idea of 'mutual interest' to society as a whole. One cannot assume that society is made up of 'mutual interests', let alone that those who benefit most from its unequal conditions would willingly engage in dialogue to change them. As a result of these kinds of criticism, Habermas made a distinction between self-reflection, and theoretical reflection, the latter producing what he calls 'rational reconstructions'.

Self-reflection is a process of bringing something unconscious, or ideological, into consciousness; in effect what is often called 'consciousness-raising'. Consciousness-raising has direct implications for life-practice, in that one would likely act differently having undergone it. Theoretical reflection, on the other hand, is something different. It is concerned with reflecting on the very conditions of knowledge itself, and thus has only an indirect implication for life-practice. Such reflection cannot specify what should or ought to be done, but details the conditions or presuppositions of what ultimately shapes different areas where the decisions about what should or ought to be done are made.

The latter form of reflection has become the mainstay of what Habermas terms 'reconstructive science', something with which he identified Critical Theory. The purpose of a reconstructive science is to reflect theoretically on the implicit structural rules underpinning different human productions. For example, Noam Chomsky has reconstructed the underlying grammar of language in general, and Jean Piaget has done the same with the structures of human cognition. Habermas's own 'universal pragmatics', developed in the 1970s, represents his attempt to reconstruct the structural detail of communicative action. The detail of Habermas's 'universal pragmatics' matter less here than the fact that he conceives Critical Theory as a reconstructive science, which is something markedly different from that of his predecessors. It acknowledges the importance of both the empirical-analytic and the hermeneutic disciplines, but develops a social scientific alternative to both.

The Undervaluation of Democracy and the Constitutional State

As part of their general pessimism over the negative effects of instrumental reason, Horkheimer, Adorno and Marcuse also had a more or less disparaging view of modern democracy and the constitutional state. They came to regard them as mere vehicles of expanding social control, and thereby no more than purveyors of instrumental reason. Habermas, since his earliest publications, has argued to the contrary, that in spite of all its limitations the modern 'democratic' state contains the germ of what a rational society should be like.

In one of his earliest books, *The Structural Transformation of the Public Sphere* (1989 [1962]), Habermas implicitly challenged the negativity of first generation Critical Theory towards the modern democratic state. He argued that the public sphere, which grew up in seventeenth- and eighteenth century Europe within the framework of a modern class-divided bourgeois society, nevertheless contained the germ of something more equitable and rational. In the seventeenth century the idea of the public sphere referred to matters dealt with by the royal court and the state, not by the people at large. By the eighteenth century there had been a shift, originating in the literary salons and coffee houses of the time. In England, Germany and France, private 'bourgeois' citizens, supported by print technology could engage with each other in matters of cultural concern. Such issues of course eventually made inroads into matters not just of cultural, but wider public concern, such as politics, even though representatives of fairly privileged groups peopled it. The public sphere had three distinct characteristics.

First, discourse in the public sphere disregarded the status of those involved. While it did not celebrate an equality of citizenship as such, it did bracket off external factors so that it was the force of the better argument that was supposed to hold sway. Secondly, discussion in the public sphere problematised issues, which up till then had been the interpretative monopoly of Church and state. As part of an emerging market economy, the increasing publication of literary and philosophical works, produced for, and distributed by the market, had a salutary effect; it made their content *accessible*. In an argument reminiscent of Walter Benjamin's on mass culture (see ch. 5), Habermas points out that even limited mass production of these works had a demythologising and democratising effect.

> They no longer remained components of the Church's and court's publicity of representation; that is precisely what is meant by their loss of aura, of extraordinariness, and by the profaning of their once sacramental character. The private people for whom the cultural product became available as a commodity profaned it inasmuch as they had to determine its meaning on their own (by way of rational communication with one another), verbalize it, and thus state explicitly what precisely in its implicitness for so long could assert its authority. (Habermas 1989: 36–7)

Thirdly, the 'same process that converted culture into a commodity' also underpinned its *in*clusiveness. However much the public sphere was actually exclusive, in the sense that it was peopled by certain (literate) sections of the population, it could not turn itself into a clique. In principle, it was always immersed in issues that were *general* in that they bore on all private people, and all private people might (one day) avail themselves of the necessary cultural commodities. Habermas is emphasising that the emerging public sphere, while empirically limited, was in the way it discussed matters aware of being an expression of the public at large. In effect, one could say that Habermas was talking about something like the 'ideal speech situation' emerging in history, long before he conceived of it in theoretical terms.

It has to be said, at this point, that Habermas is still working within the broad Hegelian-Marxist framework of his predecessors and sees reason as a potentiality unfolding through history. The last section of the book in fact shares a deal of their pessimism about the contemporary world, in that the public sphere, he argues, has become increasingly subject to the effects of the mass media. Communication in the public sphere is now structured by the mass media, and thereby shaped by the demands of advertising and public relations. However, Habermas's point is that the public sphere, with its rational-communicative potential, *has* emerged, and in spite of all the factors that distort this potential, offers an arena in which the rationality of society can be thought, considered, and discussed. In effect it is an arena with the potential for immanent critique. It is a measure of how far Horkheimer and Adorno had lost faith in the original Critical Theory programme of immanent critique, in that when *The Structural Transformation of the Public Sphere* was submitted to them, as Habermas's *Habilitation* thesis, they found it too uncritical of the Enlightenment conception of democratic public life, but also oddly too radical in its challenge to existing conceptions of public life (see Calhoun 1992: 4).

Summary and Conclusion to Part 1

In Part 1 I have presented an account of the broad contours of Critical Theory's development, the purpose of which was to capture some of the shifts and tensions in the tradition, to show that it is not a set of fixed truisms, but an ongoing search for a more adequate diagnosis of the times. Horkheimer's early theoretical ideas were based on dialectical principles that would capture the interelatedness of phenomena and reveal the tendencies inherent in history that were leading to a more rational future. However, the phenomena that were analysed did not reveal possibilities for a more rational future, but a growing irrationalism, a tendency towards a 'wholly administered' society where subjects were held economically, psychologically and culturally in thrall. Against the pessimism and contradictoriness of these conclusions Habermas has developed an alternative version of Critical Theory based on communicative rationality. On his account, because humans are language users, and because language is oriented towards common agreement, there always exists the possibility of making reason work, and generating that elusive rational society.

There is an ever present danger when you recount a tradition of thought, of unwittingly rounding up loose ends, the better to render the whole thing more coherent for the reader; something certainly out of tune with the spirit of Critical Theory. For example, the changes wrought by Habermas, described above, are themselves often taken to be a clear improvement on the work of the first generation. However, while Habermas as a theorist is encyclopedically well read as well as immensely rigorous and ambitious in his theorising, none of this makes him *necessarily* right.

In order to surpass the 'philosophy of consciousness', and overcome the instrumental implications of the subject–object relationship, Habermas developed a theory of communicative action based on the primacy of *inter*subjectivity. Yet, arguably, there are losses here, as well as gains. Adorno, Marcuse and Horkheimer all had an acute sense of how the human subject is pulled hither and thither by changes in the organisation of capitalism, even to the point where pessimism got the better of them, and, as they saw it, the subject was virtually overtaken by the system. The work of Freud was important to all three, in that it gave them critical purchase on these processes, and a sense of what was being lost via them. Both Craib (1989) and Whitebook (1995, 1996), point up the value of the first generation's use of psychoanalytic concepts, their holding on to the awkward, perverse nature of the unconscious. The unconscious, particularly for Marcuse in *Eros and Civilisation* (1955), represents a radical 'other' to the conditioning the subject receives at the hands of the one-dimensional society. It is a recalcitrant element that, at least in principle, can resist the blandishments of modern corporate capitalism.

For Whitebook (1995: 7–9, 179–196; 1996: 297–304), Habermas's work represents a falling away from the forceful, critical use, to which Marcuse et al. put the concept of the unconscious. Habermas's development of communicative action, with the stress it places on language as the medium of intersubjectivity, effectively 'linguistifies' the unconscious, reducing it to being a product of interaction through language. For Whitebook, as for Craib, contemporary authors such as Habermas (and Lacan), domesticate the unconscious, by failing to recognise that its contents are 'imagistic', not 'linguistic' representations.

What Whitebook and Craib develop is something approaching a realist view of the subject, a view they believe was a crucial strength of old-style Critical Theory. The human subject, they argue, is real in that it has an inner terrain of its own, and this *intra*psychic realm is not reducible to being the mere outcome of interaction. Indeed Craib (1997) argues (somewhat wryly) that the contemporary sociological habit of thought which sees the subject as thoroughly 'socially constructed' is a form of social psychosis! Would you trust a sociologist who told you everyone, but them, had been 'socially constructed'?

Axel Honneth (1993: 281ff), working very much in the Critical Theory tradition, and accepting Habermas's critique of his predecessors' work, also finds 'linguistification' problems similar to those identified by Whitebook and Craib. He notes that once Habermas has shifted the emphasis of Critical Theory to the reconstruction of the universal conditions of (linguistic) communication, then 'the bodily and physical dimensions of social action no longer come into view'. For all three authors, the bodily, emotional and psychic features of everyday life are crucial to an understanding of it. Habermas's development of communicative rationality was meant to anchor Critical Theory in the natural validity of everyday life in a way that was impossible following the ideas of Horkheimer et al. Yet, we do not, for example, usually experience moral offence in the everyday world as just a transgression of communicative conditions or rules, something more is invariably at stake for the subject. For Honneth (1995) the crucial normative element that is present in everyday life, but absent from Habermas's 'communicative' account of it, is the *struggle to acquire social recognition*. Honneth hopes this idea will enable Critical Theory to diagnose society's pathological conditions in a way that Habermas's rules-based critique, cannot.

Apart from Honneth's claims to have initiated a new 'post-linguistic' Critical Theory, more broadly, it could also be argued that Habermas has read the older generation rather flatly as though the task they set themselves was the same as his own; to construct a general theory of society in a non-contradictory way. The 'performative contradiction' he finds in their later work may be an expression of his aims, rather than theirs. If one reads them as not trying to create a general theory, but 'ironically', as Bernstein (1994: 1–41) suggests, then their later work can be seen more modestly as a sardonic reflection on the fact that the most advanced, modern and apparently rational societies display in almost equal proportion, the opposite.

It is not that Habermas's ideas should be thought wrong as such, but they should not be thought the only, or final ones; what comes later is not automatically better than what went before. Perhaps the first lesson of Critical Theory is to be found in one of its favourite sayings – nicht mitmachen – be out of step (see Jay 1996). This is not a recommendation to be mechanically critical of everything, but a reminder of an intuition we probably already have, that real thought always requires a certain effort and obduracy on our part.

It is not yet clear whether we can say in a singular way that a third generation of Critical Theorists has emerged, but certainly authors such as Honneth, Offe, Wellmer, and Eder in Germany, not to mention a number of North American and British authors, such as Benhabib, Kellner, Agger, McCarthy, Bernstein, and Ray, represent distinct contemporary voices working broadly within the tradition. In subsequent parts of the book, I will be concerned with the strength of some of the main arguments of Critical Theory regardless of whether they spring from earlier or later periods.

Further Reading

As indicated above, Habermas' 'Technology and Science as "Ideology"', in *Towards a Rational Society* (1971a) is fairly accessible. It introduces his distinction between work and interaction for the first time, a distinction that resurfaces in different forms throughout his later work, and represents the basis of his break with Marcuse, Adorno and Horkheimer. It is out of this distinction that his theory of communicative action emerges. Brand (1990) explores this communication theory with great clarity. Richard Bernstein's (1985) introduction to *Habermas and Modernity* provides a good, clear summary of Habermas' trajectory up to that point. Thomas McCarthy's (1979) commentary on Habermas's early work is excellent both for its detail and for the way it reveals the depth and richness of his thinking. It explores Habermas's work up to the late 1970s. Stephen White (1988) David Rasmussen (1990) and William Outhwaite (1994) deal assiduously with Habermas's later work. For an excellent summary of Habermas on the public sphere see the introduction to Calhoun (1992).

Part 2

Substantive Ideas:
The First Generation

5
Rationalisation as Reification

There is no more unfortunate creature under the sun than a fetishist who yearns for a woman's shoe and has to settle for the whole woman (Karl Kraus 1986: 97)

I now want to explore in more detail what I regard as the continuing relevance of two concepts used by first generation Critical Theory: reification and commodity fetishism. I shall refer directly to the way Adorno and Marcuse use them, but also use some contemporary examples to illustrate their case.

Two Key Concepts: Reification and Commodity Fetishism

It was Habermas (1987a: 379) who coined the phrase, 'rationalisation as reification' to capture the spirit of the otherwise diverse work of first generation Critical Theory. It is an apt term, for it expresses the ambiguity they felt towards a process that inflected every part of modern life. Reason, as they saw it, had ceased to open up the world of possibility and was now focused only on the inevitable fixity of the status quo. The idea of 'reification' refers to the mental process of making something, fixed, or thing-like, when in reality it is the outcome of a particular kind of social relationship.

When I first started doing sociology in the early 1970s, the influence of Talcott Parsons' 'systems theory' was waning, but annually, every autumn term in fact, he was, in an academic sense, 'ritually executed' (see Martins in Rex 1971). He was accused of reifying the social system, of treating its structure and functioning as something immutable, when in reality society had a dynamic about it that spoke of mutability and change and of being the product of human action. To us, as students, the dubious conservative implications of Parsons' ideas were plain. He *reified* the status quo, making it impossible to imagine things being other than they already were. I no longer think Parsons' work should be so summarily dismissed; there are powerful and necessarily systematic forces in any society, but the 'positivist' habits of thought which made them seem so thing-like and immutable, are misleading.

63

For Critical Theorists, reification meant 'thingification', but it had other connotations too deriving from the work of Georg Lukacs, who had melded ideas from both Marx and Weber. The main context for the idea of reification was to be found in Marx's account of commodity fetishism in Volume 1 of *Capital* (1961). Marx made a distinction between goods or commodities that are produced for their 'use-value' as against those being produced for their 'exchange value'. 'Use value' refers to the way we directly experience the value of a good as something useful to us. Under capitalism 'use-value' has been largely undermined by the production of goods for their 'exchange-value'. Superficially the 'exchange value' of a good is its price in the market place, but this price is determined by the nature of capitalist economic relations, more specifically something Marx explains via his 'labour theory of value'. The detail of this matters less than the fact that concealed behind the cost of exchanging goods are relations of economic exploitation: class relations. Goods appear to have a price that naturally adheres to them, when in fact it is the outcome of wider economic processes. Indeed, so well concealed are these wider processes, and so natural does the price of a commodity seem that we even come to value the commodity because it is so priced. Marx points out that in spite of being humanly produced, commodities 'assume the fantastic form of a relation between things'. What he means is that the quality a commodity has appears to us as something intrinsic to it, almost like an objective property rather than the outcome of human activity. He likens this fetishisation of commodities to religious belief.

> In order, therefore, to find an analogy, we must have recourse to the mist-enveloped regions of the religious world. In this world the productions of the human brain appear as independent beings endowed with life, and entering into relations with both one another and the human race. (Marx 1961: 72)

The following example was recounted to me anecdotally, but I believe it to be true. More importantly, even though it revolves around the modern need for niche marketing, it expresses what Marx meant when he referred to the 'mystical' properties of something as apparently 'trivial' as a commodity. A UK drinks manufacturer decided to produce a new sweet, low alcoholic drink, and was advised that there were two possibilities; either they should sell it in large bottles, cheaply, or in small bottles, expensively. The latter choice was thought likely to be more successful as customers would tend to value highly the smaller, more expensive product. If a drink product were both small and expensive, it was thought consumers would naturally think the contents of the bottle particularly admirable – like expensive perfume, if so little cost so much it must be good! This example captures both the concept of commodity fetishism and of reification. It involves valorising something that is a contrivance of market forces and relies instead on a habit of thought that reifies or 'thingifies' an object as 'valuable' independent of how it tastes.

We tend to think of fetishism as something primitive, or if it carries over into the modern world, as sexually comic, as in the quotation from Karl Kraus at the beginning of the chapter. In primitive societies, people sometimes believed that a spirit inhabited a tree and worshipped the tree-spirit as a source of meaning. In the modern world, fetishism is usually associated with the misplacement of sexual desire, where, for example, the object of desire becomes the article of clothing instead of the body that inhabits it. However, in both the primitive and modern cases the same fetishistic principle is at work, in that 'magical', larger-than-life properties are attributed to objects that don't deserve them. We still tend to exclude ourselves from such foolishness, believing that we are neither primitive nor deviant. Yet central to first generation Critical Theory is the belief that commodity fetishism and reification both lie at the heart of modern consumer society.

Despite their ambivalence towards Lukacs, Critical Theorists drew heavily on his ideas about reification and commodity fetishism. In his essay 'Reification and the Consciousness of the Proletariat' (1971 [1922]) he generalises Marx's account of commodity fetishism from being characteristic of a capitalist economy into being characteristic of capitalist society as a whole. In the process he adds another, Weberian, element to the mixture: 'rationalisation'. It is this heady brew of Marx and Weber that Critical Theory was able to use so effectively to diagnose the times.

For Lukacs, the key component in Weber's account of rationalisation was the idea of 'calculation'. The calculative mental outlook required by the capitalist to predict and control the production process, an outlook whose religious origins were made famous by Weber in *The Protestant Ethic and the Spirit of Capitalism*, had become the required outlook in all areas of society. The calculative elements in Weber's account of bureaucracy are well known and for Lukacs (1971: 98–9) they epitomized the wider condition:

Bureaucracy implies the adjustment of one's way of life, mode of work and hence of consciousness, to the general socio-economic premises of the capitalist economy, similar to that which we have observed in the case of the worker in particular business concerns. The formal standardisation of justice, the state, the civil service etc, signifies objectively and factually a comparable reduction of all social functions to their elements . . . This results in an inhuman, standardized division of labour analogous to that which we have found in industry on the technological and mechanical plane.

In introducing the idea of calculation as well as fetishism into his account of reification, Lukacs provides a bridge for Critical Theorists that will lead them to both the concept of instrumental reason (calculation), as well as a critique of consumer society (reification). What is also important to note is that in absorbing Weber into the picture, Lukacs highlights the subjective dimension of processes that Marx only described in terms of the objective movement of capitalist markets. Lukacs regularly talks of both the objective and subjective dimensions of society, and this extra, non-Marxist dimension,[13] provides fuel for Critical Theorists in their subsequent work. Reification is thus not only a process that involves 'thingification', and the calculation necessary to control those 'things', but is also a process that reaches into the very heart of consciousness, such that eventually we learn to reify ourselves. It is the manner in which consciousness is restructured through reification that Adorno et al. find so dispiriting. It is also the nub of their pessimistic defence of the autonomy of the subject.

Later on Lukacs himself became sceptical of the concept of 'reification' (and 'alienation') regarding it as too total, negative and Hegelian (1971: XXIVff). He argued that insofar as reification involved objectifying things, then one should not be entirely sceptical of it. The human capacity to objectify and manipulate things is not peculiar to capitalism, but is part of a universal ability that enables us to have some control over our lives. Certainly it would not disappear under communism. Nevertheless, we should not be too ready to dismiss the first generation's use of the concept of reification as it provides an extremely sharp tool for examining the vicissitudes of life in a modern consumer society. In many ways, it is an exemplar of how the work of two of sociology's founding fathers, Marx and Weber, can still disclose something true about the modern world. Clearly, the world has changed dramatically since they were writing; yet their grasp of some of its essentials come alive again when pressed to excess by Adorno. What these authors are able to show is how much the world has changed, yet in that difference remains the same (How 1998).

Adorno and the Commodification of Culture

Adorno, perhaps more than Marcuse or Horkheimer, extended Marx's ideas, taking the commodity form to have surreptitiously overflowed the banks of its starting point in the economy, to become a defining characteristic of culture too. In their treatment of mass culture, Critical Theorists are sometimes accused of naively breaking with their Marxist past by over-inflating the importance of superstructural elements, such as ideology, while ignoring economic factors. However, as will become apparent, the trajectory of their ideas is, if anything, the reverse of this, and towards the idea that economic factors have an overweening and malign influence in the cultural sphere.

Nevertheless, one might ask what a modern commodity is that makes it different from the cultural goods of previous, non-capitalist societies? Surely, in feudal times artists and composers were commissioned by wealthy patrons to produce musical and visual commodities, and these were no less the outcome of a commercial, 'class' transaction, than what happens today? However, for Adorno, what marks off the current situation is the way 'the culture industry transfers the profit motive, naked, onto cultural forms'. Profit is no longer an indirect element in the creation of a cultural work; it is everything. It expresses itself through the 'undisguised primacy of a precisely and thoroughly calculated efficacy' (Adorno 1991: 86).

Sometimes people argue that no distinction can be made between modern pornography and the erotic images found in pre-modern societies. It is only our Victorian attitudes that oblige us to see the worst in porn. However, regardless of the moral implications, for Adorno, what would distinguish the images of the modern porn-industry is the way they have been constructed so thoroughly as commodities. As commodities they are designed to present sexuality in the most graphic, genitally-oriented ways, to the exclusion of wider perceptions of sensuality. In short, the products of the culture industry nakedly contrive to ingratiate themselves with an audience. As Adorno put it, the typical products of the culture industry 'are no longer *also* commodities, but commodities through and through' (1991: 86).

Adorno and Horkheimer adopted the term, 'culture industry' to indicate they were talking about something different from folk culture or even mass culture, insofar as the latter suggested that the contents sprang spontaneously from the people. Their first reference to it is in the essay 'The Culture Industry: Enlightenment as Mass Deception' (1972 [1947]: 121–2). Straightway one catches a sense of the cultural shift being talked about, a shift that entails the dominatory practices of work in a mass production society being echoed in the sphere of culture.

> The step from the telephone to the radio has clearly distinguished the roles (of individual consciousness). The former allowed the subscriber to play the role of subject, and was liberal. The latter is democratic: it turns all participants into listeners and authoritatively subjects them to broadcast programs that are all exactly the same. (Adorno and Horkheimer 1972: 121–2)

In the same way that Adorno is scathing about the relationship between 'radio' and 'democracy' (above) so he regards calling something 'popular' only because a lot of it has been sold, as absurd. He is often taken to be antagonistic to popular culture generally, be it radio, film, music, or astrology columns. But what he is averse to is the spuriousness of using the word 'popular' to describe these things. To be genuinely popular, culture must spring from the lives of those who produce it, not be dispensed by an industry.

The culture industry imposed its contents on the people. Folk culture, in a broad sense, expressed the lived experience of its people, their loves, hates, sadnesses, rebellions and resistances, but when this (music) is mediated through the culture industry, it becomes something else – a commodity. Marcuse (1970: 115) noted with regard to black music that the 'crying and shouting, the jumping and playing', which once expressed a life, now is consumed as an emotional *performance*. It is a performance that takes place in a confined space such as an auditorium and is constructed for consumption. It does not take much mental effort on our part to realise that the advent of sophisticated audio-visual recording equipment makes the consumption of such performances an even greater possibility now. The pop-video, as the staple of MTV, now serves as a visual advertisement for the music that it accompanies; together they provide a brief but intense mixture of reified sex and emotion, securing the consumers attention by overwhelming it. Where Marcuse used the word 'performance' in relation to products of the culture industry, Adorno and Horkheimer referred to the same thing as the 'predominance of effect' (1972: 125). For all of them, the crucial point was that the culture industry, as an extension of capitalism at a particular stage in its development, was primarily geared to producing commodities. To be successful, to become a 'hit', cultural commodities have to be spectacular, discrete entities and thus capable of being reproduced in large numbers to meet demand.

It is the industrial techniques of mechanical reproduction that enable this kind of process to take place and which serve as a template for the kind of material that is produced. Adorno (1991: 87) did warn against taking the idea of the 'culture industry' too literally. He meant it to be understood, not just in the literal sense of, say, film production being organised on factory lines, but more importantly of cultural objects themselves bearing the mark of the process.

As already intimated, for Adorno, the culture industry is logically tied in with the emergence of monopoly capitalism. The emergence of large-scale conglomerate firms dominating the market and employing large numbers of people necessarily has a social effect. In having to commit themselves to an impersonal company in order to survive economically, people must necessarily cultivate a high degree of compliance, but as reward for this 'commitment' they will seek satisfaction in the consumption of commodities. Adorno believes the loss of an individual's sense of personal significance in this impersonal world creates fertile ground for the fetishisation of commodities. Consuming commodities compensates for the required selflessness and the monotonousness of working for a large corporation. It provides a sense of excitement, it distracts from an otherwise routine life, and acquiring commodities may even provide the individual with a sense of private purpose. Indeed, one of the main characteristics of the culture industry's commodities is the illusion of individualism they create, an illusion that serves as the natural counterpoint to the absence of real individualism in wider society.

Like his analyses generally, Adorno does not approach the culture industry in a conventionally systematic fashion. He, in particular, resisted the drive towards the 'general' or 'systematic' in intellectual work on the grounds that such extended edifices mirror the oppressive, generalised administrative forces at work in society. His Critical Theory therefore aimed to challenge the status quo, not only at the level of content, but of form as well. However, one should not misunderstand his role as gadfly for something ephemeral, there is a fierce intellect at work in the essays on the culture industry (Adorno 1991). His essays are short, terse, condensed affairs, glittering with provocative insight, and in their way as demanding and ruggedly uncompromising as the more extended works of Marx or Freud.

Standardisation and Individualisation

Two main interrelated characteristics of culture industry products surface in Adorno's writing, 'standardisation' and 'individualisation', supplemented by two others, 'schematisation' and 'stereotypes'. At first sight 'standardisation' and 'individualisation' seem to be contradictory characteristics in that to standardise means to render things the same, to individualise, means to make them different. For Adorno, the processes are opposite sides of the same coin and both reflect the wider need of the capitalist system to put an end to the 'individual' and close history down.

'Standardisation', refers to the tendencies of cultural commodities to resemble one another. It arises in part from the use of assembly-line mass-production processes, which naturally gear products towards similarity. However, there must be another more important factor at work too, for while producing cars or washing machines to a single standard is a necessary part of the mass production of those kinds of commodities, it is not the same for films or music. As Cook (1996: 40) points out, it costs no more to produce an original film or popular song, than to produce a repetitious one. 'Standardisation', for Adorno, often has a metaphorical quality about it, to do with finding more effective ways of enveloping an audience, of 'imitating' what has already held them in thrall, rather than the sheer duplication of something. The idea of 'imitation' is closer to what Adorno means by 'standardisation' than a literal sense of sameness (Adorno 1941: 21–4). It is more a question of following a cultural formula than exactly replicating a product, even though Adorno sees the former as close cousin to the latter.

We know pretty much what will happen in a film within the first five minutes, in fact if we know *who* is starring in it we can equally predict much of its content. At the present time, if Clint Eastwood is in it, it will be a 'tough guy' movie; if Kim Basinger or Brad Pitt are in it will be 'sexy'; if Hugh Grant is in it, it will be a comedy of errors. The science of prediction here is not exact, but the persona or star quality that a particular actor brings to a movie carries over and is utilised or imitated in other movies. The point being that the focus is on the power of the film, via the star, to grip its audience ahead of time, a concern with effect rather than with creative substance.

By contrast, in serious art, the parts or details resist the whole, or exist in tension with it 'as a vehicle of protest against the organisation', something that came into its own 'in the period from Romanticism to Expressionism'. This rebelliousness against the whole, Adorno argues, expressed itself in various ways; 'in music the single harmonic effect obliterated the awareness of form as a whole; in painting the individual colour was stressed at the expense of pictorial composition, and in the novel psychology became more important than structure' (Adorno and Horkheimer 1972: 125–6). However, the culture industry has put an end to this challenge, its use of 'effects' crushes such insubordination. The parts are forced into an entirely spurious harmony with the whole. The parts do not challenge the whole or undermine our expectations of the totality; they service the whole. They become 'special effects' designed to reinforce it. For example, the 'car chase', the 'sex scene', the 'fist fight', the 'shoot out' the 'explosion', have all become the staple clichés of modern commercial cinema and serve only to excite familiar responses. The whole may be a Western or a gangster movie, a chick-flick or a gross teenage comedy, a costume drama or a sci-fi thriller, but each will be bolstered by a series of clichéd characters and events, which, as if by magic, all serve to realise the whole. Indeed, Adorno (Adorno and Horkheimer 1972: 126) even declares that the whole bears *no* relation to the details, by which he means that there is no internal connection between them, in that the details are designed to fit the whole, rather than showing how things form in an antithetical, dialectical, way. He also notes a dismal political implication of the one-dimensional relationship between part and whole:

> Their prearranged harmony is a mockery of what had to be striven after in the great bourgeois works of art. In Germany the graveyard stillness of the dictatorship always hung over the gayest films of the democratic era. (Adorno and Horkheimer 1972: 126)

The fetishisation of commodities depends on 'standardisation', but also has a subjective component, 'regression'. There is a Freudian origin to this concept, but Adorno wishes his own use of it to be seen more in a sociological than a psychological light. He is not suggesting that people's listening and viewing habits have literally regressed from a mature stage to an infantile one; indeed, access to the appreciation of serious art has always been restricted, but now there is a general truncation of possibilities. Essentially, he wants to draw attention to the way commodity fetishism has structured the viewing and listening habits of modern consumers. He believes there is a certain kind of childishness in the way we home in on, and are entertained by, the reified elements of culture industry products. The catchy chord sequences and aural gimmicks of pop music, or the flashy, inflated visual tricks of cinema, leave the audience breathless with admiration for the star. Such infantile exaggeration, once appropriate for children, is now offered as standard fare for adults.

In his article 'A Social Critique of Radio Music' (1945), Adorno examines the listening habits of audiences for classical music on commercial radio. He notes that the regressive listening habits associated with light music apply as

readily to serious music when it is fed through the grill of the culture industry. Because of the quantity of recorded music available, audience listening
habits come to resemble 'those of the motion picture and sport spectatoritis
which promotes a retrogressive and sometimes even infantile type of person'
(p. 213). He illustrates this regression by way of Beethoven, whose symphonies
are highly integrated forms, where grasping the whole is vital, and the part,
that is, the melody, relatively unimportant.

> Retrogressive listening to a symphony is listening which, instead of grasping that
> whole, dwells upon those melodies, just as if the symphony was structured like a
> ballad. There exists a tendency to listen to Beethoven's Fifth as if it were a set of
> quotations from Beethoven's Fifth. (Adorno 1945: 214)

The framework in which things are heard involves 'atomistic', 'quotation'
listening. As it were, one hears things in isolation from other things, and
becomes attuned to the bright superficialities of the music, as these are
regularly quoted or 'plugged' on the radio. The listener comes to know
Beethoven's Fifth as a series of disconnected musical baubles without form
or structure. This indifference to the full potentiality of the music, he notes,
is reflected in the station's audience fan mail. Like the music, responses
have become standardised and repetitive. The audience's enthusiasm is one
of general admiration. They express thanks for having had their horizons
widened, and feel glad they no longer listen to 'trashy jazz', but no actual
music is mentioned, no particular feature referred to, no criticism made, even
though, as he notes, the programmes were 'amateurish and planless'. The audience's responses reflect the spell cast by the radio announcer, often repeating
literally what the announcer has said on behalf of culture. The audience consumes the product and expresses its satisfaction by reciting the advertisment
for it.

It is not that Adorno is claiming that serious music is *necessarily* only for the
few, or that its mass availability *has* to involve its denigration for he is quite
aware that serious, or autonomous art carries the imprint of the class-divided
societies that produced it. However, between the two poles of seriousness
and equality lies a broken middle,[14] which cannot be overcome within the
existing totality and certainly not through the blandishments of the culture
industry. In 'Theory of Pseudo-Culture' (1993: 29–30) he gives another
example of how these two halves of the equation are irreconcilable. He
acknowledges that anyone who suggests that the publication of important
philosophical texts diminishes their importance when published in paperback,
rather than hardback, is bound to be regarded as a reactionary cultural
dinosaur. Surely it would be wrong to 'secrete these texts in small and costly
editions' when economics and technology press in the opposite direction?
Surely the wider the circulation of the ideas is all to the good regardless of
how they appear?

Yet he also notes, that in spite of this there is another side to the issue. Progress in a repressive totality is not a singular process leading straightforwardly to the good, but an ambiguous, dialectical one. Progress in the modern world of pseudo-culture has a downside that is glossed over. Simply consuming culture in readily available bite-sized gobbets may not be the 'first stage of culture, but its mortal enemy' (1993: 30). Culture that is absorbed as a commodity has a toxic effect on culture proper; it becomes a kind of superstition, something to be believed in because it is 'culture', rather than something that genuinely opens life up to greater meaning. Adorno cites the example of a handyman that started to read Kant's *Critique of Pure Reason* because he yearned for something higher, and finished up reading astrology columns, as only there could he reconcile moral laws with the stars above. The point Adorno is making is not that major cultural artifacts should only be available to the few who can understand them properly, but that when they are served up as digestible commodities, their meaning and significance are lost. In his later work, he increasingly sought to show that while the poles of 'equality' and 'seriousness' are dialectically related, they cannot overcome the broken middle and should not be dialectically reconciled by theory. We have to endure their irreconcilability, and 'negative dialectics' represents his attempt to do this. The strength of genuine, autonomous art lies in its recalcitrant refusal to be absorbed by the culture industry.

In a slightly earlier, 1938 essay, 'On the Fetish Character of Music and the Regression of Listening' Adorno (1991: ch. 1) set out in much more detail, and with greater vehemence, the same kinds of argument he made in 'A Social Critique of Radio Music' (1945). The aesthetics of advertising pervade the culture industry with the result that what things mean lose their anchorage in reality. The English brewing company, Watneys, used to advertise its beer via the slogan, 'What we want is Watneys!'. It was a slogan scrawled on a chalk-white billboard that passed for the white-washed brick walls that once were common in slum areas of London and the North of England. It read like a political slogan expressing the demands of workers, but actually supplanted their interests, and converted their wants into a plea to consume the beer that the advertiser produced. The workers were now expected to *identify* with the very products they would be palmed off with anyway (1991: 42).

The process of the individual identifying with the commodity is of course also characteristic of the culture industry. In the same way that advertisements camouflage their intent by making the 'inconspicuous familiar', and the 'familiar inconspicuous', the better to insinuate themselves in the mind of the consumer, so the hit song creeps its way into the consciousness of the listener. The utter familiarity of the hit song, its standardised quality, will remain 'salutarily forgotten' only to suddenly re-impose itself and 'become painfully over clear through recollection, as if in the beam of a spotlight' (1991: 42). Herein lies the enigma of cultural commodities being both 'standardised' and 'individualised'.

The 'regressed listener' (or viewer) experiences the cultural commodity in a state of 'deconcentration'. The standardised product demands nothing of the consumer except a willingness to assimilate the familiar. No real concentration is required to absorb the product, as the audience predigests what is to come when they hear the opening chords of the pop song, or know the star or genre of the film. One can therefore listen or view in a more or less distracted way; indeed to do otherwise is impossible for there is nothing there to challenge people into thought. Of course the conspicuous bits, the aural tricks and visual special effects, the star's screen persona, are there to grip, jerk and excite the audience into life, and it is these that give the commodity its 'individualised' feel.

The culture industry generates commodities that have the appearance of uniqueness. They seem to address us personally in a way that makes a concern for our own individuality seem unnecessary. Adorno puts it thus:

> Pseudo-individuality is rife: from the standardised jazz improvisation to the exceptional film star whose hair curls over her eye to demonstrate her originality. What is original is no more than the generality's power to stamp the accidental detail so firmly that it is accepted as such. The defiant reserve or elegant appearance of the individual on the show is mass-produced like Yale locks, whose only difference can be measured in fractions of millimeters. (1972: 154)

The point of this is not just to illustrate the superficiality of the culture industry, but also to show how its reified conception of individuality stands in as a parody of the real thing. Adorno believes the relentless forcing of product, be it the 'new' celebrity talk-show host, or the film star being interviewed on the show to advertise themselves and the film that carries their brand name, discloses the absurdly amplified, but illusory nature of individualism in the current capitalist era. Modern western societies are often accounted pluralist democracies, but, for Adorno, such pluralism is an ideological illusion, necessary to conceal the system's need for homogeneity and control. The cultural commodity addresses the consumer as if it were unique, which allows the consumer to feel unique in consuming it.

Seeing Through It and Still Buying It (1)

Criticism has often been levelled at Adorno for describing consumers as passive absorbers of mass culture, without the wit to say no (Miller 1987, Strinati 1995); such a view though is misleading. Adorno makes it clear that we consumers *eagerly* consume commodities, for they are not imposed on us, but part of a way of life. We ourselves are subject to reification and thus are open to consuming reified commodities. We may 'see through' the absurdity of soap operas with the obviousness of their story lines and the artificiality of their cliff-hanging build-ups, but though we regard them with an ironic eye, we still watch them.

Seeing through something and still buying it, is a perverse tribute to the advertising industry's capacity to colonise our imaginations, so we want things even though we know their meaning is entirely artificial.

> The most intimate reactions of human beings have been so thoroughly reified that the idea of anything specific to themselves now persists as an utterly abstract notion: personality scarcely signifies anything more than shining white teeth and freedom from body odour and emotions. The triumph of advertising in the culture industry is that consumers feel compelled to buy and use its products even they see through them. (Adorno and Horkheimer 1972: 167)

While Adorno believes people 'see through' cultural commodities, he does not conceive of them as cultural dupes. To be duped implies there is another non-duped condition and is something to which we should aspire. The problem is that though the individual sees through the duplicity, he or she equally knows that consuming this or that, *is* now what it is to be an individual: there are no alternative models available. Thus, sociologically speaking, surveying or inter-viewing people about whether they recognise the way commodities are hyped would miss the point that recognising hype does not dispel it. Being familiar with what is in fashion, and what is being talked about, is now more impor-tant than ever. Where, once, ignorance of such things only meant not being able to talk about them, now, Adorno believes, there is a positive stigma in not being up to date:

> Today anyone who is incapable of talking in the prescribed fashion, that is of effort-lessly reproducing the formulas, conventions and judgments of mass culture as if they were his own is threatened in his very existence, suspected of being an idiot or an intellectual . . . People give their approval to mass culture because they know or suspect they are taught the mores they will surely need as their passport in a mono-polized life. (Adorno 1972: 79–80)

It is not therefore a question of the masses being stultified, but of them knowing full well that these are the conditions under which they live. As Jarvis (1998: 74) succinctly declares, for Adorno, the culture industry 'is not a piece of sharp business practice' but a constant 'initiation rite', an initiation into how people should think of themselves. Learning from new stars, again and again, what it is to be an individual is what is now demanded. Indeed, as Adorno sardonically remarks, 'for centuries society has been preparing for Victor Mature and Mickey Rooney' (1972: 156). It is no coincidence that he entitled one of his most famous essays, 'The Culture Industry: En-lightenment as Mass Deception' (1972: 120ff). He was not claiming that the culture industry merely deceives people, but more dubiously, parades this deception *as* enlightenment. The process of reification thus comes to complete fruition.

However, while there is no question that Adorno saw these developments in the bleakest of lights, he freely admitted that only by exaggerating things could the truth of the current situation be disclosed. He did though, in a later essay, 'Free Time' (1991 [1969]), point to evidence that audiences showed a certain reservation in their enthusiasm for culture industry products and that even the most naive of theatre and filmgoers 'do not simply take what they behold for real'. In fact, unusually he adopted briefly the language of Marcuse in pointing out that individuals are real and have real interests that 'are still strong enough to resist, within certain limits, total inclusion' (Adorno 1991:170).

Adorno is a complex figure, and not always consistent but, in that inconsistency, always seeking insight. His work can also be usefully read in context. The essay 'On the Fetish Character in Music and the Regression of Listening' (Arato and Gebhardt 1978: 270–99) responds to the essay by his friend and sometime colleague, Walter Benjamin, 'The Work of Art in the Age of Mechanical Reproduction' (1973: 219–53).

Benjamin versus Adorno

Walter Benjamin's essay can be read as a criticism of Adorno's overly negative ideas on the culture industry. Benjamin, it is said, has a more optimistic, democratic view of the culture industry, particularly film, and the potential it has for enhancing progress (see Wolin 1994). The reader, though, should beware of seeing Benjamin's and Adorno's views as polar opposites. As I have described above, Adorno's views are more complex than first appears, and Benjamin's are far from simply being in favour of the culture industry.

As the title of his essay suggests, Benjamin is concerned with the nature of art in the contemporary age, when artworks are capable of mass reproduction. It might seem as though the artwork itself does not change regardless of how many times it is reproduced. Modern photographic and recording techniques enable high levels of reproductive accuracy to be achieved, but for Critical Theorists the meaning of art has changed over time. What an artwork as such means is bound up with the conditions of its production and reception, though it is not a merely relative phenomenon because of this.

For Benjamin, western art has its origins in cultic or religious belief. In the Middle Ages, painting and music expressed divine inspiration and were integral to religious ritual and ceremony. By virtue of this divinity, art had a unique 'aura' that could not be reproduced. The original was the authentic work, and it was the meaning of this, inherent in the single work, that was reverently passed down as tradition. Even during the Renaissance, when religious motifs were partly replaced by secular ones, an 'aura' of authenticity clung to the original work. In the nineteenth century, the autonomy of the work of art reached its high point in the secular world with the growth of the doctrine of 'art for art's sake'.

In the modern age of mechanical reproduction, however, the meaning of the artwork changes. In film, for example, the use of close-ups, or slow motion images, reproduce things that the naked eye could never see. The capacity of films to bring extraordinarily disparate images together for an audience to show them the minutiae of their everyday lives, for Benjamin, effectively valorises those lives and has an intrinsically liberative effect. By the same token, the situations in which an artwork is viewed or heard also changes. The art gallery and the concert hall lose their 'sacred' quality, in that artworks can be reproduced and experienced in a variety of mundane situations. The immediate effect of this process is to diminish the significance of the artwork's aura. If the aura of the work depends on the latter's uniqueness, then the availability of many copies necessarily reduces that aura.

Benjamin is aware that the process of mechanical reproduction does not involve a straightforward break with the irrational elements of auratic art, and may, in a commodified way, echo it with the impression made by a 'star':

> The film responds to the shriveling of the aura with an artificial 'build-up' of the personality outside the studio. The cult of the movie star fostered by the money of the film industry preserves not the unique aura of the person but the 'spell of the personality', the phoney spell of a commodity. (1973: 233)

In spite of this less than progressive feature, Benjamin believes it more important to recognise the virtues of different kinds of art, such as film and photography, which result from the advent of different kinds of production process. The virtue of the modern system of mechanical reproduction lies in the fact that it does away with too much reverence for art, it breaks with the elitist 'auratic' tradition by making art available to everyone. Benjamin describes the egalitarian implications of breaking an artwork's anchorage in tradition thus:

> To pry an object from its shell, to destroy its aura, is a mark of a perception whose 'sense of the universal equality of things' has increased to such a degree that it extracts it even from a unique object by means of reproduction. (1973: 225)

In other words, the mass reproducibility of objects, including art objects, has had an effect on perception; it makes us aware of the transitoriness of objects. In the age of mechanical reproduction, an object in being an object is, in a sense, no more or less fabricated than any other object In modern parlance we might say its meaning is 'socially constructed', and cannot be mysterious in the way that unique works of art supposedly are.

There are other subtle differences that separate the mechanically reproduced artwork from the auratic one. In cinema films, as opposed to theatre plays, actors have no opportunity to adjust their performances for the audience, which allows the audience to take up a certain critical distance towards them. Everyone in the cinema audience, he notes, becomes something of an expert on the film they have seen. When we watch cinema newsreels, because it is our world that is set before us, we know we could have been there, transformed from 'passer-by to movie extra'. Cinema audiences watch films with a certain degree of inattentiveness that makes them receptive to revolutionary visual innovation. Where many people's reactions to the fragmentary images painted by Picasso were negative, visual fragmentation in a Chaplin movie was accepted as progressive and enlightening. What is important to Benjamin is the change of 'political' attitude that flows from these material/cultural changes. It may or may not express itself directly in a different attitude to specific political issues, but represents a subtle shift towards an irreversibly more democratic world-view.

Benjamin's essay is often taken to be a valuable breakthrough in Critical Theory, a move away from Adorno's thoroughly negative view of things to a more differentiated understanding of mass culture and one that also allows us to see some potentially progressive, interactional elements in its reception. This evaluation springs not only from second generation Critical Theory, but is also at the heart of much contemporary media analysis. However, while it is not my task here to side with one or the other, it is worthwhile recalling Adorno's responses to Benjamin's ideas, as a reminder of their continuing force.

Benjamin saw in an audience's distraction or inattention towards things, a chance for them to break from the irrational grip of an artwork's aura, a space in which the audience's critical faculties could be brought to bear without the overbearing effects of tradition being present. By contrast, Adorno saw this same distraction as a symptom of regression. People consumed their films or music in a distracted way because their lives were not their own, but dependent on adhering to the strictures of monopolistic companies. The commodities they consumed as solace were vacuous, requiring no concentration, only absorption. Far from evoking critical thought, they rendered thought itself unnecessary. The fact that everyone has a view on the latest blockbuster is a tribute only to how much money has been spent on it, and how effective has been its publicity and merchandising.

In a letter to Benjamin in 1939, Adorno was critical of the way he undialectically ran the mythical-religious artwork and the modern authentic artwork together, by virtue of the fact that both had an 'aura'. Benjamin had contrasted the auratic artwork per se, with the contemporary mechanically-reproducible work, finding in favour of the latter by virtue of the fact that it had shed its 'aura' and acquired some universal potential. Adorno is unconvinced by the argument. The 'aura' of the modern authentic artwork may have its origins in religious belief, (something both he and Benjamin regarded as irrational), but this tells us nothing about its quality, about the disclosive power of the work, how well it reveals reality to us. In other words, the authentic modern artwork is a progressive force and should not be denigrated by virtue of having an 'aura', which anyway is subject to dissolution in the modern age (Adorno in Bloch et al. 1977: 121). Moreover, as Adorno points out, it is surely now the modern cinema film which most thoroughly exudes 'aura', albeit the ersatz 'aura' of a fetishised commodity. The cult status accorded the fabricated 'stars' of film and pop music is also a measure of how much the culture industry is a regressive force in that, for many, the images of such 'stars' have such an evocative quality as to make them totemic.

Similarly, to regard cinema as progressive because it can surprise its audience with its 'shock-like seduction', for Adorno, is mere romanticism. Much of 'the laughter of the audience at a cinema . . . is anything but good and revolutionary . . . it is full of the worst bourgeois sadism' (Adorno in Bloch 1977: 123). Anyone who has watched a 'revenge' movie in recent times and felt irresistible pleasure at the bloody outcome will know what Adorno is talking about. Adorno believed the nub of the issue lay not in the particularities of changing production techniques as Benjamin suggested, but more broadly in the mode of production. The latter required all modern art, both auratic and reproducible art, to submit to the commodity form. It is the dubious effects of the capitalist mode of production that should call forth the critical spirit of Critical Theory, rather than the hope that new reproduction techniques would spontaneously produce a more critical-democratic outlook in the masses.

Much of Adorno's criticism of Benjamin has a second target in mind, the playwright, Bertold Brecht. Adorno always regarded the influence of Brecht on Benjamin as malign. Brecht was a Marxist author, but Adorno saw his work as manipulative, and though it had a liberative, left-wing intent, the fact that it was manipulative meant it reiterated the features of the culture industry that Adorno found regressive. The Nazism of the mid 1930s may have aestheticised politics by making violence seem stylish and invigorating, but producing art for the sake of left-wing political ends is only the other side of the same coin. Both are symptoms of the insidious growth of instrumental reason.

Adorno and the 'Autonomous' Work of Art

As the reader might gather, the ground for Adorno's critique of Benjamin as well as the culture industry, lies in the possibility of there being an 'authentic', or as he usually calls it, an 'autonomous' work of art. The autonomous work of art stands in contrast to lesser products that owe their existence entirely to the system of commodity production. Adorno's views on art are complex and the range of his interests wide. In terms of music, he has written on amongst others, Mahler, Schoenberg, Wagner, Beethoven, and Stravinsky; in literature, on Joyce, Kafka, Beckett, Baudelaire, and Proust. I shall not therefore attempt to deal in detail with these views, but present only a very general picture of them, a picture that is shared, with some variation, by Marcuse and Horkheimer.

Like Marcuse and Horkheimer, Adorno believed in Marxist fashion that art, both autonomous and mechanically reproducible, bears the imprint of the (class) society out of which it was produced. Despite the transcending effects of its aura, it is not a transcendental entity because impressed in the body of the work are the taken-for-granted assumptions of a particular set of historical circumstances. Unlike most Marxists, however, Adorno believed equally that authentic art displayed qualities of autonomy in being able to exceed the conditions that produced it, and in a unique fashion revealed the truth of those conditions. Genuine, autonomous art was undoubtedly a product of society, but that was not all it was. Furthermore, written into the disclosure of those conditions, albeit negatively, was the possibility of perceiving an alternative reality.

Autonomous art has a subversive quality which challenges the status quo, in contrast to products which merely express or reaffirm it. The challenge of autonomous art is not though, just a matter of railing against the times, of declaring oneself to be for this or against that; if that were the case the abstract nature of music would disqualify it as art. Adorno is concerned with how the *form* the artwork takes stands in relation to society. Schoenberg's (early) dissonant, atonal music, for example, stands as a challenge to the musical 'resolutions' standardly provided in the classical music canon. It resists the tendency to reify musical 'resolutions' and arrive at 'harmony'. In doing this, Schoenberg resists musically society's tendency to reify false resolutions to contradictions and echoes Critical Theory's challenge to the false harmony society achieves through affluence. The task of music thus parallels the relationship of Critical Theory to society (Adorno 1978: 130).

In contrast to the glittering superficiality of culture industry products, the radicality of Schoenberg's music lies in the way it reverses the relationship between essence and appearance:

Richness and plenitude are to be made the essence, not mere ornament; the essence will no longer appear as the rigid framework on which the music is draped but rather as concrete and evident in its most subtle traits. What he [Schoenberg] designated as the 'subcutaneous' . . . breaks through the surface, becomes visible and manifests itself independently of all stereotyped forms. The inward dimension moves outward. (Adorno 1981: 153)

What Adorno means is that the familiar structures around which musical appearances are wrapped, recede, allowing the inner richness of the music to appear in its own right. Schoenberg refuses to offer listeners familiar aural categories to organise their responses, compelling them to take an active, almost compositional attitude to his acutely spare music. It is very much the opposite of the culture industry's approach, where constantly changing musical ornamentation is everything while the framework remains rigidly the same. For Adorno autonomous art, such as Schoenberg's, negates the status quo and produces in its wake a genuine kind of praxis, though one quite different from familiar instrumental notions of political praxis. One should not mistake the role of autonomous art as a call to the barricades!

In the essay, 'Commitment' (Arato and Gebhardt 1978: 300ff) Adorno applies the same ideas to literature. He implicitly continues his debate with Benjamin through an overt critique of Brecht and Sartre. Once more the argument is that the form the artwork takes in relation to the status quo is what defines it as autonomous and radical, not the overt message of the work. He believes that Brecht (like Sartre) is too didactic, too much the educator, not enough the artist. Samuel Beckett and Franz Kafka, on the other hand, despite having no overt political message to pass on, are more authentic artists and more deeply politically committed because of the *form* reality takes in their work. Beckett's plays, with their desolate characters that unremittingly fail to communicate, or even achieve the coherence and consistency needed to present a 'self', are more truly an expression of the 'abdication of the subject' in the modern world than more overtly committed work. For Adorno, 'Beckett and Kafka arouse the fear that existentialism merely talks about' (p. 314), a fear that this is how things really are now. The autonomy of such work lies in its ability to disclose the truth of reality from the inside.

Of course Adorno's ideas should not be placed above critical suspicion. His admiration for only the most challenging artworks sits rather oddly with his belief that audiences' tastes are now so 'regressed' as to be beyond the call of art. He recommends Benjamin become more dialectical and less simplistically oppositional in the way he counterposes auratic to reproducible art. Yet, as second generation Critical Theorist, Albrecht Wellmer (1991: 32–4) points out, there is something of the pot calling the kettle black in this. Benjamin may well have overestimated the virtues of mechanically reproduced art, and underestimated the virtues of autonomous art, but is Adorno's case any more dialectical? Adorno certainly *appears* to recommend the importance of both autonomous and mass art:

> The reification of a great work of art is not just loss, any more than the reification of the cinema is all loss . . . Both bear the stigmata of capitalism, both contain elements of change . . . Both are torn halves of an integral freedom, to which however they do not add up. (Adorno in Bloch et al. 1977: 123)

However, the torn halves of the broken middle were *never* likely to add up, Wellmer believes, because Adorno never really found any value in one of them: the culture industry. Adorno always measures the products of the culture industry against standards that make them seem 'inane or cynical', whereas Benjamin is prepared to be theoretically less secure and risk a certain amount of contradictoriness in order to see how a new *aesthetic* might be emerging. Indeed, Wellmer suggests that rock music might serve as an example of the folk music of the industrial age, with 'just as much positive potential for democratization and the unleashing of aesthetic imagination as there is potential for cultural regression' (Wellmer 1991: 33). It is the doubtfulness of such possibilities, that Adorno famously and bluntly dismissed with regard to jazz (Adorno 1981), that Wellmer thinks we should defend.

Wellmer's case is a complex one involving a reorientation of Adorno's ideas about the truth content of auratic art as against its lack in mass culture art. He utilises Habermas's communicative orientation towards truth to make his case. It is beyond the scope of this book to pursue the issue, though Jarvis (1998) provides important insight while broadly defending Adorno. My own view is that at face value it is difficult to see how rock music, or any other part of the culture industry, could serve the optimistic ends after which Wellmer hankers. Such industries are as, if not more, committed to commodity production now than they ever were, and audiences as prone as ever to their apparent novelty. Moreover, even if Adorno's dismissal of traditional jazz grates for various reasons, his arguments about the nature of autonomous art are nuanced enough to be applied to modern jazz and to find in its favour, as has been done by Nesbitt (1999).

Marcuse, Language and Ideology

While Adorno's work, particularly in the area of aesthetics, has received an increasing amount of attention, Marcuse's has received less. Although Marcuse worked with broader strokes of the brush than Adorno, we should not ignore the particular and continuing relevance of his work, something I want to illustrate with a contemporary example.

One Dimensional Man (1964), like the work of other Critical Theorists, gnaws away at the discrepancy between appearance and reality. Modern industrial societies seem to be the most open and thoroughly liberated of societies, and yet from the angle of Critical Theory they are subtly but decisively closed. Indeed, their apparent openness is a function of their closure at a deeper level. In Chapter 4, 'The Closing of the Universe of Discourse', Marcuse focuses on the political implications of a subtle change in the way we talk about things, particularly in the public sphere. He notes that there has been a gradual elimination of a critical dimension in the use of language. Increasingly, the overbearing language of advertising has become the norm for public discourse generally, swamping and transforming matters of public concern into the language of commerce – what now would be called the politics of the 'sound-byte' and the 'spin-doctor'. Because ordinary language is used in this way, there is no longer a space in which the receivers of messages can properly 'think' alternatives and take up a critical attitude towards things: from being interlocutors in a discursive process they are increasingly asked to be mute consumers of images. The healthy, dialectical tension between appearance and reality is tending to disappear in favour of a culture of nothing but appearances.

Marcuse uses the terms 'operationalism' and 'functionalization' to describe what is happening to the ordinary language of public discourse. Concepts, which properly speaking should give us some critical distance in understanding the facts, their significance and so forth, are dissolving into the facts. How something functions at the level of factual appearances is becoming the whole story. Identifying something with the way it functions is unproblematic when we are dealing with technology. If you are setting up new software on a computer it is important that the instructions are unambiguous and that you adhere to them. When it comes to other areas of life though, such technological reasoning is much more problematic. Marcuse (1994: 92) uses an example from *Time* magazine where the use of 'the inflectional genitive makes individuals appear to be mere appendices or properties of their place, their job, their employer, or enterprise':

> Georgia's high-handed, low-browed governor . . . had the stage all set for one of his wild political rallies last week

The function of the governor, along with his moral characteristics and political practices are 'fused together into one indivisible and immutable structure which, in its natural innocence and immediacy, overwhelms the reader's mind' (pp. 94–5). There is no space for the reader to differentiate elements, or develop critical thought, the whole package moves as one sealed unit, in this case, defined more or less as a human interest story. Another irrational effect of this syntactic overload is to slide past the reader, as harmonious, factors that are contradictory; notions such as 'precision bombing' or Ronald Reagan's description of the Inter-Continental Ballistic Missile as a 'peacekeeper' (Ingram 1990: 84).

Marcuse identifies the abridged use of language as a carry over from the world of commerce and advertising and as something that produces an automatic response in people. However, his examples are taken from political journalism in the USA in the 1960s, and one might ask whether the same thing applies in other areas of public life, and if it still applies today? Peter Womack (1999) does not refer to Marcuse, but echoes the latter's ideas in his account of the current trend for British universities to have 'mission statements'. A 'mission statement' is a broad public declaration of what the University stands for and is something that is meant to orientate the ideas of other policy-makers in the institution. Womack's 'mission statement' is from the University of East Anglia, but could have emanated from almost any other higher education institution, including my own.

UEA Norwich is a premier research and teaching university. We are dedicated to the advancement of learning and the increase of knowledge both to satisfy the aspirations of individuals and to contribute to economic, social and cultural progress at regional, national and international levels.

Apart from its vagueness, he notes two particular characteristics. First, something he calls 'repletion', which like any advertisment, seeks to overwhelm. The number of *ands* ensures that every eventuality is covered; research *and* teaching, learning *and* knowledge, social *and* cultural, national *and* international – nothing escapes, the statement is beyond critical challenge, at UEA they do everything!

Secondly, there is an abundance of what he calls 'superegoic' verbs, verbs that speak too much of everyone's good. He notes, that in a fairly short sentence, 'we are dedicated, we satisfy, and we contribute; and somebody or other advances, increases, aspires and progresses'. The result of saying all this is not a feeling of well-being, but of nausea. We cannot fault the selflessness of the claims, but if they were uttered by an individual we would certainly distrust their sincerity. We would feel uncomfortable with them, for anyone who claimed to be so virtuous would likely be unstable. All negativity has been eliminated; there is no hint of irony, or scepticism, protest or challenge, only an unrelenting declaration of one's own virtue. The odd thing is that, traditionally, universities have fostered clear-minded scepticism as part of their academic raison d'être. Nor is the absurdly positive style of writing peculiar to 'mission statements', as Womack points out, anyone who has knowledge of the many documents currently produced by universities, will be aware how much this 'overstocking of the syntactic shelves' now permeates academic life. Reality matters less than getting the right style of prose, indeed the implication is that the right style of prose creates 'reality'.

The idea that reality flows from the way we talk about it, from the way our concepts construe it, bears much in common with the ideas of sociological postmodernists, such as Jean Baudrillard. However, where they conceive the process uncritically, as a fact of postmodern life, and even as a kind of free-wheeling liberation from traditional notions of reality, for Marcuse it represents the opposite: the triumph of one-dimensional ideology. Though Critical Theorists are sometimes accused of overplaying the importance of ideology, they do not follow postmodernists down the anti-realist path. For them, reality is not socially constructed in a contingent way, but to a significant degree is tied in with economic relations. The reality of commodity production, the process of reification, the pre-eminence of instrumental reason, impose themselves on human subjects from the outside, even though, in the more pessimistic accounts, they ultimately transform the inside too.

In Chapter 1, I drew attention to the importance of the speculative element in Critical Theory, how it informed its opposition to empiricist/positivist outlooks with their emphasis on observable facts. For the latter, 'justice' (for example) could only consist in what an observable society considers justice to be. Critical Theorists, by contrast, (following Hegel), argue that linguistic concepts have a universal claim built into them, and it is the universalising potential in the idea of justice which should be used to challenge what actually passes for justice in a particular society. Reason contains a natural dialectical tension between what is and what ought to be, something which is increasingly disappearing in a world dominated by what *is*, alone.

For Marcuse, even modern, ordinary language philosophy slid into the habit of ignoring the proper dialectical tension between the particular and the universal. In different ways, authors as varied as J. L. Austin, Gilbert Ryle, and Ludwig Wittgenstein reduce meaning to the factual and particular, ignoring the way concepts have a potential to speak in a universal way. For those influenced by ordinary language philosophy, the meaning of particular expressions is to be found in the way they are used. It is the context in which they are found that determines what the expressions can mean. There is no transcendental meaning to the concept of justice, its meaning is a function of its context. Ordinary language philosophy saw its task as bypassing (metaphysical) discussions about transcendental meaning and instead clarifying the situated use of the concept. For Marcuse, this eliminates the crucial speculative and critical elements that are natural to ordinary language.

Marcuse's critique was concerned with the then current development of ordinary language philosophy, but such an outlook is not peculiar to philosophy. In sociology, symbolic interactionism and ethnomethodology both insist that meaning is situationally produced, and general sociological concepts, such as class, have no purchase on social reality, except insofar as actors use them in their daily lives. Similarly, in the history of ideas, the work of Quentin Skinner (1969, 1970, 1974) is well known for its emphasis on discovering what the concepts in a text meant to a particular audience at a particular time, even if possible, on a particular occasion. In each case, it is a description of what *is* the case, the status quo at that point, and nothing else that drives the work forward.

For Marcuse, this kind of outlook echoes the ideological foreshortening of language found in wider society. Ordinary language, he argues, should not be reduced to its descriptive function, for it contains an equally important, *prescriptive* implication. For example, the concept of 'democracy' has a prescriptive or evaluative dimension that is implied in its everyday usage. When we talk of democracy we imply something more that just the facts of supposedly democratic regimes. Built into the word is the evaluative idea of governance via a rational and freely achieved consensus. It is this latter dimension which is in danger of subsiding in the modern world, and which Marcuse wants to bring into critical conjunction with the facts of democratic life. Only then, through immanent critique, can the facts of how democracy actually works, be tested against the way it should work, how well it does freely achieve a rational consensus. One might add that the role of 'sound bytes', 'spin doctors' and 'popularity polls' in achieving modern political consensuses makes Marcuse's insights still seem highly pertinent.

Seeing Through It and Still Buying It (2)

It is not just in the area of language that Marcuse sees the insidious effects of one-dimensional ideology. Like Adorno, he identifies the consumption of commodities as a key element in the quietening of the masses; like Adorno he draws on Freud's work to make his point. People buy into their own control by consuming ever larger quantities of goods on the promise that such consumption equals liberty. He coined the term 'repressive desublimation' to capture the irrationality of this process.

Freud used the term 'sublimation' to refer to the way sexual energy is redirected away from a primary (sexual) object towards a something else, perhaps writing a novel or playing sport. The substitute satisfaction is found in the creative outcomes of such activities. Freud does not denigrate these activities; indeed, in a sense civilization has grown out of our capacity to re-channel this energy in creative ways. Marcuse too believes that authentic art, which involves sublimation, has made an important contribution to the development of human happiness and stands in opposition to the one-dimensional society. In fact he celebrates sublimation as one of the great creative forces in society. To be sure, sublimation as expressed in art may reflect the barriers to the gratification of instincts, but at the same time it 'preserves the consciousness of the renunciation which the repressive society inflicts upon the individual, and thereby preserves the need for liberation' (1994: 75). However, he also believes that in the modern world a process of *repressive desublimation* is going on.

The idea of *de*sublimation sounds as though it is part of a sexually liberated society where the sublimation of our instinctual drives is no longer necessary. For Marcuse though, it represents a very different story. The emergence of explicitly sexual material into everyday life appears to be a kind of liberation from repressive Victorian values, but actually involves a new kind of repression. The allure of sex is now used to sell so many commodities that we scarcely notice how much it figures in our lives. The heightening of the sexual in so many areas of life, as it were, calls out our libidinal energy with the promise of instant gratification, but then channels it into the illusory satisfaction of buying the commodity. We may know that buying those tight designer jeans will not bring us true erotic fulfillment, but we buy them anyway because they promise so much. We know that watching beautiful film stars performing larger than life sexual feats on screen will not bring satisfaction to us, but we are riveted with admiration for them, and will seek out their next movie. The result of this commercial amplification of sexuality is a crude focus on 'sexiness', ultimately genital sexuality, and a diminishment of deeper sources of happiness in eroticism and a wider feeling of sensuousness. Marcuse gives an example of what this difference might mean:

> compare love-making in a meadow and in an automobile, on a lover's walk outside the town walls, and on a Manhattan street. In the former cases, the environment partakes of, and invites libidinal cathexis and tends to be eroticised . . . In contrast a mechanised environment seems to block such self-transcendence of the libido . . . libido becomes less 'polymorphous', less capable of eroticism beyond localized sexuality, and the *latter* is intensified. (1994: 73)

Marcuse's claim is that lovemaking in natural surroundings offers human possibilities that do not exist in our urban world. It is as though in making love in an 'un-natural' urban environment we become obsessed by genitals, because in them lies our last connection with nature as a source of happiness. Whereas making love in natural surroundings allows us the possibility of transcending our ordinary lives in experiencing what we share with nature. Under these circumstances libidinous feeling is not artificially focused on genital sexuality, but allows us a more expansive feeling of sensuousness to the point where even our surroundings are eroticised.

Marcuse's example is rather unusual in terms of *One Dimensional Man*, which is a broadly political book, but it does illustrate his concern both with Freud and with the idea of happiness. In *Eros and Civilisation* (1955) he makes a distinction between repression and surplus repression. He follows Freud in acknowledging that all societies require some repression of instinctual life in order to function. However, unlike Freud he recognises that the kinds and levels of repression required, vary historically. Levels of repression are related to the *scarcity* of goods that condition the way a society functions. More repression of instinctual life is needed when conditions of great scarcity exist, this ensures that what materials are available are used in as disciplined and effective way as possible. The advance of technology in modern capitalist societies has enabled them to overcome scarcity to a significant degree, but there has not been a corresponding decline in levels of repression. People continue exist in a state of economic fear in such societies. The reason for this is that capitalist economic relations and commodity production are organised on a repressive basis; they require that individuals not only submit to a capitalist work ethic, but be simultaneously tied into it via the spurious rewards of commodity fetishism. The contemporary 'workaholic' culture, ever greater consumption of commodities and the globalisation of capitalism serve to illustrate the continuing relevance of Marcuse' point. A state of *surplus repression* may underlie our conception of progress and that surplus serves not the needs of individuals, but the needs of the system.

Marcuse's example also hints at another theme, that of human happiness. The idea of happiness is not fashionable in the social sciences. For the most part, when they focus on moral issues, they focus on the concept of justice.

They are concerned with how equitable or not certain situations are. Certainly much of Habermas's work has been geared towards grounding the idea of justice. In 'On Hedonism', Marcuse (1968: ch. V) though, recognises the importance of happiness and that an opposition exists between happiness and more rationalistic principles, of which justice would be one.

We can imagine people being happy in an unjust society, as well as people being unhappy in a just society, yet Marcuse argues, that with a wider conception of Reason (with a capital r) we can see that the two principles involve each other, and neither should be neglected. He attacks the idea that happiness is a subjective condition internal to the individual, arguing instead that the freedom to enjoy sensual satisfaction is something that underpins happiness and has a universal potential. It is when happiness is restricted to the sphere of consumption, that it is experienced only as a private internal phenomenon, dependent on what we are able to consume. Of course enjoying happiness depends on having the freedom to satisfy one's needs and this requires not just greater affluence, but a radical reorganisation of how we experience the world. It involves a restructuring of the production process as well as consumption. In this, he anticipates what we now call 'soft technology' and 'green politics'. The broader point, though, is that for human beings to fulfill their potential a simple move to a more equitable, possibly communist society will not suffice. Our vision must be more utopian still, and draw more thoroughly on our sensuous, libidinal nature. The rational society would be both just and happy.

Like Adorno's ideas, Marcuse's are open to criticism in that they rely on a too singular view of the nature of instincts, and their capacity to generate a utopian future. Nevertheless, his ideas on the significance of happiness as something physically 'embodied', and our need for sensuousness as something repressed under the apparently rational conditions of modern capitalism, remain an important challenge to conventional assumptions.

Summary and Conclusion

The work of first generation Critical Theory has been subject to a variety of criticisms, usually based on its failure to provide a nuanced enough account of reality. Adorno is thought to be too negative and pessimistic and lack a sense that actors can, and do, evaluate the products of the culture industry. Marcuse is thought to be a mite more positive, but then only to produce misleading hopes of a utopian future based on a simplistic view of the psyche as driven by libidinal instinct (Leledakis 1995: 177–8). However, I believe their strength lies precisely in the uncompromising account of the way our system of production and consumption permeates other areas of life, especially the effects it has on the human subject. Under these circumstances, the current poststructuralist fashion for ideas such as the 'death of the subject', or 'subjectless discourse', seem ideological. To find intellectual value in seeing the subject constituted by discourse, and having no essential nature other than that created by discourse, only confirms a status quo in which the subject has indeed been taken over. Adorno and Marcuse's account of the processes of reification, commodity fetishism and rationalisation are timely reminders that social reality may have been 'constructed' through a discourse, but not freely, and not for the benefit of the people who inhabit the discourse.

Oliver James (1998, 2000), a contemporary clinical psychologist, with no connection to Critical Theory, confirms the picture drawn up by Adorno and Marcuse that our most affluent consumer societies impoverish us emotionally, with direct physical and psychological consequences. The use of technology in a purely instrumental fashion has damaged the environment in a variety of ways, 'there is not much doubt that the use of hormones, antibiotics and nitrophosphates in the food chain is weakening the human immune system'. But added to the physiological effects upon the brain, such as low levels of serotonin, James believes that there is a yawning gap between the promise of happiness implied in consuming commodities, and the reality of life. The mismatch between the two leads to constant disappointment and a measurable increase in levels of general depression, exacerbated by the use of medical and non-medical drugs to relieve the condition.

The complicated nature of social status in contemporary society adds to the situation. We all need the recognition of others, that who we are and what we do, is worthwhile. When Max Weber was writing in the early twentieth century, hierarchies of status were relatively stable, but now the picture is more complex and ephemeral. The shifting sands of social prestige may be a cause for celebration for postmodern authors, but do not provide firm ground for actual people to live meaningful lives. Capitalism requires a flexible workforce that accepts the instability of employment and ever more novel work practices; in return it offers only the thin fare of designer clothes and mobile phones as indicators of worth. I have noticed how currently in Britain second generation mobile phones are being advertised not for their technical value but their appearance. To be caught in the company of friends with an old fashioned phone, so the advertisements tell us, is shameful.

Under these circumstances, the human subject may well now show more clearly the signs of deformation spotted by Adorno et al. some fifty years ago: the narcissistic personality as the corollary of capitalist development. In the next chapter, I shall explore how Critical Theory saw the impact of capitalist development on family life and the changes it evoked in human relationships.

Further Reading

The best way in to Adorno's work, as indicated above, are the essays in *The Culture Industry* (1991) and *Minima Moralia* (1974); *Prisms* (1981) also offers the same possibility. Deborah Cook's *The Culture Industry Revisited* (1996) provides a careful interpretation of Adorno's ideas showing they are more nuanced that his critics suggest. A recent challenge to the idea that 'commodification' is now universal can be found in Williams 2002. Jarvis's (1998) introduction to Adorno is excellent, providing a carefully written account of 'negative dialectics', but it is not for the faint hearted, any more than is Gillian Rose's *The Melancholy Science* (1978), which is nevertheless more matter of fact. Richard Wolin in his *Walter Benjamin: An Aesthetic of Redemption* (1994) writes, what I think is the best and clearest account of this most cryptic Critical Theorist. Anyone interested in the Benjamin–Adorno debate should read Chapter 6. Wellmer (1991) provides a critique of Adorno's views on aesthetics from a second generation Critical Theory point of view. However, Marcuse's *One Dimensional Man* (1994) still provides the best and most accessible way into his use of the concepts of reification and commodity fetishism. For a good introduction to both Adorno and Marcuse see the relevant chapters in Turner and Elliot's *Profiles in Contemporary Social Theory* (2001).

6

Critical Theory, the Family and the Narcissistic Personality

In the last chapter, I dealt in some detail with Adorno and Marcuse's critique of culture for which they are renowned. In this chapter, I want to deal with Critical Theory's less well-known views on the decline of the modern family and the kind of emergent 'individual' that is symptomatic of this trend. I shall illustrate Critical Theory's claims by referring to the work of Christopher Lasch who also links changes happening at the level of culture with changes in family life. Lasch and Critical Theorists have been criticised by feminists and others for their patriarchal, backward-looking assumptions and for having a passive view of the subject. I shall argue that their concepts actually give us far greater purchase on modern family life than the vast array of new ones coined by authors such as Anthony Giddens.

The key element in Critical Theory's understanding of the family is that the latter stands in a pivotal position between the individual and society. For Critical Theory, the kind of individuals that emerge via the family express what is required by society at a particular stage in its development. Whether we can say society calls the shots in quite as deterministic a way as this implies is another question. Certainly, Fromm became less convinced by the amalgam of Marx and Freud that Marcuse and Adorno used to analyse things, preferring a more active, interactional view of things, a view also preferred by second generation Critical Theory. Other contemporary authors sympathetic to the first generation's ambitions also raise doubts about a rigid locking together of Marx and Freud that virtually eliminates 'autonomy' from the subject (Benjamin J, 1977, Craib 1989: ch. 6, Whitebook 1995: 24–41, Castoriadis 1997: 310–18). Nevertheless, as Craib acknowledges, Critical Theory's analyses provide an important building block for a wider understanding of things, and a timely reminder that behind the current promotion of the late-modern 'reflexive subject' by Giddens, lie real human relations. It is on these I wish to dwell.

Horkheimer and the 'Bourgeois Family'

In his seminal 1936 essay, 'Authority and the Family', Horkheimer set out his view of the family as sustaining society (1972: 98):

> The family, as one of the most important formative agencies, sees to it that the kind of human character emerges which social life requires, and gives the human being in great measure the indispensable adaptability for a specific authority-oriented conduct on which the existence of the bourgeois order largely depends.

Although Horkheimer seems to express the family's relation to society in functionalist terms, he has a less harmonious, more dialectical view in mind than one would get from a straightforward functionalist account. For Horkheimer, the family exhibits the contradictory tensions of wider society. In the same way that the middle-class family of the period of competitive capitalism (roughly 1850–1920) sought to echo the characteristics of aristocratic families by ostentatious displays of wealth, so the working-class family takes the middle-class family as its model for behaviour. However, in both cases the structural conditions of society make such imitation contradictory. The worker's family is necessarily pressed into wage slavery, which precludes it from achieving its middle-class ambitions. However, the structures of personality emergent within both bourgeois and working-class families, according to Horkheimer, are the same; both are oriented to the 'rightful' authority of the patriarchal father.

What is important to Horkheimer is the symmetry between the characteristics of the father-figure and the economic characteristics of competitive capitalism. He makes the link via the concept of instrumental reason. Critical Theorists followed Weber in believing that modern reason had been reduced to its bare technical essentials. Weber had captured the idea in his concept of 'Zweckrationalität', or goal-oriented reason, where the emphasis is on reason as an abstract, disinterested calculation of the most effective means of achieving a given goal or end. He contrasts this with the more substantive value-oriented forms of reason that are found in pre-modern societies. It is the modern emphasis on the *means* of achieving things, even to the point where means become ends, where we do things just because they are technically possible that gives modern reason its peculiarly instrumental quality (Weber 1978 [1922]: 85–7). We have come to experience the world as a variety of objects available for manipulation. Our concerns are with how effectively we can manipulate things rather than with the validity of the purpose or goal of that manipulation. Zygmunt Bauman (1989) gives a graphic example of what this can mean. In the Second World War in the Nazi concentration camps, gas became the preferred method of extermination because it was a more efficient way of achieving the given goal. Bullets were expensive, and anyway being asked to shoot innocent people tended to upset the soldiers. The over-

whelming brutality of this kind of rationality, let alone the action, is striking
because there is a perverse kind of logic to it: it is the logic of instrumental
reason where the validity of the ends recede entirely behind the emphasis on
means.[15]

Horkheimer implicitly draws on Weber's famous account of the emergence
of capitalism in the *Protestant Ethic and the Spirit of Capitalism*. The calculative, instrumental qualities required by the spirit of capitalism produce a deper-
sonalised form of interaction and a human (male) subject capable of rigid
self-discipline, of acting independently of others, in effect of treating himself
as an instrument for achieving goals. To be sure, there is some ambiguity for
Horkheimer and Adorno as to whether this way of going on originated with
capitalism, or has been part of western thought since ancient Greek times
and has only been amplified by capitalism. Nevertheless, this sociological idea
is then melded with a Freudian account of the structure of the human
personality.

The father-figure emerges as a strong autonomous being whose psychic
structure has profound effects upon others in the family. Capitalism has a
need for calculative, competitive entrepreneurs and produces an 'ideal' male
individual whose controlling, authoritarian outlook is internalised by other
members of the family. There are obvious sociological reasons for this, notably
the family's economic dependence on the male breadwinner, but the process
is more pervasive. Protestantism regarded the father's superior strength not
only as a natural fact but as a moral one too, and mothers and children learnt
to hold that superiority in high esteem (Horkheimer 1972: 100). There was
a progressive element in this:

> The self-control of the individual, the disposition for work and discipline, the ability
> to hold firmly to certain ideas, consistency in practical life, application of reason, per-
> severance and pleasure in constructive activity could all be developed, in the cir-
> cumstance, only under the dictation and guidance of the father whose own education
> had been won in the school of life. (1972: 101)

Nor were these progressive tendencies confined to 'constructive activity'.
Where the father's pressure was not too harsh, and was softened by maternal
tenderness, then there was the possibility of producing individuals who were
aware of their faults, and who, in following their father's example, developed
an 'attitude of independence, a joy in free dispositions and inner discipline;
who could represent authority as well as freedom and could practice these'
(Horkheimer and Adorno 1973: 141). Of course Horkheimer was not
unaware that individualism was unevenly distributed. The lives of women, by
virtue of their economic dependence, were thoroughly shaped in a negative
way by a patriarchal society. It was not just a matter of women needing to gain
access to money via men; there was also a range of other factors that left
women at a disadvantage. The spheres of education, culture, religion and leg-

islation were all overlain with masculinist assumptions about women's relative inferiority and thereby closed to them (1949: 385–6). Nevertheless, despite her subordinate role, the mother, by virtue of her structural position inspired a certain opposition to the father, necessary for the development of individuality. Also, because of her exclusion from wider society it fell to her to cultivate ideas of love, warmth and solidarity. Thus, while the virtues of bourgeois individualism have to be set against the background of social causes, such as the needs of the free market, and not dressed up ideologically in religious or metaphysical terms, they do contain an important element in the construction of the individual's sense of autonomy and well-being.

The growth of individualism, even under the distorting conditions of capitalism, is important not only because it marks the emergence of the individual from the grip of tradition, but also because it is the source of future possible rebellion. Individuals who were aware of the rightness of their autonomy had the potential to resist conditions that denied it. The problem was that the male-oriented individualism of early capitalism was under threat, not from working men seeking economic liberation, but from a new form of capitalism that restructured the individual as an altogether more compliant creature.

Monopoly Capitalism and the 'Fatherless' Society

In two essays, 'Authoritarianism and the Family Today' (1949), and 'The Family' (Horkheimer and Adorno 1973 [1956]), Horkheimer sharpened up the view that the authority once exercised by the family and the father-figure, was being supplanted by the impersonal authority of the system. In the name of instrumental reason, it was the system that now had to be obeyed, not the father-figure. The idea that the family was in crisis has a contemporary ring to it, but even when Horkheimer was writing, it was a familiar theme and a cause for regret amongst conservative thinkers. Horkheimer also felt regret, but it sprang from the fear that the family was being undermined as an implicit bastion of resistance.

For resistance to be possible, the authority of the father had to be internalised and rebelled against, yet under the conditions of monopoly capitalism men were obliged to see themselves as functionaries of conglomerate corporations, where flexible compliance with the corporation's commercial needs were uppermost. In a fairly strong sense, fathers had nothing to teach their children, except perhaps the implicit value of compliance to economic authority.

Quite rapidly nowadays succeeding generations regard the previous as 'old fashioned', as though issues of how best to live are only matters of transient fashion, so fast do the conditions of life change. Currently on British daytime television there are a variety of shows which explore, and offer quasi-expert advice on, matters of an extraordinarily personal, intimate kind. It works on the basis that everyone now craves advice about their inner lives from an authority *outside* the family. Indeed, the programmes expose the family as normally dysfunctional.

Under earlier conditions men knew themselves through and through by what they were, a master or a servant, something that was 'linked to a place and a past, a destiny'. Under the conditions of mass society they are isolated atoms, known only through their qualifications, or what they can consume, things that serve as external labels of identification. While this splitting of the individual from a more organic sense of unity has involved our liberation from the rigid hierarchies of tradition, it has a downside too.

Mothering, Horkheimer notes, has become subject to instrumental reason, with the nurturing of children seen as a professionalised activity. Women still love their children, but now plan their upbringing in a detached 'rational' way, ensuring the child has access to the best professional advice available for their health and education. In terms of upbringing, women even deliberately treat the child with a 'well balanced ratio between reprimand and friendliness as recommended by the popular psychological literature', such that even 'love is administered as an ingredient of psychological hygiene', with motherhood becoming a kind of profession (Horkheimer 1949: 387). As with men, so with women, relationships proper to the market now inflect relationships within the family.

The fate of fatherhood is similarly dispiriting. Fathers may still show signs of authority, but the child 'soon discovers that the father is by no means a powerful figure'; he is no longer 'the impartial judge, the generous protector he is pictured to be'. Unsurprisingly, the child takes a realistic view of the father's 'socially conditioned weakness' and ceases to identify with him as a source of moral autonomy. Instead, the growing child looks further afield for more powerful images of 'superfathers', which in Horkheimer's time were furnished by fascist imagery. The combination of 'rationalised' love from the mother and socially conditioned weakness from the father, Horkheimer believes, leaves the child's ego directly vulnerable to wider society. The internalisation of authority which once led to the individuation of the child and ultimately the formation of a strong autonomous ego had been eclipsed by direct conformity to external pressure. The result of this is that the child seeks adulthood prematurely, and in fact 'behaves as a scheming little adult with no consistent independent ego but with a tremendous amount of narcissism' (Horkheimer 1949: 390). Horkheimer believed that where once the child might have identified with the father's independence, now the only yardstick had become 'that of success, popularity and influence'. In short, he believed that children now identified with anything that is societally powerful. What he has described are the historical-sociological conditions, albeit rather general ones, which from a psychoanalytic point of view underpin the emergence of the narcissistic personality as a general feature of modern life.

Psychoanalysis and the Culture of Narcissism

Critical Theorists regularly used Freudian concepts to describe the implications of societal change for the structure of personality. Indeed this aspect of their work was originally driven by a desire to explain the lack of revolutionary potential amongst the working class, but they were not explicitly systematic in the way they applied these concepts. There will therefore be a certain amount of extrapolation on my part to show how their ideas feed into the broader thesis of what Christopher Lasch (1979) called the culture of narcissism, and how this is related to Freud's work.

One of the contradictions of Critical Theory to which Jessica Benjamin (1977) has drawn attention is that in a book such as *Dialectic of Enlightenment*, Adorno and Horkheimer identify the process of western 'enlightenment' with the development of instrumental reason, the main characteristics of which are manipulation and authoritarianism. Yet, in their work on the family, they seem to be regretting the loss of a form of family life based on the *authority* of the father-figure and the capacity of children to internalise and reproduce it. I leave this issue to one side for the moment, but it does express a tension in their work, though not one of which they were unaware – given Adorno's efforts to develop a negatively dialectical view of reason to which I referred in an earlier chapter.

Whether or not Adorno and Horkheimer secretly hankered after the authoritarian personality as a model for real individualism, it is as Cook (1996: 21) points out, the concept of narcissism that is the psychological key to how they analyse the damage done to individuals by changes in the capitalist system. Adorno himself described it as 'among Freud's most magnificent discoveries' (Adorno 1967/68: Part 2: 88), and his use of it can be seen in the essays 'Freudian Theory and the Pattern of Fascist Propaganda' (Arato and Gebhardt 1978: 118ff), and 'Sociology and Psychology' (Adorno 1967/68), though not in *The Authoritarian Personality* (Adorno et al. 1950).

The idea of the narcissistic personality has its origins in Freud's theory about the processes of mental growth from childhood to adulthood. Put rather baldly, the baby gradually has to learn to differentiate itself from its mother; it has to move from being at one with, and wholly dependent on its mother, to a state of recognising its separateness and potential autonomy. Anyone who has had small children will know how distraught the young child can become if the mother even disappears from the room for a moment – no amount of consolatory words seem to soothe its fear and anger. Coupled with this is the baby's voracious need to have its appetites assuaged via food, warmth and amusement, as though it was the centre of the world, and the world, its mother, there solely to satisfy these needs. This display of omnipotence Freud regarded as normal infantile narcissism. The word 'narcissism' derives from the Greek god Narcissus, who looked into a pool of water and was so enchanted with his reflection he fell in love with it. From then on he could find nothing to value except that which was a reflection of himself. However, while the baby has to come to terms with reality, growing to realise, rather painfully, that it is not at the centre of things, but one ego amongst others, adults under some conditions show signs of 'pathological narcissism', which is a kind of regression, or more accurately the re-emergence of narcissistic elements first displayed in infancy.

Freud argued that growing into adulthood was a process that went through stages. These stages involved the individual dealing with issues such as fear, anxiety, love and hate that occur in different forms at different times. The stages should not be seen in too clear cut a fashion, not least because the resolution of issues at one stage does not involve a simple leaving behind of the problems encountered there. In early childhood, roughly before the age of three, the child goes through the oral, anal and phallic stages, before encountering the oedipal stage, where sexual difference between boys and girls comes to the fore.

Central to the development of narcissism is the Oedipus complex, a group of problems and resolutions the individual finds at that stage. Freud maintained that early childhood was not asexual as common sense suggests, but a time of implicit sexuality, providing the ground from which the child gradually learns to become male or female. Up to the age of about three, the child is bisexual, his or her sexuality is not yet organised around the formal male/female distinctions we know in adult life. At the oedipal stage, both boys and girls, having been soothed and nurtured for three years, regard their mothers as objects of love and desire. Little boys will often express the wish to marry their mothers when they grow up, but the boy's desire for his mother is bound to be thwarted by the father, whose adult strength and general superiority is obvious. The boy cannot supplant his father in his mother's affections, but must wait until he is an adult to seek alternatives. As a counterpoint to this, it is often noted that fathers, apparently rather oddly, feel jealous towards their sons who suddenly receive all the love and attention they thought was reserved for them (Craib 1989: 43).

The boy must give up his desire for his mother or he will run into conflict with his father, who can appear as something of an ogre, the disciplinarian who admonishes the child for being tied to his mother's apron strings, while pointing out that he needs to face the hard world of reality to be a 'proper boy'. According to Freud, at the level of phantasy, competition between father and son can entail a fear of castration on the boy's part, a fear that unless he accepts the father's position vis-a vis the mother, he runs the risk of having his penis cut off. In order to relieve these fears the boy must relinquish his desire for his mother and start to identify with his father and all that he stands for. The boy then represses his desire for his mother and learns to control his behaviour. Developing an ego-ideal based on his father, he learns to identify with the father-figure. This ego-ideal, or what the child wants to be like, becomes the foundation for a strong, autonomous ego in later life.

As feminists have pointed out, Freud gives a certain logical priority to the development of boys, though the developmental processes that girls undergo are no less difficult. Girls can identify with their mothers up to a point, but sooner or later must direct their desire towards a father-substitute, ultimately perhaps a baby. However, while this has critical implications for how we value the traditional family, what was important from Critical Theory's point of view, and even more so from that of Christopher Lasch, is what now appears to be the *waning* of the Oedipus complex (Loewald 1980: 384–404), particularly in relation to the historical role of the male.

If the ego-development, and ultimate autonomy of boys, depends on early conflict followed by identification with a strong independent father-figure, what becomes of that process if changing economic relations requires the adult male to be not independent and strong, but subservient and flexible to the needs of the system? The answer, in short, is the emergence of the narcissistic personality along with the ground on which it flourishes: the culture of narcissism.

As already mentioned the resolutions to the various stages a child goes through are not clear cut affairs, but involve the recurrence of similar issues at later times in life. Elements of the Oedipal stage, for example, reappear during adolescence, when the relationship between parents, children and wider society come into focus. Lasch focuses on the characteristics of the adult narcissistic personality in relation to the decline in the authority of the family. He notes that the classic symptoms of neurosis and hysteria that Freud identified as resulting from too much repression in the family are no longer the symptoms that patients present to psychoanalysts. Instead they now come with a much vaguer sense of disquiet, with feelings of emptiness, a kind of inner numbness that is experienced in spite of the person being apparently successful and popular in the outside world. Because the child in a 'fatherless' society has never had to come to terms with the anger and jealousy generated during the oedipal stage, he or she is robbed of the inner sense of purpose and self-direction that the internalisation of authority would have provided.

The male narcissist lives superficially, he may be promiscuous, popular and generally successful, but fears genuine intimacy and commitment, as it raises the spectre of the anger he originally directed towards his parents, and which they were unable to resolve and he redirect. As the messiness of real intimacy is too threatening, the narcissist cultivates a shallow attitude towards things, seeking only to be part of what will show him in a good light, to be an example of what is powerfully popular. It is the uncritical attraction to things that *appear* powerful that Adorno felt underpinned the popularity of fascism. In effect, where the traditional authority-centred family may have suffered from too much repression, the modern family, ironically, suffers from too little, but nevertheless produces a personality type amenable to authority.

In 'Freudian Theory and the Pattern of Fascist Propaganda' (Arato and Gebhardt 1978), Adorno does not directly link the decline of the patriarchal family to the rise of fascism, nor does he try to say that narcissism caused fascism, but that the tendency towards narcissism provided the psychological ground for its development. One of the curiosities of fascist propaganda is its lack of any rational content. There is no programme that would pass muster at a political level, yet its appeal seems to overwhelm its followers. The appeal, Adorno believes, is best explained by reference to more primitive unconscious needs. Instead of dealing with the objective causes of problems, fascism's appeal is made directly through the power of an overwhelming leader, who 'is apt to reanimate the idea of the all-powerful and threatening primal father'. Such a figure serves group psychology, where the lack of identification with actual father-figures via the Oedipus complex has declined enough to leave a vacuum. The imagery of fascist propaganda, in a sense, *must not* be rational, for to fill the vacuum it must draw on a regressive unconscious need to be at one with an all-powerful parent.

The narcissistic aspect in this is also apparent. The leader's followers experience his persona to be so much at one with them, that no other vision of the world is possible. The fascist group's view of things is not open to question, because like the god, Narcissus, only its own image is worth looking at; 'the follower, simply through belonging to the in-group, is better, higher and purer than those who are excluded'. In fact any kind of criticism, any challenge from a group perceived to be outsiders is likely to be met by a violent reaction, because it will be experienced as a 'narcissistic loss' that 'elicits rage', from an angry child that has had its omnipotence threatened by being deprived of its love-object (Adorno in Arato and Gebhardt 1978: 129–130).

But how does this account of mid-twentieth-century fascism serve our understanding of contemporary western societies, where life appears distinctly free and unencumbered by authority? Adorno makes the point that a given social structure 'selects' psychological tendencies but does not 'express' them, by which he means that different historical circumstances draw on different psychic formations in the human subject, but the correspondence between a society's psychology and its social structure is not direct (Adorno 1967/68: 89–90). Critical Theory has always been wary of trying to explain one level of reality in terms of another. Thus, while the political conditions that characterised Nazi Germany were very different from those we find today, the human subject may have psychological properties similar to those that Critical Theory saw emerging in the 1940s and '50s. Certainly Adorno felt that the nature of fascist propaganda and the products of the culture industry were popular because they appealed to the same narcissistic elements in the human subject.

For Lasch (1979), what makes modern culture narcissistic is its overwhelming emphasis on *appearances*. The appearance of things, of success, of sexiness, of celebrity, is what matters more than its substance. Indeed, in a sense the appearance of success has now become its substance, there is no success except that found in what appears popular, desirable, and so forth.

I was struck recently, while watching a BBC television production of Jane Austen's *Pride and Prejudice*, how different dancing was in the nineteenth-century, compared with now. The rigid formality of nineteenth-century dances seemed so repressive compared with what goes on today. Yet contact of both a physical and emotional kind was possible then, albeit gripped within an inflexible framework of politeness. Today, in contrast, formality and politeness have gone, and have been replaced by what appears to be an altogether more free and easy form. However, the modern form in its way is no less rigid, demanding the appearance of sexiness from the dancers, but ironically with no physical contact possible. It is as though the dancers are now dancing on their own, performing to aggrandize themselves in the eyes of others. The dancers seem to saying 'look at me', 'look how sexy I am', 'don't you envy me, wouldn't you like to have me, though you can't'. Of course this is not to say that less sex happens now than in the nineteenth-century, quite possibly the opposite, but like dancing, sex for the modern narcissistic personality involves avoidance of, not embroilment in intimacy.

The rigidity of the nineteenth-century form ensured a degree of equality between the dancers, but the modern form is ruthlessly competitive, with the sexiest dancers making their way to the centre of the floor so they can display themselves to best effect. The poorer dancers have to content themselves with shuffling back and forth around the edges. This is not a democratic environment where all have an equal chance to participate, but one where each individual must desperately compete to be envied by the others. Where once dances were an opportunity for interaction to take place, as a prelude to establishing something more personal, they are now designed to preclude it. Not only do modern dancers avoid holding a partner because such holding would restrict self-display, but also the volume of the music is so great that it even prevents talk between people. The purpose of such an environment is thus not to foster personal relations, but to inhibit them. The narcissistic personality is fearful of risking him or herself in the awkwardness of a personal relationship, preferring to develop what Lasch (1979: 37) calls 'a careful protective shallowness'. As a student remarked to me, 'love now seems to consist of manipulating others into admiring you'.

It does not of course mean that everyone who dances in a club is, in Freudian terms, pathologically narcissistic. There is a danger that in trying to map an inner condition on to society one ignores the complexity and specificity of that society. Nevertheless, I believe the value of Critical Theory lies in providing broad building blocks for diagnosing the times. The trend Critical Theory identified fifty years ago towards ego-weakness, and the compensating trend toward pseudo-individualism, is evidenced in the kind of account Lasch provides. In some degree, as Lasch (1979: 34) points out, 'every culture reproduces itself . . . in the individual, in the form of personality'.

Like Critical Theorists, Lasch believes that the decline in the patriarchal family has left unresolved tensions deriving from the oedipal stage of development. The inability to identify with a strong parent has left individuals to act out their conflicts rather than sublimating or repressing them. The child's sense of anger towards his or her parents is internalised, and later, in compensation, projected onto the outside world 'with fantasies of wealth, beauty and omnipotence.' At a cultural level this trend can be seen in various ways. For example, the management of personal impressions in the business world is now seen as of vital importance. Rather than focusing on problems to be solved, the young executive must appear to be a winner. S/he must cultivate the playful attitude of a 'gamesman', travelling light emotionally and morally, the better to ooze the potential that others will envy.

Lasch refers to studies dating from the 1970s, but the same kind of development is described in more recent work. Richard Sennett in his *The Corrosion of Character* (1998) shows how changes in work patterns have affected the character of company employees. Sennett draws a distinction between character and personality. He argues that the more superficial qualities of 'personality' have replaced the more fundamental qualities of 'character' in our lives. Jobs in the new 'disorganised capitalism' require employees to have 'personality', not 'character'. Employees need to be immensely flexible in their work practices and be willing to move from job to job frequently and opportunistically'; this requires 'personality not 'character', and is something that impacts on our sense of commitment in other areas of life. One may wish to pass on to one's children the moral virtues of loyalty, trustworthiness and responsibilty, but if 'the conditions of the new economy feed instead on experience which drifts in time, from place to place, from job to job', then this short-term outlook will be at odds with that wish. In the long run, it corrodes not only the ties which bind people together, but also those features of everyday life that sustain our sense of self. If we cannot live in a regular, persistent kind of way, we cannot know who we are.

What Lasch and Sennett share in common with Critical Theory is a sceptical attitude towards society's appearances. A belief that what appears to be the case, such as the emergence of a new, flexible, freewheeling personality, liberated from the constraints of tradition, is neither a liberated individual, nor the product of benign forces. The issue is not new to sociology either. Alvin Gouldner in his famous, *The Coming Crisis of Western Sociology* (1971), takes Goffman's interactionism to task for a similarly failing to move beyond appearances. In books such as *The Presentation of the Self in Everyday Life* (1971), Goffman had dwelt on the way individuals manipulate themselves to produce the desired effect on those around them. The implication was that individuals are no more than lightning calculators of their own appearances and function without emotion. Goffman's mistake was to assume that this modern super-reflexive creature was the model for how we should understand all human subjects. For Gouldner, what Goffman had described, was in fact the self-manoeuvring of the modern American company man, someone who had no choice but to manoeuvre.

Lasch also sees Goffman as one who has described but not challenged the assumptions of reflexivity in the modern subject. For Lasch, the need to calculate and control one's behaviour inhibits spontaneous action, and is ultimately the result of a 'waning belief in the reality of the external world' (1979: 90). In other words, reality in a narcissistic culture seems so much to be a reflection of how we choose to think and act, so much socially constructed by us that the idea of something being externally real and independent of us, appears to be the illusion. Life seems to consist only of a network of social relations that we self-consciously negotiate, to present ourselves hopefully to good effect in our various 'roles'. And for this 'performing self', the information gleaned from advertising, films and mass culture generally, provides the informational props needed to polish up the performance.

In a slightly different but related way Marcuse (1955: 44) refers to the 'performance principle' as something that has emerged under the specific conditions of modern capitalism. He accepts Freud's idea that the development of civilisation has required the repression of instincts. In Freudian terminology, the Pleasure principle must come to terms with the Reality principle, the libidinal, pleasurable side of life must be mediated by the demands of living in the real world, where work and so forth are necessary for life. However, he disagrees with Freud in arguing that the Pleasure and Reality principles are historically variable. In capitalist societies, for example, the Reality principle takes the particular form of a Performance principle. In pre-modern societies, because material goods were scarce, high levels of repression were necessary to ensure that food and shelter were available. In modern societies such scarcity no longer exists, the great merit of capitalism has been to generate hitherto unimaginable levels of wealth. However, because capitalism is organised on an exploitative and repressive basis, it cannot allow this wealth to weaken its grip on people. Capitalist reality must continue to impose itself, which it does through the Performance principle. It must modify our instinctual lives so we become more and more acquisitive and seek satisfaction through the consumption of ever more goods, which in turn allows capitalism to expand more or less indefinitely. In short, we must learn to perform as narcissistic subjects both in terms of production and consumption.

Lasch provides numerous examples of what cultural narcissism means, how it speaks to the same personality trait in people and he sometimes directly adopts Adorno's claim that the culture industry uses 'super-ego introjects'. Because the narcissist is incapable of identifying with 'good' parents or other authority figures in the first place, the often violent, malevolent, and grotesque heroes of popular film reanimate the fears and needs generated by the earlier, unresolved challenge. We, in a sense, consume the stunning performative style of film characters such as Rambo, Robocop and Terminator, who in their barely human way can be seen to represent the avenging 'primal-father figure', so that the audience can feel both discomfited and excited.

In *Haven in a Heartless World* (1977: 177), Lasch refers to the content of comic strips, television comedy, and crime films. People often ask why we relish crime stories so much. The answer, he suggests, is that:

> The melodrama of crime brings to quasi-consciousness a sinister father image, buried but not forgotten in the disguise of a criminal, a 'lord of the underworld', or a law enforcement officer who commits crime in the name of justice. In *The Godfather*, the identification of the father with the master criminal becomes unmistakable.

The content of crime films arguably has shifted so much that the criminal often takes on heroic qualities. In Britain, the Kray family, who were famous in the 1960s for their protection rackets and the way they murdered or intimidated anyone who got in their way, still holds attention. National newspapers and television still record the large ostentatious funerals that follow deaths in that family and films and television still examine the lives of the main characters, with a fearful but intent gaze. It is as though the ruthless omnipotence of such gangsters bypasses our concern for justice and triggers in us a deeper mixture of horror and admiration. No such interest is shown towards the policemen who arrested them and secured their conviction.

Even the policeman who breaks the law to achieve his goal is set up in films and television to be admired for style and singularity of purpose; this in itself is seen as justification for his behaviour. We all know it is an unsafe and amoral world, thus performing stylishly in it has become both the right and only thing to do. Of course the psychoanalytic explanation for this trend is not the only one possible. Kellner and Ryan (1988) and Kellner (1995), from a broadly Critical Theory standpoint, have shown how films such as the Rambo series are heavily tinged with the American sense of failure following the Vietnam war, but their account complements rather than runs counter to the one I have drawn from Adorno and Lasch. Ryan and Kellner's account is pitched at the level of ideology, and directed towards cultural mood, which they see as an indirect reflection of political and economic trends, such as New Right Liberalism and Reaganism.

For Lasch, the admiration of 'power' and 'celebrity' shows up not only in show business, but in politics too, as a symptom of a desire by people to see themselves as an extension of those who have such 'power' and 'celebrity', real or imagined. Because the narcissist is unable to identify with the 'good' authority figure, he or she is unable to identify with the justified fame that some figures might deserve. Instead 'celebrity' is admired for its own sake. Hence we sometimes declare that celebrities are often just 'famous for being famous'. The trend is serviced by politics, as it becomes more a matter of spectacle than substance. When politicians find themselves becoming unpopular in the opinion polls they seek not to question the policies, indeed different policies seem almost literally 'unthinkable', but to repackage them. They assume that the only thing wrong is that their policies have not been presented attractively enough.

It is not only in the public arena that cultural narcissism is apparent, there is now a veritable industry of therapies designed to help the individual achieve self-fulfillment. As Lasch (1979: 92) puts it:

> All of us, actors and spectators alike, live surrounded by mirrors. In them we seek reassurance of our capacity to captivate or impress others, anxiously searching out blemishes that might detract from the image we intend to project.

Lasch is referring not only to beauty therapies, but also to a broader idea, that for both women and men 'the creation of the self has become the highest form of creativity', and that people have become 'connoisseurs of their own performance'. They seek reassurance about their identity, through therapies that promise to fill an empty space, the one left over from an earlier stage by the inability to find parental objects with which to identify.

Lasch, in Critical Theory fashion, challenges the idea that the desire for self-improvement is an expression of capitalism's interest in our potential for human development. In fact, for the narcissistic personality, it is as much about self-hatred as self-admiration. The narcissism that is fed by these cultural developments compensates for unresolved infantile rage by providing fantasies of omnipotence and perfection. The fantasies, though, service our self-concern, our need for admiration. They cultivate what Craib (1994: ch. 9) calls the 'false self of late modernity', rather than doing anything else. They are an expression of the problem, not part of the solution. Lasch and Craib, like Horkheimer and Adorno are sceptical about the authenticity of individualism in societies that trumpet it most loudly.

The Feminist Critique

Lasch has developed and applied some Critical Theory ideas in a particularly vivid way. He has been able to show how prophetic Horkheimer and Adorno's insights were in the context of modern American life. His examples are plentiful, though one weakness is that they are too plentiful and re-reading *The Culture of Narcissism* I find myself wishing he would dwell longer on, and explore more thoroughly, fewer examples. The collage effect leaves me wondering whether all the examples fit the thesis equally well. Certainly his claims, like those of Horkheimer and Adorno, have been criticised.

Feminist writers such as Barrett and McIntosh (1991), and Doane and Hodges (1987), question the negative assessment of family life that Lasch's narcissism thesis has produced. They argue that from the point of view of women, the more loose-limbed and fragmentary nature of modern family life has had distinct advantages. The traditional patriarchal family designated

women a subordinate role that distorted their lives to such an extent that to
talk, even implicitly, of it being a better model for human development, is wide
of the mark. They rightly ask, better for whom? Lasch, they argue, betrays an
uncritical nostalgia for a well ordered 'masculine' world, where people knew
their place, and found the identifications and commitments necessary for their
psychic well-being. In doing this, he constantly plays down the negative side
of such family life: its oppression of women.

Barrett and McIntosh also point out that when Lasch criticises the fact that
the welfare state has undermined the authority of the family, by robbing it of
some of its functions he overlooks the material advantages this has brought.
It can just as easily be seen as a victory for the working class over a capitalism
that exploits it, but which it nevertheless needs. It has brought to millions a
level of health and material security quite unknown in earlier times. Certainly
there is some lack of dialectical awareness in Lasch's work, and a corresponding failure to see anything progressive in the modern world. However, while
Barrett and McIntosh's argument is an important reminder of the fact that the
welfare state has improved the material lot of large numbers of people, it does
not invalidate Lasch's point that one of the unforeseen consequences has been
the changes he describes.

Similarly, while Lasch does use the patriarchal family as a kind of norm
against which to judge the current state of affairs, he is never simply an advo-
cate of it. He uses it to try and make sense of the current situation and to
challenge the idea that the apparent democracy and lack of 'authority' in the
modern family is not all it is cracked up to be. Behind the scenes it produces
often unhappy people directly vulnerable to the illusions of capitalism, and
thereby more amenable to its requirements, either in terms of 'consuming' or
'performing'. In this, his work, like that of Critical Theory, retains an important radical thrust in developing the ground for a social psychology of
conformity.

Jessica Benjamin (1977, 1978) draws attention to similar patriarchal assumptions in Adorno and Horkheimer's work. The essence of her criticism is
that their work is contradictory. They are arguing, she maintains, that the only
way we can resist authority is by first internalising and accepting authority,
something paradoxical: they cannot have their cake and eat it too.

> Those aspects of consciousness where this resistance might be located – critical
> reason, individuation, integrity and ultimately resistance itself – are tied to the
> process of internalizing authority. As a result, the rejection of authority can only take
> place through its prior acceptance. Even though the subjective dimension of domi-
> nation is found to be in the way authority is internalised (*the reification of con-
> sciousness etc.*), the only possible resistance to authority is located in the same process
> of internalization. (Benjamin 1977: 42, italics added)

She is referring to Critical Theory's claim that during the era of competitive capitalism, at least the possibility of individual autonomy emerged, but

under more recent conditions individualism has deteriorated into a facade for 'seamless conformity'. Because Critical Theorists see the process of domination as being directly imposed by the one-dimensional society, while the role of the family diminishes, they are obliged to look back nostalgically to the (male) authority of the traditional patriarchal family as a source of autonomy. Without the effects of the traditional family working at the level of individual psychology, the struggle for social emancipation cannot be waged.

Benjamin, like second generation Critical Theory, asks whether the potential for emancipation would be better grounded in 'an intersubjective theory of personality, rather than an individual psychology of internalization'. She has in mind the perspective in psychoanalysis known as object-relations theory. In this perspective, ego development is explained in terms of interaction with other peoples rather than an individual's libidinal struggle for autonomy against overwhelming odds. The weakness of Adorno's account is to see the development of the ego as something society allowed to come into existence, but thereby something it can eliminate. The intersubjective realm, with its more reciprocal notion of personality, allows for a more nuanced account of the relation between a society's psychology and its social system than does the concept of narcissism, which is dependent on the waning of the Oedipus complex.

From a feminist perspective in a slightly later paper, Benjamin (1978) argues that there is a serious flaw in Horkheimer's insistence that autonomy depends on the internalisation of the *father's* authority. This view implies that the nurturant part played by the mother does not contribute to the autonomy of the child, and she asks,

> what is nurturance if not the pleasure in the other's growth? if not the desire to satisfy the other's needs, whether the need to cling or the need to be independent? (1978: 54)

To hold to Critical Theory's version of individual autonomy means to emphasise an undialectical, patriarchal view of freedom where the isolated individual is seen as the desirable end state, something with which women would find it difficult to identify. Critical Theory's weakness, again, is to miss the active intersubjective element in the process of growing up. Adorno and Horkheimer may lament the decline of the nurturant side of things, but have no place for it in their account of freedom. What accounts for the diminution of ego-autonomy, for Benjamin, are the privatization of family life, the break up of kinship ties and other local networks of relationship. The decline in affective support once provided by these factors has left mothering an isolated activity. This is likely to make the mother more dependent on the child, and to 'demand that the child perform according to the reified standards she imbibes from the media'. She wants the child to reflect well upon her as a mother, but because of her isolation contents herself with the appearance of self-reliance in the child, rather than with a true sense of independence:

Benjamin's criticisms are telling, particularly in view of Critical Theory's claim to be a dialectical theory. However, whether they are decisive is another matter. Cook (1996) cites textual evidence to show that Adorno was aware of psychoanalytic explanations other than the Oedipus complex for the decline in ego-autonomy, but I think Benjamin is right in pointing out the one-sided emphasis Critical Theory places on it. Nevertheless, her emphasis on changes in family life as a source of declining ego-autonomy is not at odds with Adorno and Horkheimer's claims, but a revision of it. It is the same changes in social-economic conditions that have produced a more pliable ego, whether it is conceived in terms of a 'fatherless society' (Critical Theory), or the influence of instrumental reason upon motherhood (Benjamin). The problem for both parties is the lack of ego-autonomy rooted in conditions that have altered the structure of family life and thus the dynamics of individuality. Adorno and Horkheimer may appear to give normative value to the patriarchal family, but Benjamin does something similar in searching for the more authentic, nurturant relationship between mother and child that modern conditions have undermined.

Giddens' Critique

In *Modernity and Self Identity* (1991) Anthony Giddens takes Lasch's narcissism thesis to task for underestimating the power of agency in the human subject. He develops the idea that what characterises late, as opposed to post-modernity, is its reflexivity. He uses the term 'late modernity', as opposed to 'postmodernity' as he sees its characteristics as an extension of the modern world, rather than as a break with it.

There are three main characteristics of late modernity: the 'separation of time and space', the 'disembedding of social institutions', and 'reflexivity'. The separation of time and space refers to changes wrought by the ability to coordinate 'social activities without necessary reference to the particularities of place'. The instantaneous nature of mass communication in the late modern world means that we no longer feel tied to the reference points of a particular place for our understanding of the world. In everyday terms, we can communicate on a global basis, undertaking personal or financial transactions at the click of a computer mouse, which means that people and places that were once distant can be brought into our lives instantly. Unsurprisingly our commitment to a particular moral locality is lessened. This, in effect, is what he means by the disembedding of social institutions, which he describes as the 'lifting out' of social relations from local contexts and their rearticulation across indefinite tracts of time and space.

The third characteristic, reflexivity, refers to the susceptibility of most aspects of social activity and material relations with nature, to 'chronic revision in the light of new information or knowledge' (1991: 20). What he means is that we constantly have to revise our lives according to changes in knowledge. Where it was the hope of the Enlightenment to secure true knowledge once and for all, we now have to accept a lack of certainty about knowledge, that it is an open-ended process rather than one of final discovery. The recent crisis in Britain over 'mad cow disease' could stand as an example. Rather oddly, Giddens distinguishes between this kind of reflexivity and its more usual sociological usage as the self-monitoring of the human subject. Odd, because what he describes so plainly relates to what happens to people.

Nevertheless, he develops the implications of 'globalisation', which in essence is what he is talking about, in terms of what it means for human relationships. The breaking up of tradition has allowed the 'pure relationship' to emerge. The pure relationship is one based solely on intimacy and trust, unencumbered by traditional bolsters of family, kinship, and economic considerations: 'it is, as it were free-floating' (Giddens 1991: 89). The commitment between people depends wholly on the investment each puts into the relationship and exists 'only for what the relationship can bring to the partners involved'. It is also reflexive in the sense that it requires regular monitoring; a kind of continuous examination of how worthwhile it is for both parties.

His critique of Lasch is based on these observations about the 'pure relationship', which he tacitly applauds. He criticises Lasch and by implication, Horkheimer and Adorno, for the way they see the individual as 'passive in relation to overwhelming external forces'. Lasch's outlook fails to grasp the nature of human empowerment, the way people 'react against social circumstances they find oppressive'. We may live in a 'risk' society, but that does not mean we cannot intervene in it. He cites the work of Judith Stacey (1990) on ties amongst working-class families in Silicon Valley in California. The social environment of married life, he notes, has indeed become 'disturbing and unsettling'; marriage is not particularly stable, certainly not traditional. Yet, in the face of this, people do not withdraw, as Lasch suggests the narcissist would, but establish new forms of relationship. They actively restructure 'new forms of gender and kinship relation out of the detritus of pre-established forms of family life' (1991: 176–7). This development, Giddens argues, flies in the face of Lasch's claim that the narcissist uses relationships as a defence mechanism to compensate for feelings of emptiness and lack of self-esteem.

It is difficult to see how Giddens' claims count against Lasch. Lasch, like Adorno, is not claiming that the narcissist withdraws from the world in an ordinary sense. In fact, quite the opposite, narcissists are highly involved in worldly affairs, they take pride in their appearances, the skill they possess to evoke the admiration of others, and they certainly have a creative attitude towards relationships, being able to move 'creatively' from one to another. They are very much *in* the world, if not exactly of it. They use what the world has to offer to protect themselves from it, rather than using it to change the world or themselves.

When Giddens argues that the restructuring of family life along non-traditional lines contradicts Lasch's claim that cultural narcissism induces a waning sense of historical time, a closure of our sense of there being a past and future as we immerse ourselves in the present, he contradicts himself. Not only does Stacey's work suggest that the instability of the working environment in Silicon Valley produces a much looser, less long-term sense of what a relationship might be; his own views about disembedding from locality, time–space separation, and the emergence of the pure relationship, point in the same direction. Our commitment to time and place, and other people has become a fragile affair.

Giddens also criticises Lasch, for paying too little attention to the relation between the self and the body. Giddens believes that the body can no longer be just ' "accepted", fed and adorned according to traditional ritual', it must now become a core part of the reflexive project of self-identity. This is because the processes of fragmentation, characteristic of late modernity, have undermined tradition. How we should look and what we signal by it, is now a lifestyle option. For Giddens, lifestyle options concerning the body, the impression we make in wearing particular clothes, our body image and muscle definition, all entail us making choices between alternatives. It is the fact that we do make choices that leads him to the view that human subjects are actively involved in the creation of self-identity, and therefore not narcissistic. Again, Lasch and Adorno do not deny that the narcissist will actively seek out the best image to project, more important for them is the perceived *need* of the subject to project an image to establish his or her identity, as though identity was as temporary and frangible as a new outfit, and not the messy, sometimes tortuous affair that Freud's work suggests.

Indeed, Giddens momentarily recognises that we have *no* choice but to make a choice. As he puts it 'deciding between alternatives is not itself an option, but an inherent element of the construction of self-identity' (1991: 178). It is not that Giddens is descriptively wrong, but that his account is partial; there is surely much more to identity than the creation of appearances. The fact that we *have* to pursue a self-image, rather than have it supplied by tradition, class, or gender *appears* to be a kind of liberation, but only in a fragmentary world peopled by isolated consumers. The idea that this condition might be a deeply ideological one that serves the interests of capitalism eludes Giddens.

Giddens is not unaware of some of the psychological implications of the fragility of modern life. He does, for example, deal with the 'ontological security' of the subject under late modern conditions (1991: ch. 2). Ontological security refers to a strong sense of our own reality and the legitimacy of our own being. Given the fragmentary nature of our experience, our surety with regard to this can become problematic. Giddens has a distinctly social-interactional view of the problem of ontological in/security. He describes our capacity for such security as dependent on 'acquired routines and forms of mastery associated with them ... they are constitutive of an emotional acceptance of the reality of the "external world"' (1991: 42). In other words, for Giddens, it is the routines of everyday life that sustain our sense of trust in reality. Yet social routines take many different forms and presuppose different motives (Layder 1997: 62–6). Do health routines that demand ever-thinner bodies or ever-larger muscles sustain our sense of reality or distort it?

Giddens seems to suppose that interaction per se will secure us, because ontologically speaking, human subjects *are* reflexive interactionists, and if we have enough interaction we will become ontologically secure. I don't think this is entirely mistaken, but 'reflexive interactionists' is not all we are. We have an inner world that shapes what we do in our interactions. Giddens draws on the work of R. D. Laing in his discussion of ontological security. Laing has argued that chronic ontological insecurity underlies mental illness (schizophrenia), in that schizophrenics are so insecure about who they are, so unable to sustain their autonomy, that they lack all sense of personal identity. Yet, in *Sanity Madness and the Family* (1968), Laing's argument is that there are certain kinds of *routine interaction* in family life that actually precipitate mental illness. Moreover, Laing's work is influenced by Sartre's and Heidegger's existentialist philosophy, which emphasises that ontological security is not a solid achievable condition, but exists in tension with ontological *in*security, which is the source of our freedom and autonomy. Layder (1997: 67) describes this as a dialectic between our sense of relatedness and separateness. In some degree, even mentally healthy people as part of their normal condition, oscillate between feelings of being overwhelmed by others, and of wanting to connect with them. The point he is making is that we have an inner life, which is not simply made up of interaction with others. Interaction with others may make us feel secure, but equally it may not. And as Craib (1992: 176) points out, anyway, ontological security is not the same as feeling safe, but more to do with the ability to deal with change than with following routines.

There is much in Giddens' work that catches the eye. His description of new social phenomena is partially accurate and a useful, almost phenomenological guide to what is going on. But like phenomenological accounts generally, it often reads rather like a 'just-so' story; this is the way the world is, and that is all that can be said about it. Of course we have to start from how things are, but that does not mean that is all there is, or that that is where we have to finish up. There is a stoical acceptance in Giddens of the way the world is, and a dwelling on the creative responses actors make to it, something that is the basis of his structuration theory. The task of sociology, as he presents it, is to describe the world as it appears, and the array of forty-one concepts he includes in the glossary to *Modernity and Self-Identity,* seems to do this. But he does not invoke concepts that might question its validity by explaining how it came to appear that way. The latter view is the one that Lasch and Critical Theory stand for.

Indeed one might suggest that the sheer volume of concepts Giddens uses is a symptom of the narcissism he denies in society. There is no reason to assume that the effects of cultural narcissism do not intrude into social theory itself, providing an unconscious way of producing the appearance of explanation while covering up the lack of a more substantial account of how the world works. Of course, anyone who has read Lasch's *The Culture of Narcissism* might point to a similar tendency towards impressionism, a collage effect, produced by making a wide range of examples serve his thesis. Yet, it seems to me that while not all these examples work equally well, they are underpinned by an explanation. It is that changes in the intrapsychic structure of the individual, evinced by larger social-historical change, are related to, and have reciprocal effects at, the cultural level. There is also a danger that one might read into Lasch's work the assumption that everyone in society is 'pathologically narcissistic'. Certainly he marshals psychoanalytic literature concerned with this pathology in support of his case, but also refers to 'borderline narcissism' in general discussion. He is thus able to use the idea of narcissism as a kind of ideal type against which we can gain an understanding of a variety of cultural phenomena.

Summary and Conclusion

One of the difficulties with Horkheimer, Adorno and Lasch is that their ideas are pitched at a high level of generality, making the need for further more detailed accounts necessary. Lasch's remarks about the changing content of Hollywood film expressing an unconscious need for an all powerful 'primal father-figure' are very suggestive, but need to be worked through in a more comprehensive way.

Nevertheless, I have argued that first generation Critical Theory provides us with a general explanatory framework through which we can make sense of changes at the level of family life and at the level of wider cultural life, rather than seeing things only in their immediacy. The case brought by Critical Theory is that the changing nature of modern capitalism has brought with it a change in the nature of the subject. The decline of the male-centred (patriarchal) family has wrought a more compliant individual whose identity is tied in narcissistically with a consumerism that is the corollary of large-scale mass production. Whilst feminists have drawn attention to a nostalgia for a more well-ordered masculine world in this thesis, I believe that Horkheimer et al.'s ideas are important because whatever the virtues or vices of the earlier, 'authoritarian', family may have been, they are right to point out the doubtfulness of assuming that the modern individual has been liberated by the process of change.

Giddens' challenge to Lasch is based on the importance of interactional routines to the way we sustain reality, but downplays the importance of forces outside interaction – including the inner workings of the subject. The implication of Critical Theory is that interactional routines may be ideological when seen in light of these workings. The changes described by Critical Theory suggest that an individual whose inner life is more compliant and dispersed, functions very well at the level of interaction, but not without real losses to a strong sense of individual identity. This is not to say that our inner lives are not in a sense generated by interaction with others, notably our parents, but that the inwardness of the psyche is something that exists in its own right and exerts its *own* force at the level of interaction.

If this is the case, then recent discussions about 'globalisation', the 'risk society' and the 'decentring of the subject', which exclude or minimise such matters, are partial, and ideologically partial too. From fifty years ago, Critical Theory still speaks to us, reminding us to be wary of the idea that the most advanced societies have liberated their members into a golden age of individual freedom.

Further Reading

Critical Theory writings on the family are not very thick on the ground, hence my extrapolation via the work of Lasch (1977, 1979). Apart from the essays by Horkheimer et al., referred to in this chapter, I would suggest looking at Craib (1989) and Craib (1994). Both of these explore amongst other things the connections between Lasch, Critical Theory and the family.

Part 3

Substantive Ideas:
The Second Generation

7

Overcoming the Impasse: Habermas's Reconstruction of Critical Theory

In the previous section I have tried to show the resonance of first generation Critical Theory particularly in relation to its concern with the reality of the human subject. I now want to change tack slightly and examine how the second generation, notably Jürgen Habermas, sought to overcome what he saw as the weaknesses of Horkheimer, Adorno and Marcuse's work; their too-individualised notion of the subject and their Marxist view of history.

If one relies on an idea of the subject as an individual consciousness and then describes its oppression in terms of the reification of consciousness, you necessarily block from view all those areas of life where people act creatively *with* others. You push to the margins the common ground they share and the value they place on it, the resistance they have to the status quo, such as the jokes they make about pop stars and politicians and the decisions they make about what is or is not worth buying. Similarly, if you adhere to a Marxist view of history, noting especially the 'incorporation' of the working class, you necessarily find nothing worthwhile in the modern world and view everything negatively as an expression of the capitalist system.

Habermas's reconstruction of Critical Theory ranges far and wide and, in order to make this long chapter more digestible, I have divided it up into three large sections subdivided into smaller ones. First, I shall be concerned with the way he uses Hans-Georg Gadamer's 'hermeneutics' to make up the 'inter-actional deficit' of his predecessors. Second, I shall be concerned with how he reworked Talcott Parsons's 'systems theory' and third his reconstruction of Marx's 'historical materialism'.

Habermas Goes Hermeneutic: The Context

Habermas's engagement with hermeneutics (interpretation) can be traced back to the role he played in the so-called 'positivist dispute' in German sociology between Adorno and the philosopher of science, Karl Popper (Adorno et al. 1976). The title of the dispute is misleading as both Adorno and Popper resolutely denied they were positivists. The details of the debate do not matter here, though they are well worth the attention of the reader, and have been recounted in various places (Frisby 1972, 1974, Wilson 1977, Holub 1991, How 1995: 101–16). The fact that both of the main protagonists refused the 'positivist' label was a symptom of the lack of engagement between the two men. Their ideas seemed like ships in the night, passing by unaware of each other's existence. It fell to Habermas, for Adorno, and Hans Albert for Popper, to flesh out the differences between the two outlooks.

Habermas's position at this time was relatively unformed, for although he defends Adorno's ideas he clearly adds his own twist to them introducing the idea of hermeneutics as a counterweight to the equally important sociological systems theory: two bodies of knowledge about which Adorno had nothing good to say. In fact much of Adorno's sociological work is pitched against what he sees as the false harmonies of systems theory, as well as interpretations of the lifeworld that see it as anything but thoroughly reified.

The concept of the lifeworld (Lebenswelt) is derived from Husserl's phenomenology and refers in sociology to the everyday world as experienced by men and women; both it and Parsons' systems theory were bodies of knowledge about which Adorno had little good to say. In fact, much of Adorno's sociological work is pitched against what he sees as the false harmonies of systems theory, as well as interpretations of the lifeworld that see it as anything other than thoroughly reified.

At the time of the 'positivist dispute' in the early 1960s, Habermas did not explore the possibilities of hermeneutics in any detail. This came a few years later in two books: *On the Logic of the Social Sciences (1988)* and *Knowledge and Human Interests (1971b)*. His concern in these books was epistemological, with marking off Critical Theory's view of knowledge from the then dominant paradigm of positivism. The assumption made by positivists was that real knowledge was produced by science and that other disciplines should aspire to use the same methods to achieve the same kind of success. The goal was a 'unified science' to which all disciplines would adhere.

Habermas Contra-Positivism

In the appendix to *Knowledge and Human Interests*, Habermas argued that knowledge was not one thing but several. Different kinds of knowledge were governed by what he called different 'cognitive interests', each with its own in-built assumptions that determine the kind of knowledge it produces. There were three broad types of knowledge, empirical-analytic, hermeneutic, and emancipatory. The empirical-analytic disciplines (essentially the natural sciences) were guided by an interest in manipulation and control. The concepts they used, the data they collected and the explanations they generated were oriented by the assumption that knowledge would enable us to control the world of nature.

The hermeneutic or interpretive disciplines (essentially the humanities) were guided by a 'practical' interest in reaching an intersubjective understanding, rather than control. Literature, history and art were analysed in terms of how they opened up our common horizons to show us what we were like in our shared humanity. They were oriented by the need to communicate with, and convince others about, what our community or tradition was really like.

The emancipatory disciplines (essentially Marxism and psychoanalysis) were guided by a reflexive interest that enabled human beings to have greater autonomy and self-determination.

The weakness of the positivist view was that it assumed that the empirical-analytic interest in control was the *only* purpose of knowledge and that other forms of knowledge were effectively non-knowledge. It lacked the capacity to reflect on the limitations of its own view of things, seeing everything in terms of causal mechanisms. Very crudely one might say that it reduced a work of art to being the effect of someone's brain chemistry. However, the hermeneutic view was also flawed in that it failed to see that there were external forces at work in the cultural sphere, and that these functioned as causal factors impacting on our common horizons without our awareness.

The emancipatory disciplines, into which category Habermas wanted to place Critical Theory, drew from the assumptions of the other two, accepting the importance of both 'causality' and 'hermeneutic understanding'. Habermas did not wish to denigrate either empirical-analytic or hermeneutic ways of going on, each 'epistemology' in its own way produced different, but equally valid kinds of knowledge. His purpose was to locate Critical Theory and social science generally, on a wider map of knowledge.

For Habermas the problem was that while the empirical-analytic and hermeneutic disciplines had produced extensive and influential bodies of knowledge, Marxism and psychoanalysis looked fairly thin in comparison; both had established a place in the social sciences but neither represented a dominant paradigm. As a result, Habermas's idea of an 'emancipatory' interest appeared too speculative to be convincing as a full-blown category in its own right.

There was a further problem. Habermas, like his predecessors, wanted his ideas to be *grounded* in something substantial. He rejected their adherence to a Marxist view of history. However, if social classes were not moving through history towards a communist future, he had to find a replacement. He argued that 'cognitive interests' were not just intellectual categories, but were 'quasi-transcendental', by which he meant that while they may have emerged historically, they were not temporary historical phenomena. He has sometimes used the phrase 'anthropologically deep seated', to capture the idea of 'interests' as something more or less given with human nature, with the result that academic disciplines naturally draw on them to produce knowledge. Thus, he could quite reasonably claim that humans have a deep-seated need to control the natural world to ensure their survival, a need which ultimately produces science. He could also claim that humans are social beings and therefore have a need to work cooperatively to ensure their well-being, a need that is met by the common norms and values of a society's lifeworld. This was something that academically culminated in the hermeneutic concerns of the humanities. However, it was less convincing to claim that human beings had a categorically separate need for emancipation. The desire for emancipation was likely to spring from interpretation at the level of interaction, and therefore be a hermeneutic concern.

Habermas (1971b: 314) tried to ground the 'emancipatory interest' in language:

> Through its structure, autonomy and responsibility are posited for us. Our first sentence expresses unequivocally the intention of a universal and unconstrained consensus.

There is nothing obviously wrong with this claim; we do find our sense of what is to count as responsible and autonomous behaviour through immersion in our natural language and we do expect, in communicating with others, to reach a common (universal) agreement. However, language is very much the arena of the well-grounded 'hermeneutic interest' rather than a separate interest in emancipation. It was the realisation that the hermeneutic tradition was knocking at the same door as Critical Theory that led Habermas to engage more thoroughly with it and to draw what he wanted from it. It was to the work of Hans-Georg Gadamer that Habermas looked for answers he could use.

Habermas and Hermeneutics

Before I came across Gadamer's work via Habermas and Janet Wolff (1975a, b), I was unaware that there was a hermeneutic tradition, though it has been recounted in various places (see How 1995: 7–10). The word 'hermeneutic' is thought to have its origins in the activities of the Greek god, Hermes, who was the messenger of the gods. It was Hermes' task to transmit god-knowledge to ordinary mortals who would otherwise be unable to understand it. According to legend he wore a helmet that enabled him to disappear and reappear at will, at night or during the day. He had wings on his sandals that could transport him rapidly over great distances, and a wand that could send you to sleep or wake you from slumber. He was a trickster, the god of thieves and highway robbers, and could bring sudden good or ill luck. He was also the god of crossroads and boundaries, and led the dead across the frontier into the underworld (Hades). These elusive, quicksilver characteristics stand out more clearly when we realise that his other (Latin) name was 'Mercury'. Hermes was the god that mediated or interpreted the truth of the world in a form that would resonate with people in the conditions of their ordinary lives. True to his character, the knowledge that Hermes brought would always be subtle, partial and tacit; it would enlighten people, but resist completion. Thus, while hermeneutics is concerned with revealing the meaning of things, meaning that may be hidden from view, or concealed in a text; it also accepts that it will never come fully into view. We are historical creatures, bound by our 'finitude' and as such, meaning will vary with the circumstances of the life that we live.

In the Middle Ages, biblical hermeneutics rested on a tension as to whether the Bible was to be understood in a literal fashion as divinely inspired words, or interpreted in a way that resonated with the times. In the modern, nineteenth-century world, hermeneutics became the basis of the *Geisteswissenschaften* or human sciences. Gadamer's work placed itself in this latter framework, seeking to draw out the conditions under which all human understanding took place.

Gadamer's *Truth and Method* (1989 [1960]) is divided into three sections; the first is concerned with the nature of aesthetic understanding, the second with the historical nature of understanding, and the third with language. I shall be concerned only with the last two, as it was these aspects of hermeneutics that Habermas sought to incorporate into Critical Theory.

Understanding has a Forestructure

Central to Gadamer's hermeneutics is the concept of understanding. Max Weber's recommendation that sociology needs the concept of *Verstehen* to be effective in analysing the social world, is based on the idea that the social world is symbolically pre-structured and that social 'objects' are embedded in complexes of meaning to which the social scientist has basically the same kind of access as everyone else. The social scientist has to understand what is there, as it were, before analysing it. For nineteenth-century hermeneutic authors, such as Dilthey, as for much interpretive sociology, this tended to mean imaginatively stepping into the shoes of other people to see 'objectively' what their world was like. For Gadamer, this psychologistic approach is inadequate because it fails to recognise what we bring to the situation *in* understanding something. A better way of conceptualising what should, and anyway *does* happen to those who are aware of the process, is the 'fusion of horizons'. The horizon of our understanding has to be brought into conjunction with that of the historical text, or the social practices of an alien culture, and through a to-and-fro process of question, answer and revision, a more adequate understanding of what things mean comes to light. Things that are alien or 'other'

to us cease to be passive objects of observation, and become sources of inex-
haustibly greater self-understanding. Every new historical horizon we inhabit
has the potential to show us something new about the historical text or alien
culture, which in turn reveals something more to us about ourselves.

In *Truth and Method*, Gadamer develops the idea that understanding has an
inescapable forestructure that our horizon has bequeathed us. We cannot shed
this forestructure, indeed one of the main characteristics of understanding is
its *projective* quality. We project onto the world a set of concepts that shape
what we find in an automatic way, we never come across the world in a con-
ceptless way, but locate things within a framework of meaning, so we always
see something *as* something. This does not mean that we are passive conduits
for what society has taught us, for the process of understanding is also a circular one of constant revision (Gadamer 1989: 266–7). When we read a novel,
for example, we automatically project meaning onto the text, we anticipate
what we are going to find there, but this has to be revised in light of what we
discover in the various chapters, which in turn is affected by how we conceive
the overall story, and so on. The 'hermeneutic circle' was originally conceived
(epistemologically) in terms of understanding texts, but Gadamer describes it
(ontologically) in terms of how we exist in the world.

Gadamer's Rehabilitation of Prejudice, Authority and Tradition

While Gadamer places emphasis on the dialogic nature of understanding, he
equally emphasises that the *forestructure* of understanding never allows us the
luxury of pure, presuppositionless knowledge. Our dialogic understanding is
animated by our preconceptions, or prejudices, as he provocatively calls them.
As he puts it, 'prejudices are the biases of our openness to the world', they
shape us from the past in a whole variety of subtle and mostly unexaminable
ways. If we did not have prejudices we would, in a sense, not find anything in
the world, for it is our biases towards the world, which orientate us to what
is there. Using his vocabulary, we might say that our prejudices come with our
'being-in-the-world', without them there would be no 'world'. He uses the
word 'prejudice' to mean our first judgment on things, which has to be revised
dialogically in light of further evidence. Nevertheless, his use of the word,
'prejudice', is deliberate, as he wishes to stress the fact that all our understanding of things is preceded by the prejudices of tradition. In fact, so embedded are we in our tradition that we cannot step outside it and disinterestedly
view our prejudices, at least not all of them. So much modern reason, he
believes, has sought to elude the implications of 'prejudice' that one could
even characterise Enlightenment reason as having a prejudice against prejudices. (1989: 271–77).

For Gadamer, it is only since the Enlightenment that we have had an entirely
negative attitude towards prejudice, seeing it automatically as a distortion of

things and thus something that needs to be eliminated. This 'faith in perfection' is an illusion, as we cannot get rid of prejudices, but need to see them in a positive light, to explore them more thoroughly and see how much we are embedded in them; only then can we understand ourselves more thoroughly. In more general terms, we need to recognise that 'history does not belong to us', but that 'we belong to it'. He summarises the point:

> The self-awareness of the individual is only a flickering in the closed circuits of historical life. *That is why the prejudices of the individual, far more than his judgments, constitute the historical reality of his being.* (1989: 276–7)

We can intuitively see what Gadamer means in thinking back on our own lives. We often think we know who we are and what the world is like in relation to us. Yet in recalling what we were like a decade earlier, and how much we along with the world have changed, we realise how much has shifted and that we are deeply historical creatures. We are pushed and pulled by the winds of history far more than we are able to control them.

Tied in with the importance of history is the authority it exercises over us in the form of tradition. We tend to think of the authority of tradition as something that is wrongly imposed on us behind our backs, and that in exercising modern, objective (Enlightenment) reason we can slough off its effects. Gadamer wants us to see authority in a positive light. He rejects the simple opposition between reason and the authority of tradition in part because of the role prejudices inevitably play in structuring our understanding, but also because he sees positive virtues in it. In fact, he sees authority as *not* 'to do with blind obedience to commands', but 'rather with knowledge'. This is quite a difficult idea to grasp, particularly if you are a student of social science, where much of the work done seeks to challenge the legitimacy of authority.

Gadamer is not trying to say that all authority is justified, but that when we obey it we do so because we intuitively know that the views of someone who has a wider or better knowledge, should hold sway. True authority cannot be bestowed; it has to be earned and rests on the kind of superiority that we quite reasonably acknowledge. I have tried to illustrate this point in relation to the authority of the classic authors of the sociological tradition (How 1998). It seems to me that the work of Marx, Weber and Durkheim, and perhaps Simmel too, still warrants our careful attention because it has been able to show us aspects of social reality in ways that the work of say, Auguste Comte and Herbert Spencer, has not. The accumulated authority of classic texts springs from our knowing that they enable us to see the world they open up clearly as still our own. While their continued authority may derive in part from the fact they are 'imposed' on undergraduates at regular intervals, this is a separate matter from their validity as authoritative knowledge.

Gadamer believes that Enlightenment reason, with its opposition to the authority of tradition has gone so far as to deny any validity to authority. He recounts an anecdote, that his secretary made a mistake over the word, 'author-itative', which she mistook for 'authoritarian'. She assumed he meant the latter because she had never come across the former, and was unaware that the words referred to different things (1996: ch. 9). The point is that we have become so used to seeing authority in a negative light, of always seeing it as authoritarian that we fail to recognise that it could be legitimate. Of course authority can be dogmatic and authoritarian, but this is not its real nature. Its real nature lies in our ability to recognise the finite, limited nature of our own understanding, and to recognise that the views of others might be more adequate. The child intuitively knows that the parent has a more extensive knowledge of things than he or she does, as does the student in relation to the teacher. In both cases there is a justified acceptance of authority.

Clearly the left-wing sensibilities of Habermas would be roused by the conservative implications of Gadamer's account of prejudice, authority and tradition, but another aspect of Gadamer's work, his views on language, were even more important.

Hermeneutics, Language and Reality

It is through language that prejudice, authority and tradition are mediated to form our understanding of the world. In fact Gadamer describes language in ontological terms, as something upon which being, or reality, depends. To have a language, Gadamer argues, is to have a 'world'. Language goes ahead of us giving shape to the world. There is no 'pure' world lying behind language, though we can of course speculate what the world might be like if there were no languages. However, such speculation would entail thinking of a 'wordless' world *through* language.

Language may appear to be an all pervasive phenomenon for Gadamer, but equally it is not a closed system that is imposed upon us; its real nature lies in its dialogic character. Gadamer uses the concept of play in his discussion of the experience of art, but it is also confirmed in his discussion of language, where language is seen to have a game-like quality. In games of any kind, whether as players or spectators, we are drawn into the play of things, and though in taking the game seriously we try to put our mark on it, if it is too one-sided it is pointless. In fact, a one-sided game is no game at all, because it has lost its playfulness, and thereby its purpose. So, also with language, there is an essential reciprocity involved. He captures this in using the model of conversation:

> We say we 'conduct' a conversation, but the more genuine a conversation is, the less its conduct lies within the will of either partner. Thus a genuine conversation is never one that we wanted to conduct. Rather, it is generally more correct to say that we fall into conversation, or even that we become involved in it . . . No one knows in

advance what will 'come out' of a conversation . . . All this shows that a conversation has a spirit of its own, and that the language in which it is conducted bears its own truth within it – i.e. that it allows something to 'emerge' which henceforth exists (1989: 383).

In emphasizing that language has a constitutive role in forming reality he is making a point that is fairly familiar in sociology and social psychology. We are used to hearing that reality is socially constructed, and that language is a key element in this. However, Gadamer equally insists that because of its dialogic character it is also 'self-transcending'; something emerges from it. By this, he means that because language and the prejudices enmeshed in it have a projective, forward-leaning quality; they are not stuck in the formal rut of one horizon, but have a natural boundary-overstepping capacity. They constantly mediate between what is familiar and what is alien to us, allowing us to enlarge our understanding, though never to the point where our horizon knows it all. Understanding always remains a product of our finite existence and open to change.

What Habermas Takes and What He Leaves

Habermas's engagement with hermeneutics was a critical one, but one from which he absorbed much. He was critical of its too accepting view of prejudice and tradition. He regarded both 'science' and 'reflection' as having the power to breach prejudice and tradition in a way that Gadamer did not allow. His view of the hermeneutic account of language was more conciliatory. He accepted much of its anti-positivist implications regarding the impossibility of presuppositionless (objective) knowledge. But more important for him, because language constitutes the common ground of our mutual understanding and is dialogic in character, it means that through language we can establish further common ground. In effect, it provided Habermas with the basis for his theory of *communicative action,* the mainstay of his later work.

I want now to consider how Habermas uses 'science' and 'reflection' as a route out of 'tradition', while sustaining a connection with the hermeneutic view of language.

Science versus Tradition

Habermas is sympathetic to Gadamer's hermeneutic account of the pre-structured nature of understanding in breaking up 'objectivism', but thinks he has understated the significance of scientific method. Gadamer's book, *Truth and Method* could, he believes, be accused of presenting the social sciences with the stark choice – truth *or* method. Gadamer's views so emphasise the way truth is the product of dialogue, the hermeneutic circle, and the fusion of horizons as they function *within* tradition, that they bypass the value of 'controlled distantiation' (method). They ignore the significance of adopting the objectivating attitude that is an essential part of scientific method.

Habermas has always been sympathetic to the achievements of social scientific authors, such as Talcott Parsons, Jean Piaget, and Lawrence Kohlberg, admiring the methods they use to reveal the systematic features of social reality. Where hermeneutics claims that tradition allows us to see certain things and not others, the systematic application of method allows us to see things that are not apparent 'in tradition'. It allows us to see the way systematic elements of reality go on external to tradition and more or less unbeknownst to the actors involved. The 'objectivating' attitude of (social) science enables it to take up a more challenging, less accepting view of tradition.

Like Gadamer, Habermas (1971b: 301–17) sees our understanding of things as prestructured, but prestructured around 'human interests', one of which is an interest in the control of nature and the wider world generally. The natural, or empirical-analytic sciences have enabled us to gain some purchase on this aspect of reality and represent a more or less inevitable feature of human life. Unless we had this capacity we would not survive. The social sciences have to recognise that although hermeneutics equally provides knowledge of human life, it is not the only contender. In fact, the social sciences are nearly always involved with material that has a foot in both camps. Its 'object' is both factual and normative, and is therefore open to both empirical-analytic and hermeneutic outlooks.

There are factors external to tradition, such as 'work' and 'domination', (or labour and power in the Marxist sense) that structure tradition and function towards its smooth running, yet do not appear in it as such. For example, in the UK, increasing competition in international markets in the last 20 years has produced the demand for a more 'flexible' workforce. As a result of the increasing instability of employment and the 'flexibility' demands made on those in work, employees talk about their lives in much more transitory terms than before. The conditions under which people work in the new freewheeling 'disorganised' capitalism reflect the demands of the free market. Firms have to be able to move and change direction quickly according to the transient nature of market conditions. Employees similarly must adopt an entirely flexible, indeed opportunistic attitude to their own careers to be successful (Sennett 1998).

Sennett's examples show people torn by the demands to be geographically and emotionally flexible, yet unable to marry up their fragmentary lives with any clear sense of purpose. When it comes to convincing their children of the value of doing a job well for its own sake, of the importance of responsibility to others, trust, and so forth, there is a yawning gap between what they say and what they do. In other words, the language of everyday morality sounds increasingly hollow in the face of behaviour structured by a capitalist economy.

Of course there is a 'libertarian' language that has accompanied these economic changes. The idea of 'flexibility' has an emancipatory ring to it. It suggests that the individual has been liberated from the fetters of constraint and can move freely to express him or herself. But this way of talking about things has not sprung *spontaneously* from language's natural open endedness, but from a 'tradition' that has external economic forces at work on it.

Thus language can serve the interests of economic power in screening off the origins of a particular ways of looking at things. Language is ideological, not in the sense that there is a deliberate piece of deception going on *in* it, but that a more impersonal deception is going on 'with language as such' (Habermas 1988: 172).

The more detached objectivating approach of Parsons' 'systems theory' will provide Habermas with the conceptual tools to suggest that a 'hermeneutically informed' functionalism should serve as the framework for Critical Theory. Nevertheless, the hermeneutic view of language opened up another possibility for Habermas. In that human beings are language users, no amount of reification can extinguish a certain communicative possibility for intersubjective agreement. The task then for Critical Theory becomes one of examining whether a social consensus is genuine, or whether it is distorted by external factors such as economic power.

Language, Reflection and Prejudice

Habermas accepts Gadamer's account of language as superior to others in the social theory canon, but uses it to out-Gadamer Gadamer. The hermeneutic account of language is a dynamic one showing us that when we are socialized into the norms and values of our own society, we do not merely assimilate them, but re-interpret them as well:

> the language-games of the young do not simply reproduce the practice of the old. With the first basic linguistic rules the child learns not only the conditions of possible consensus but also the conditions of possible interpretation of the rules, which enable him to overcome and thereby also to express a distance. (Habermas 1988: 148)

In other words, Gadamer's own account suggests that language *enables* us to take a critical stance towards tradition. All thought may happen within tradition, but the boundary-overstepping capacities of language mean that we can challenge tradition rather than just reinforce it.

In a similar vein, Habermas accepts the significance of 'prejudices' in our understanding, but asks whether their inevitability should lead us to accept their validity. What he rejects is Gadamer's tacit rehabilitation of prejudices as such, as though their inevitability was sufficient to make them something to which we *have* to submit as part of our tradition. The power of reflection enables us to retrace the origins of our current understanding and take up a different, more critical attitude, towards it. Reflection gives us the means to take up a different attitude towards things we previously accepted in an automatic way.

Habermas is arguing that Gadamer does not recognise the truth of his own argument. If tradition, like understanding, is dialogic, then its natural back and forth movement should allow reflection to offer the hope of emancipation. It is only Gadamer's conservatism that refuses to see that reflection can break up assumptions that have been inculcated by tradition. A prejudice that has been made transparent by our reflection on it can no longer function as a simple reinforcement of tradition.

The logical framework of psychoanalysis further provides Habermas with a general model for how Critical Theory might work at a sociological level. It is both hermeneutically sensitive and aware of how external (unconscious) forces 'cause' different behaviours at the level of everyday life. If it is successful, it breaks up those distortions by bringing them to consciousness, allowing individuals to be more self-determined and less governed by external factors in what they think and do. Like hermeneutics, psychoanalysis involves a circular process of interpretation, but psychoanalysis introduces a level of *theory* into the equation, the better to explain elements that are a function of external factors. Where the hermeneut is tied to interpreting a text against his or her prejudices, the psychoanalyst can utilise a *general* framework that will explain the causes of a patient's behaviour. Psychoanalysis is pertinent because it acknowledges that unconscious forces 'bear the cloak of causes', they function as invisible causal factors shaping people's lives. Unconscious forces are (humanly) purposive, and therefore hermeneutic in character, but they are also the product of factors outside the awareness of the actor and have to be explained that way. Working on this basis, Habermas argued that Critical Theory would have to engage with Parsons's systems theory as a model to explain phenomena at a societal level.

While Habermas's engagement with hermeneutics enabled him to make up Critical Theory's 'interaction deficit', his engagement with structural-functionalism in the context of the evolution of society would enable him to make up the deficit lost by its commitment to Marx's 'philosophy of history'.

Habermas and Structural-Functionalism

In the 1960s, Habermas's interests had been epistemological; during the 1970s and 1980s they shifted to social theory per se, to a concern with the general workings of the social world rather than with the methodological assumptions we should use in the process of studying them. The weakness of hermeneutics he identified as its failure to consider the way society's structural 'externalities' such as money and power imposed themselves on the lifeworld of actors. The remedy lay in reworking the path opened up by Talcott Parsons and a contemporary German systems theorist, Niklas Luhmann (see Holub 1991).

From the outset, Habermas was not uncritical of systems theory. The sociological use of an 'organic' model, which draws on an analogy between biological and social systems, he thought misleading. The boundaries of biological systems are observable entities, whereas the boundaries of social systems are symbolic in character and therefore much less easy to discern. They have to be understood in a different way. In a similar vein, the habit of systems theorists seeing 'equilibrium' as the end-state to which social systems naturally tend is problematic. What might 'equilibrium' mean in the context of a social system? The larger systemic elements may work well together and thus the system continues to reproduce itself as if it were a biological system, but this tells us nothing about whether its members are happily integrated into it.

Much feminist criticism of Parsons's account of the nuclear family is pitched against his view that it is the model best suited to meet the requirements of an industrial society. For example, Parsons assumed that women are best suited to meet the 'expressive' demands of family life as housewives, while men are best suited to meet the 'instrumental' requirements by going out to work. Feminists rightly claimed that while this arrangement may suit the system, it conceals a much less harmonious, indeed oppressive situation at the level of personal life. The distinction between system integration and social integration, which originated with Lockwood (1964), is drawn on by Habermas in support of the development of his own system–lifeworld distinction. He does this, not to dismiss Parsons' ideas, but to broaden them. In fact a Parsonsian account based on the changing needs of the system could probably now be invoked to explain the decline of the nuclear family. As the demands of the economy for male labour in heavy industry have declined and been replaced by the need for female labour in the service sector, so the need for a traditional male-dominated nuclear family has also declined (Mitchell 1987). Parsons' account is not wrong, but partial and needs to include the distinctive features of the lifeworld.

In *Legitimation Crisis* (1976) and *The Theory of Communicative Action,* Volume 2 (1987a) Habermas developed a dualist theory of society where system and lifeworld were interwoven, but where one was not reducible to the other. In not wanting to conflate system and lifeworld, he shares much in common with the sociological ideas of Derek Layder and Margaret Archer. His ideas thus bear on contemporary issues over structure versus agency and micro versus macro sociology, the kinds of issue that separate Layder and Archer from Anthony Giddens's structuration theory, where structure and agency are pressed together.

System, Lifeworld and Social Evolution

The concept of the lifeworld is derived from the tradition of phenomenology and refers in Habermas's hands to the meaning horizon of social actors. The lifeworld provides the context in which actors come to know themselves, where they ask questions of each other raising 'validity claims' about what is true or false, right or wrong, about what should or should not happen.

Like Parsons he recognises the lifeworld as a pre-patterned world of norms and values that has become differentiated out into a societal subsystem. As a subsystem it is also subdivided into further subsystems. It encourages certain kinds of social integration, certain kinds of cultural assumption and particular kinds of personality type. Unlike Parsons, though, he sees it as an interpretively active and changeable site where people can make a difference, for it is the place where 'communicative action' takes place. Communicative action is based on the peculiarly human capacity to dialogically reach a consensus through language, something Habermas took from his engagement with hermeneutics. When actors engage communicatively with each other they reproduce/reinterpret culture, social integration and the formation of personality. What is important for Habermas, *un*like Parsons and Luhmann, is that herein lies the potential for emancipation and greater self-determination (Habermas 1987a: 185–6).

If the lifeworld is the intersubjective context for communicative action and has to be understood from the point of view of a 'participant', a switch of view to that of an 'observer' reveals something different. It shows how elements of the lifeworld are functionally related to the workings of the wider system. Parsons' strength was to show this connection, though his weakness was to blank out the specific workings of the lifeworld, its tensions, alienations, and unpredictability. His 'observer's' standpoint allowed him to see the lifeworld as *only* a differentiated set of subsystems, existing to maintain society as a whole: as derivative of the system and without its own internal logic. (Habermas 1987a: 153–4). What Habermas wants to do is bounce off the emancipatory potential inherent in the lifeworld against the demands of the system. To see how one affects the other they must be kept analytically separate even if they are interwoven in everyday life.

By 'system', Habermas means the larger institutionalised features of society, such as the economy, the polity and the state. Again, he partly follows Parsons' ideas about social evolution involving a process of systemic differentiation that culminates in 'modernity'. For systems theorists, the idea of increasing differentiation describes the way modern societies have become more complex. A simple analogy would be the way thirty years ago if a car owner had problems with the brakes, tyres or the exhaust system, he or she would take it to the local garage. Now, these tasks have become 'differentiated' out; one can go to separate quick-fitting exhaust or tyre centres, or to brake specialists. So it is with the social system; the economy, polity and state have become relatively separate entities with their own internal rationale.

Certainly it is important for Habermas that the system be seen as *ultimately* springing from the lifeworld in the sense that society is a product of human interaction both between subjects and with the outside world. Nevertheless, what characterises modern society is the way the systemic elements have become *uncoupled* from the lifeworld and now exist 'externally' to it, feeding back into it from the outside. In fact, not only have system and lifeworld become differentiated from each other; both have also become differentiated within themselves so the workings of the economic sphere may now challenge those of the political, and vice-versa. Given his Marxist credentials, it is not surprising that Habermas sees the 'steering demands' of the capitalist economy, what it needs to maintain itself, as the most imposing factor, not least because it distorts the emancipatory potential of the lifeworld. However, his argument is complex as he sees the uncoupling of system and lifeworld in both a positive and a negative light.

Never one to limit the range of his theory he set his account of the emergence of system and lifeworld in a schematic anthropological history of the world, divided into three broad stages. He argues that in terms of social evolution pre-modern societies were largely undifferentiated. In primitive (or Neolithic) societies there was one organising principle, that of kinship, all (tribal) activities were centred on the influence of this one factor, age and sex roles were fixed and unproblematic. In sociological terms, he is referring to something like Durkheim's concept of 'mechanical solidarity', characteristic of societies with a low division of labour and a closed world-view built around rituals and taboos (Habermas 1976: 18).

In neolithic societies, nature and culture are interwoven and though they show some signs of differentiation it is only with the appearance of 'traditional societies', roughly between the eighth and fourth century BC that we can say this changed and the evolutionary process of 'rationalisation' proper gets underway. Habermas's 'traditional societies' include ancient Egypt as well as the more developed traditional societies of ancient Greece, China and Rome. What characterises these is a shift towards class domination as the main source of social integration rather than kinship. As these societies become more internally differentiated, particularly in terms of their economies and the ownership of the means of production, there emerges a latent tension between system and lifeworld, or between how the system is integrated and how people are socially integrated into it. A system that develops its economy has to legitimise its economic inequalities more explicitly. It requires social institutions that will justify things to its subjects and ensure their compliance. The crucial point for Habermas is that this evolutionary step *did* require a higher level of justification to sustain social cohesion. Roman Caesars may have had mythical qualities but Roman law was based on rational principles that could be applied to Caesar. Once a system has to justify itself it is open to challenge from its subjects who can, in principle, challenge its 'validity claims'. In short, the possibility of communicative action emerges.

With the advent of early modernity, roughly after the fifteenth century, system differentiation becomes sharper and though the mythical role of monarchs is still significant in terms of social integration, there is a gradual process of demythicisation and thereby of the emergence of rational social legitimacy.

In modern industrial societies the process of differentiation and demythicisation continues, with Habermas arguing that the overall evolutionary process of 'rationalisation' is a good thing because it enables human beings to see how different aspects of their society really work. It enables people to recognise that in some degree society is their own creation, not that of divine intervention or just an inevitable fact of life. However, there is a clear (Marxist) downside to the process. The 'rationalised' modern world has come into existence via capitalism and the exploitative demands it makes on people. It is the *capitalist* system that has become uncoupled from the communicatively shared experience of its subjects. Instead of this 'rationalised' society being coordinated through the language-based consensus of the lifeworld it is coordinated through the system-media of money and power. Indeed, so far has the process gone that Habermas talks of the 'colonisation of the lifeworld' by system imperatives. So while modern society has a potential for thoroughgoing rationalisation in the spheres of both system and lifeworld, the system feeds back into, and has come to dominate the lifeworld to the point where it is difficult though not impossible for people to think of alternatives. It is difficult for people to see their lives as anything but dependent on the exigencies of the market.

I could again illustrate the implications of Habermas's (1976) account of how the system colonises and overloads the lifeworld by Richard Sennett's book *The Corrosion of Character* (1998), where he shows how modern work practices can 'de-moralise' the workforce. But David Smail's *The Origins of Unhappiness* (1993) serves the same purpose. Habermas's picture of the various kinds of relationship existing within and between system and lifeworld is complex, though he is clear that their uncoupling allows capitalism to be openly, if not brutally, dynamic while at the same time it makes it prone to crises.

We tend to think of crises as something dramatic, something that might result in revolution or war, but Habermas's account alerts us to the constant tensions of a dynamic system such as capitalism. A crisis may originate as an economic one, but if it is insoluble in market terms it may be displaced to the state apparatus as a 'rationality' crisis. If adequate decisions are not forthcoming from the state, because traditional political solutions are not up to the job, it may become a crisis of 'legitimation' involving a withdrawal of popular support and a general scepticism towards the state's ability to resolve problems. A 'legitimation' crisis in its turn may involve a 'motivation' crisis where the requisite amount of meaning to support the system is absent from people's lives.

A rough and ready example (mine) will serve to illustrate. During the late 1970s, Britain underwent a series of economic crises involving balance of payments deficits, high inflation, industrial unrest and problems of financing the welfare state. The political rationality of the time was sometimes called 'butskellism' after the Conservative Party leader, R. A. Butler and the Labour Party leader, Hugh Gaitskell. They established a political consensus in Britain in the 1950s, whereby the Conservative Party, contrary to its usual principles, accepted the importance of the welfare state. The Labour Party, contrary to its usual principles, acknowledged the economic importance of free markets. The Conservative Party agreed not to dismantle state welfare provision, and the Labour Party agreed not to undertake a large-scale nationalisation of the private industry that underpinned the workings of the free market. The inability of Labour governments to solve the economic crises of the 1970s led to a crisis of 'butskellist' rationality and to doubts about the legitimacy of the state. The formation of the new-Right rationality known as 'Thatcherism' in the 1980s entailed seeking popular legitimacy by shifting economic problems into the motivational arena of the lifeworld.

'Thatcherism', as a term, is derived from the ideas of the then Conservative Prime Minister, Margaret Thatcher. However, we are not here talking about individual actors but something much broader and abstract: the workings of a system where a crisis in one area pulled other system elements into a new formation. Nevertheless, one can, for simplicity's sake, say that the upheaval wrought by the spread of 'Thatcherite' free-market principles into all areas of life to establish a new legitimacy, created a motivation crisis. The patterns of motivation associated with 'butskellism' were no longer adequate. At the level of the lifeworld, people's cultural assumptions and personality types had to be restructured along more individualistic and opportunistic lines to meet the steering needs of the system and without the solace of the welfare state.

I have described the process of a system crisis in a rather simple and mechanical fashion, as though it always went straightforwardly in one direction, from the system (economy) to the lifeworld (motivation). Habermas makes it clear that this is not so. All kinds of tensions, contradictions and resistances exist *within* as well as between the elements of a system. Nevertheless, his abiding concern is with the distorting effects of the colonisation of the lifeworld by other system imperatives.

Smail exemplifies the negative psychological effects of this kind of crisis-displacement. For Smail (1993: 129), the 1980s were particularly significant:

> since it was in this decade that all pretence of society's being for people was abandoned: it was now up to people themselves to survive the rigours of the 'real world' and no provision was to be made for 'lame ducks'. In fact those who, without

suspecting it, were injured by the times were far from 'lame ducks' – often they were people whose sensitivity, social responsibility and sense of moral integrity rendered them particularly vulnerable to the dishonesty, superficiality and callousness of Business Culture.

Smail looks at the lives of several individuals who came to blame themselves for their inadequate 'motivation' and general inability to manage new circumstances, when in fact it was the effect of system demands quite outside their control that distorted their lives.

Dave (a pseudonym) was an accountant who experienced some unpleasant physical symptoms such as stomach pains and numbness in the chest. He also developed a fear of driving on motorways, something his new job required. So bad was this fear that when he drove 'his back went rigid, his legs and feet ached so much he couldn't use the pedals properly' (2001: 131). As an accountant, he was fairly successful having risen to a relatively senior position in charge of a team of accountants. When his firm was taken over by an international conglomerate in the 1980s, his world changed. The new organization was 'leaner', 'fitter' and altogether more image conscious. Dave had no hesitation in describing the new senior management as 'bullshitters'. His job increasingly became that of attending high-profile meetings and compensating for the ignorance of senior managers with his technical know-how. His discomfort at having to service this artificial world of 'image-making' and 'presentational skills' was amplified by the fact that he now had to act differently towards those below him. He had to 'badger and cajole, bully and threaten people who had previously been his friends and colleagues' to produce results for which no adequate time was given (2001: 134).

Dave's torment arose not from his own inadequacy, though he blamed himself, but from finding that structural and ideological changes had inverted all sense of personal integrity. He now had to be respectful towards a world of bosses he did not respect and callous towards those below him whom he did. Smail is not arguing that the dynamics of Dave's family background played no part in his unhappiness, but points out that he was managing his life with a modicum of success until it was turned upside down by 'invisible' societal factors outside his control.

Habermas is inviting us to see modern society as a tug-of-war between (capitalist) system and lifeworld, with the lifeworld mostly being pulled out of shape by the system. At the level of the lifeworld, communicative rationality has endlessly to struggle with the instrumental rationality that the system imposes on its subjects. Because Habermas develops the idea of a seam existing between system and lifeworld, he is better able than his predecessors to grasp the nuanced nature of modernity's social pathologies. Where they tended to see the modern world as covered by a blanket of reification with no way out of the impasse (*sic*), he is looking for a way of conceptualising the variety of effects the system can have on the lifeworld. However, there are critics of his concepts of system and lifeworld who regard the account as still too singular to capture the complexity of things.

Critical Comments

When Habermas talked of the switch of viewpoint from 'participant' (lifeworld) to 'observer' (system) revealing a different set of relationships, some authors believe he confused a methodological switch for a real difference in reality (Giddens 1987, Mouzelis 1992). Giddens and Mouzelis argue that the two sets of relations, (especially system integration and social integration), are only the outcome of a methodological decision, so that if you adopt one perspective you come out with one set of results, if you adopt the other something else results. However, as Layder (1997: 102) argues, there is something unconvincing about this because if the distinction is analytically useful, which Giddens and Mouzelis admit, then it surely points to a distinction *in reality*, not just to a different set of methodological assumptions: there is something *there* to be analysed separately. One might say that we as human beings have an emotional life made up of all the pains and pleasures with which we are familiar, but this does not mean we do not also have a biological life that affects our emotions but is quite separate from them; something that goes its own way pretty much independent of our emotions. It seems to me that reality is stratified whether we are talking about emotion, biology, system or lifeworld, and that these are not arbitrary distinctions, not merely the outcome of the way we look at things, but point to real differences in the way reality is.

However, Layder (1997) and also Honneth (1993) question the 'purity' of Habermas's distinction between system and lifeworld. Habermas tends to find all the good things in life in the lifeworld and all the bad things he attributes to the system. The lifeworld offers us the chance, albeit only theoretically, of perfect communication, of achieving a consensus through the 'ideal speech situation', whereas the system offers us only the chance of being colonised by its imperatives, of being subjected to its power. The choice seems too stark.

Layder and Honneth have a point. In his efforts to develop a normative benchmark for Critical Theory, a universal norm to which humans should aspire, Habermas does tend to see the lifeworld as a power-free zone where a true consensus could be reached. Power on his account imposes itself on actors malevolently from the outside, as something that systematically distorts communication. Instead, it may be that power is tied into actors' lives in all kinds of subtle ways. For example, following Freud we could suggest that the unconscious has power over the conscious in that it can shape thoughts, actions and reactions without our knowing it. One cannot treat this unconscious power as derived from the (capitalist) system, nor is it necessarily a negative power.

One might also note that the conception of power developed by Michel Foucault, which he termed 'disciplinary' power, suggests that the modern human subject only exists within, and is produced by, a discursive force-field of power. Thus, power is not something that is imposed from an external source such as the system. Of course Foucault's views are not above critical suspicion, not least because they are based on the presumed 'death of the subject'. However, like Freud's ideas they do raise fruitful questions about conceiving power only in a negative way.

Similarly, Habermas represents the system as a norm-free zone, driven only by its own mechanical imperatives. As Layder points out, empirical research has shown that even in industry and government bureaucracies, where system imperatives would seem to dominate, there is evidence to show that *communicative* practices play an important role with all kinds of tacit norms being negotiated. However, while Habermas does describe lifeworld and system in almost oppositional terms he does not deny that in any empirical situation they will be entwined.

Whether Habermas's distinctions are satisfactory or need further refinement is an open question. But I share with Layder (1997: 103) a belief that Habermas's great theoretical achievement is in finding a rapprochement between two intractably opposed sociologies. One should not downplay this achievement because problems still exist with it.

Habermas and the Reconstruction of Historical Materialism

While embracing both hermeneutics and structural-functionalism to reconstruct Critical Theory, Habermas also has a third target in sight, Marx's 'historical materialism'. Historical materialism had many virtues but was lopsided in its emphasis on 'material production' as the key to progressive change. Progress at the level of applying science and technology is something fairly easy to gauge. If one machine does a particular task more speedily and effectively than another we regard its use as 'progress', and societies that have developed this form of progress as the most advanced. However this tells us nothing about what progress at the level of everyday life might mean.

For Marx, progress meant the development of a society's productive forces, its capacity to develop instrumental forms of knowledge the better to control and manipulate the natural world to its advantage. Baldly stated, Marx's case was that the dynamic of all social development was to be found in the conflictive relationship between a society's forces of production (science and technology) and its relations of production (social classes formed by the way the ownership of the means of production is distributed). Habermas believes there is a misleading 'technologistic' bias in this account. Because humans have to get food and shelter to survive Marx assumes that the development of the forces of production, which give us greater control over our physical environment, is the natural driving force behind *all* development. As we get better at controlling nature, new forms of social (class) relation are called into being and this will culminate in a communist society. However, the expansion of productive forces cannot explain the development of our *intersubjective* capacities.

As with Parsons, Marx misses the irreducibility of the level of interaction. He fails to see that it has a developmental history of its own, with the result that historical materialism has a poor 'predictive' record. Societies are not 'totalities' that are determined by their productive forces but are stratified entities that develop according to different rationalities. The lifeworld has an interactive or communicative rationale of its own, it is the locus of moral-practical knowledge, of meaning shared by families, of ideas shared in workplaces, of the shifting nature of cultural mood. Habermas captures the specificity of what he means in an early work (1971a: 92):

> By 'interaction' . . . I understand *communicative action*, symbolic interaction. It is governed by binding *consensual norms*, which define reciprocal expectations about behaviour and which must be understood and recognized by at least two acting subjects . . . While the acceptance of technical rules and strategies depends upon the validity of empirically true or analytically correct statements, the validity of social norms is grounded only in the intersubjectivity of mutual understanding of intentions, and secured by the general recognition of obligations.

Habermas (1979: ch. 4) does acknowledge that problems in the development of a society's productive forces, that is the development of new technologies to exploit the material world, *may* trigger problems in forms of social integration (lifeworld), but for the most part a mode of production will have to draw on the dynamics of moral-practical (interactive) knowledge to run effectively; indeed, sometimes social norms may be the pacemaker of change. What he has in mind is Max Weber's insight that the 'capitalist spirit' *presupposes* the 'protestant ethic'. As it were, capitalism, with its manipulative ways of going on, only emerged because certain religious beliefs about seeking salvation through the calculation of virtue, already provided the accumulated moral-practical potential for capitalist development.

Habermas repeatedly comes back to the importance of the lifeworld as something that may be 'systematically distorted' and may never become completely rational, but nevertheless is the foundation of society. He is always on the lookout to counter any reductionism that would see society as the product of instrumental responses to system demands. What is central is that the lifeworld has a 'communicative' *logic* of its own which can be reconstructed. It can be reconstructed in two dimensions. 'Horizontally', it has universal communicative properties, something he calls 'universal' or 'formal pragmatics', while 'vertically' it has a history that he conceives in terms of the moral development of the human species. Both of these dimensions are part of his reconstruction of, if not complete move away from, Marx's ideas.

The Horizontal Dimension: Universal Pragmatics

Partly as a result of the problems that arose with the 'interest in emancipation' as well as his reading of Gadamer, the locus of Habermas's concerns becomes that of language, which he sees as being at the heart of our communicative capacity to create the social world. However, he also wants something more determinate and critical than 'interpretation' to be at the heart of analyses of the lifeworld. He wants to stay at the level of communication but locate universal elements that go beyond any particular subject matter and can be used 'critically' to evaluate that subject matter.

He draws on both Chomsky's structural linguistics and Piaget's psychology of cognition to move beyond hermeneutics. Structural linguistics does not reflect on the meanings found in language, but reconstructs the rules that structure how things can be said. It reconstructs 'the rule system that underlies the production of all the various grammatically correct and semantically meaningful elements of a natural language'. Using the idea that language has an invisible structure that is presupposed in any use of it, Habermas seeks to apply the same idea to human communication. As Chomsky reconstructed what is tacitly presupposed in language use, Habermas seeks to reconstruct what is tacitly presupposed in *communication,* something slightly different from language. He believes that while actors are plainly 'communicatively competent', in that they have the skill and general know-how to perform complex communications, they do not know the rules they are applying. Beyond the hermeneutic realm of interpretation there is a pre-conceptual realm that is only accessible through the rational reconstruction of its underlying rules. The realm that underlies communication he terms 'universal' or sometimes 'general pragmatics'. 'Universal', because it applies to all human communication through language, and 'pragmatic' because it refers to the automatic ways we orientate ourselves towards the world in different situations.

Habermas makes the same point in relation to the work of Jean Piaget, arguing that cognition also has an underlying structure that shapes our understanding of things independent of language. While the categories of 'space, time, causality, and substance' come into language in everyday life, they do not originate in language, but are superimposed on it. Piaget's work shows that cognition goes through stages of increasingly complex development, and these are not amenable to interpretation, but actually precede our interpretations. If we can reconstruct the rules underlying language and cognition, and see how these processes *should* work, then in principle we can do the same with 'communicative competence'.

In normal communication we conform in myriad ways to the language-oriented rules of everyday life. Because we can distinguish between a verbal symbol and what it refers to, we are able to distinguish between self and other, subject and object, internal and external, public and private. Similarly, in normal communicative situations we are able to shift the meaning of the concepts of 'causality, space and time' according to whether the discursive framework refers to physical objects or human beings. We do not 'realistically' refer to physical objects such as cars as having motives. If we give a car personal name, and refer to it as being in a mood this morning because it won't start, everyone knows we are cracking a joke. The success of the joke depends on everyone's ability to know that we have deliberately switched discourses to produce an amusing effect. What makes it funny is that people know how personally irritating cars can be when they won't start, and understand why we might suddenly talk to them in this way. There would be no joke if cars really did have motives, and we would be very worried by someone who seriously believed their car was in a mood.

It is the idea that the perception of reality is not only prone to interpretation, as hermeneutics suggests, but has a universal structure that guides interpretation, that attracts Habermas. His aim ultimately is to uncover the universal features presupposed in any communication about reality. To this end, he introduces the concept of the 'ideal speech situation'.

Though he is not wedded to language in the way hermeneutics or interpretive sociology is, a central intuition of all his work is that what is distinct about the human species is that it maintains itself by working cooperatively through the medium of language. The reason our species persists in this way is because built into human language is the possibility of achieving a consensus. Of course, consensus is not a straightforward affair, there are all kinds of extraneous factors affecting it, but the *possibility* of agreement is always present in any communication. This possibility can be theoretically expressed in the ideal speech situation where all extraneous factors, such as systematic distortions, inequalities and ideologies, are suspended and only the force of the better argument holds sway. In this purely theoretical circumstance all people in the communicative situation have an equal chance to present their views.

At first sight, the idea of the 'ideal speech situation' seems rather fanciful, certainly to those working in the social sciences, where the empirical existence of such a situation seems laughably unrealistic. Habermas's point, though, is that this is only a virtual ideal, implicit in any actual communication, not something that actually exists, nor probably ever could exist. It is intriguing because it captures the idea that the point of language, no matter how it is actually used, is to convince others of something and reach a consensus. Even dictators, such as Hitler or Stalin, did not just impose their policies, but sought to justify them, to find 'good' reasons why people should believe them.

The purpose of the 'ideal speech situation', for Habermas, is to provide a universal, normative centrepiece for Critical Theory, and to show that the realm of norms and values is, in principle, as rational as the factual realm of physical objects. In principle, we can be as objective about assessing the validity of social norms, as about the existence of physical objects. In pursuit of this idea, he develops the concept of 'ideal speech' in terms of what he calls the 'validity claims' (or claims to the truth) we raise in ordinary speech.

Validity claims are those claims we implicitly raise when uttering something; they are what will enable the utterance to be believed. For the most part they are implicit in everyday interaction, but they are open to challenge and thoroughly intersubjective. Habermas (1970) argues that in all linguistic communication we raise, either singly or more usually in combination, four validity claims: that what we say can be understood, that it is true, that it is right, and that it is a sincere expression of the utterer's feelings. Each one of these could be challenged by a partner in dialogue, with the implication that we would then have to redeem the claim by further justification in order to reach a consensus. Of course, Habermas knows that what actually happens rarely matches up to the ideal speech situation, but insists that it is more than a fiction. It is something that implicitly happens every time we utter something.

The detail of his argument here, and in the subsequent 'What is Universal Pragmatics' (1979: ch.1) is pretty formidable, but matters less than the purpose of the work. Habermas's aim is to establish that both the natural *and* the social world are prone to objective evaluation. If we take the second and the third validity claims, we can see how this works. When we make a factual or propositional statement, the implication is that we could justify it by producing evidence that would support it, and that it would be found acceptable by the other person. Of course, not any old facts would do, they would have to be understood as being relevant to the issue, and be recognised by both parties as acceptable evidence about the situation. Similarly, if we make a value statement, the implication is that we could call up norms acceptable to the other party, ones that would count in its favour. Thus if we declare that such and such a film was very good, we could call up value judgments concerning the quality of the cinematography, the direction and the acting, which would be couched in the common norms concerning judgments in these matters. Validity claims take different forms according to the order of reality, or 'world relation' we are addressing, but they each refer to the possibility of reaching an intersubjective agreement about the truth of the matter.

Critical Comments

Habermas is claiming that there is a normative basis to the underlying rules of communication and that these rules orientate us to reaching agreement. For the lifeworld to become more rational, ever more validity claims must be made explicit and a consensual resolution found to them. However, he equally recognises the corrosive effects that the capitalist system's steering mechanisms, (money and organisational power), have in distorting the lifeworld. His gloomy adage, 'the colonisation of the lifeworld' captures this well. It is not that a pessimistic attitude is necessarily wrong, his predecessors in some ways had good reason to be so, but Habermas has set his cap at constructing a theory that is much less negative in tone while many of his conclusions seem to point in the opposite direction.

Part of the reason for this may be the distance between what actually happens in interaction and the idea of a disturbance to the underlying rules of communication. Axel Honneth (1999: 328) approves of the development of Critical Theory along the lines of a 'communicative paradigm', but asks what moral experiences are supposed to correspond to distortions of these rules:

> (individuals) experience an impairment of what we can call their moral expectations, that is their 'moral point of view', not as a restriction of intuitively mastered rules of language, but as a violation of identity claims acquired in socialization.

The logic of Habermas's argument over underlying communicative rules may be good, but if it seeks purchase on the moral experiences of those involved it is less convincing. If we refer back to the example of 'Dave' and his new relation to those above and those below him following the takeover of his firm, we can see what this means. Dave's physical and emotional discomfort resulted from his being required to be callous to those below him in order to ingratiate himself with those 'bullshitters' above him. He did not experience this as an illegitimate breaking of the rules governing interaction; indeed he accepted the new interactional order and blamed himself for not being able to deal with it. He internalised his difficulties as his own fault. What he experienced was a violation of his own moral identity and intuitive sense of justice. It was not communicative validity claims that were at stake here, though those concerned with sincerity or factuality were doubtless being contravened, but respect and recognition for the dignity of others.

For Honneth, Habermas is not wrong, but his emphasis on the tension between system and lifeworld should be refocused onto 'the social causes responsible for the systematic violation of the conditions of recognition' (p. 330). Honneth, as a developer of third generation Critical Theory, is keen to shift attention from the power of autonomous systems to the actual damage caused to relations of social recognition, which he sees as at the heart of the social world (Honneth 1995).

While Habermas's language in these matters is notoriously convoluted and slippery, and many of his ideas problematic, their fruitfulness lies in the effort he makes to reconstruct the rules that make everyday life possible. He applies the same reconstructive principles to try and discern the universals on the 'vertical dimension' of the lifeworld.

The Vertical Dimension: Moral Development and Social Evolution

As in his work on 'universal pragmatics', Habermas makes a sharp distinction between the interactional properties of communicative action and the instrumental qualities of purposive-rational action. Where Marx was concerned with the revolutionary changes in the mode of production (purposive-rational action), Habermas's concern with the specific properties of the communicative realm enables him to suggest that the history of worldviews has a moral-evolutionary logic of its own. To bring this idea into focus he draws on the work of Lawrence Kohlberg (1971).

Kohlberg's work hinges on the idea that an individual's moral development goes through stages of increasing levels of adequacy. These stages are not the product of a stimulus-response model of behaviour but the outcome of active learning. For example, the child will learn that deliberately breaking some small thing is more morally reprehensible than accidentally breaking something more important. The idea that an accident radically affects how we conceive of events, and what rightfully should follow from them, captures the idea that moral learning is a process of 'integration' and 'differentiation'.

'Differentiation' refers to the idea that at higher stages we can recognise a moral judgement from some other value judgement. In this case, we can recognise the importance of the accidental nature of the breakage in contrast to the value of the object broken. 'Integration' refers to the degree to which we can integrate conflicting claims about the accident. The more points of view we can bring to bear on the situation, the more we can recognise its moral complexity. Thus, even if it was an accident, we should have been more careful given the importance of the object for the other person.

Kohlberg's work demonstrates two things that attract Habermas. First, that the underlying structure of moral development can be reconstructed, and shown (empirically) to be universal (sic). Secondly, that the higher stages can be shown (philosophically) to be superior to the lower stages. In an audacious move, Habermas (1979: ch. 3) seeks to apply these insights into individual moral development to the evolutionary development of society. The idea is that a 'world-view' contains the structure of the moral-practical realm of that society. Thus, he suggests that an historical reconstruction of societal 'world-views' shows an homology exists between the stages of individual moral development and what happens at a societal level. In effect, he wants to claim that progressive, evolutionary elements can be identified at the level of the life-world as readily as at the technical level of the system.

Habermas's account of social evolution is underdeveloped and has been subject to a variety of criticisms. Strydom (1992) and Eder (1998) point up the doubtfulness of transferring a model of individual moral development to the level of collective development. McCarthy (1982) argues that Habermas's views on social evolution are based too readily on what has happened in the western world and are therefore culturally biased. However, while as with his reworking of systems theory, Habermas's ideas are not above critical suspicion, they do have the happy knack of provoking thought and opening up areas of further possible investigation (How 2001).

Summary and Conclusion

I have only been able to sketch out some of Habermas's ideas as they relate mainly to sociology. The situation is made more complicated by the fact that he frequently presents the reader with a moving target. Ideas raised at one point, reappear later in a different form, or disappear altogether; this can be disheartening for a reader who wishes to grasp the full package.

Nevertheless, I have tried to show how Habermas drew on Gadamer's hermeneutics to fill the 'interaction' gap left by first generation Critical Theorists, and that this 'linguistic turn' formed the basis of his 'communication theory'. Certainly, it is something that has been at the heart of his subsequent work on 'discourse ethics', 'law' and 'democracy'.

In appropriating Gadamer's work, Habermas used 'immanent critique', albeit in a different way to that of Horkheimer et al. His approach was to adopt Gadamer's ideas, but to press their logic to the point where they revealed an alternative, more rational, and less conservative view of things. He accepted Gadamer's view that there was no such thing as presuppositionless knowledge, and that, particularly in the social sciences, prejudices or prejudgements are a crucial element in our understanding of the world.

However, our reflective capacities do not commit us to the mere continuity of tradition, they also provide us with the potential for breaching tradition. Prejudices, once revealed, no longer have to function as blind prejudices, as we have the capacity to transform ourselves in response to them. Moreover, this potential is confirmed, for Habermas, in the hermeneutic account of language. If Gadamer is correct in saying that language is naturally oriented to mutual understanding, then under the right conditions we can arrive at a rational consensus. Of course, the conditions have to be right, and at this point Habermas introduces the concept of the ideal speech situation.

Given that language is essentially dialogic, the conditions that underpin dialogue have to be 'ideal': they have, in principle to allow unconstrained dialogue between interlocutors. Such conditions may not ever exist in actuality, but they have a virtual existence every time we communicate via language. Every time we speak with others (even if we are lying) we ask to be believed, we expect the 'truth' to be accepted, and in so doing are obliged to raise 'validity claims'. Validity claims are those underlying assumptions that orientate us to the world in different ways. Validity claims are geared in different ways to different 'world relations' and their framework conditions the normality of our communications.

In developing 'universal pragmatics', Habermas formalises his move away from hermeneutics. Universal pragmatics accepts that language and reality are entwined, as hermeneutics suggests, but moves beyond the embrace of linguistic tradition by reconstructing the rationale of the conditions through which *all* utterances are made. In making these theoretical moves Habermas seeks to breach tradition as well as striving to find a plausible moral centrepiece for Critical Theory. He acknowledges that one cannot directly critique what happens *in* the world on this basis; that requires participation in the specifics of particular situations, but reconstructing the universal conditions which shape different orders of reality should enable us to *indirectly* critique a consensus that has been spuriously achieved.

As a theorist, Habermas works at a high level of abstraction, and a reader could rightly ask how all these (and many more) elaborate theoretical moves bear on the reality of everyday life? How can the social scientist apply them? There is no easy answer. He seems sometimes to want others to apply his insights, while he ploughs on with further theoretical investigation. Nevertheless, this should not deter us as there is a wealth of material to work on, and his own 'hypothetical' approach encourages challenge and counter argument.

He is very much aware that tradition no longer governs ordinary people's lives, and that amidst the transient and fragmentary nature of this 'postmodern' world, people increasingly have to rely on their own 'communicative performances'. To the extent that this is the case, then uncovering the grounds of *rational* communication, at least offers an academic challenge to the nihilistic postmodern view that reason has died under a welter of alternative narratives, and communication just a matter of rhetoric. Certainly Habermas is critical of Gadamer's notion of tradition, but is much more so of the postmodern view that we should now applaud the coming of the traditionless society.

Further Reading

Habermas's first engagement with hermeneutics is to be found in *On the Logic of the Social Sciences* (1988: ch. 8). His subsequent challenge to the 'universal' claims of hermeneutics can be found in either Bleicher (1980: reading III or Mueller-Vollmer (1986: ch. 10); these translations differ slightly from one another. Gadamer's 'universal' claims for hermeneutics can be found in Gadamer (1977: ch. 1), his responses and challenges to Habermas in Gadamer (1977: ch. 2) and Ormiston and Schrift (1990). These essays are rather daunting for a reader unfamiliar with the work. Holub (1991: ch. 3) offers a clear introduction to the issues that lay between Critical Theory and hermeneutics, as (I hope) does the more extensive treatment given to it by How (1995) in *The Habermas–Gadamer Debate and the Nature of the Social*. Habermas developed his ideas about Parsons and the importance of the distinction between system and lifeworld in the second volume of his, *The Theory of Communicative Action: The Critique of Functionalist Reason* (Habermas 1987a). Apart from the references I give in this chapter, the only other secondary source I know that deals with Habermas and systems theory is Holub (1991: ch. 5), which is concerned with Habermas's debate with the famous German systems theorist, Niklas Luhmann.

8

Critical Theory and Postmodernism

Introduction

In this chapter I explore the contemporary postmodernist challenge to Critical Theory via two of its leading protagonists, Jean Baudrillard and Jean-François Lyotard. First, with regard to Baudrillard, I shall compare his account of the elimination of the subject as an active agent in mass society with that of Marcuse and Adorno. Using the concept of human need, I shall show that Critical Theory retains an important sense of the reality of the subject; something notably absent from Baudrillard's work. Secondly, I shall examine in detail the counter-challenge to postmodernism brought by Habermas in his essay 'Modernity: An Unfinished Project'. In this, he reminds us that the hopes generated at the time of the eighteenth-century Enlightenment for human progress and emancipation have not been fulfilled, but that this is no reason to reject the whole project, as postmodernists do. Postmodernism's failure lies in its over emphasis on the importance of the aesthetic sphere at the expense of other systemic factors which play an equally influential part in our lives. I shall then consider the work of Lyotard who regards our grand modernist 'stories' or 'metanarratives', such as 'progress' and 'emancipation', as illusions, concluding that Lyotard has misunderstood Habermas's claims and that if we have hopes that social science might contribute to a more rational future, we should look to Critical Theory for illumination.

The term 'postmodernism' is one of the most elusive terms currently in use in the humanities and social sciences. It came to prominence during the late 1970s and, though its popularity has waned in recent years, its effects are still being felt. When I first came across it I was struck by how contradictory it sounded. How could something come *after* the modern, when the modern referred to things that were right up to date? I learnt that this sense of contradictoriness was very much in the spirit of the term: it was deliberately provocative. The provocation came not just from the term itself, but in the way it, as an outlook, undermined so many of the assumptions that Critical Theory held dear, including the reality of 'truth', 'progress', 'history' and the

143

'subject'. One of its implications was that Critical Theory, with its emphasis on the reification of the subject (Adorno), or the possibilities of undistorted communication between subjects (Habermas), was old hat, and that radical thought was now the province of postmodernists.

The diffuseness of postmodernist thought makes if difficult to describe in a straightforward way. It is a close cousin to a number of other 'posts', such as 'post-empiricism', 'post-industrialism', 'post-Fordism', and 'post-structuralism'. The latter term, particularly, overlaps with postmodernism. Poststructuralism is associated with authors such as Derrida and Foucault, who, drawing on the linguistics of Saussure, emphasise the idea that what words mean derives from their relations with each other, not from that to which they refer. In fact the thing to which they refer, derives *its* meaning from the relationship between words. Thus, there is no reality that is outside 'language'. Post-structuralism differs from its predecessor (structuralism), in that it denies there are fixed, deep-lying structures which function like laws of nature. Rather, the emphasis is on the changing forms of reality as they are produced by language or discourse. Even the modern, reflexive subject, Foucault (1979) argues, is a product of discourse.

What is Postmodernism?

Postmodernism is a broad term, which refers to twentieth-century cultural changes in art, architecture, literature, music and film. Like poststructuralism it attends to the lack of fixity in the meaning of things, dwelling playfully, sometimes ironically on life in a consumer society, but generally celebrating the advent of this new kind of life. In sociology, it focuses on music, shopping and film, on the increasingly fluid nature of gender definitions, or on the way social identity now depends on the consumption of commodities and what they signify, rather than social class or other traditional factors. More abstractly, and drawing on the poststructuralist idea that reality is a linguistic construct, it undermines the validity of modernist notions of 'truth', 'reason', and 'progress', arguing that they are western inventions and thus the product of a particular view of what counts as reasonable, truthful or progressive, not the supra-historical, universal ideas the West claims.

Although it fell to Habermas (1987b, 1996) amongst Critical Theorists to defend the legitimacy of 'truth', 'reason' and 'progress' against its relativisation in the hands of postmodernists, the work of first generation Critical Theorists also stands in opposition to it by virtue of the latter's critique of mass culture. The main thrust of their later work was that capitalism had reached a point where oppositional forces had been incorporated into the system in such a thoroughgoing way that society had become one-dimensional. They argued that the consumption of the products of the culture industry, the gradual commodification of all aspects of life and the accompanying reification of consciousness, had rendered the human subject so 'happily' helpless that the potential for an historical change to a better life had been all but eliminated. In effect, capitalism had induced a kind of historical stasis for the purpose of maintaining itself.

Baudrillard's Postmodernism

I shall treat the work of Jean Baudrillard as representative of the postmodernist outlook as it expresses in a most decisive fashion the claims of the oeuvre. The very features of life that Critical Theory identified negatively are held in almost the opposite light by postmodernists such as Baudrillard. For Baudrillard, to impute to the subject (Marxist) concepts such as reification of consciousness, commodity fetishism and so forth, is a habit of thought that has no purchase on reality as it wrongly assumes the possibility of a pure, self-determining, unalienated subject. Rather, subjects are always the product of an era, and the idea of a wholly self-determining subject is an illusion fostered by western metaphysical thinking, not something intrinsic to being human.

Baudrillard's writing stretches over four decades and although he is best known for his apolitical postmodernist views, his early work had a radical left-wing tinge to it. In the 1960s, he was associated with the Situationist International and the work of Guy Debord in particular. The Situationists were a quasi-anarchist group that drew their ideas from the world of radical art. Surrealism and Dadaism provided the touchstone for a movement that sought to transform the deadness of urban landscapes through dramatic interventions with live music and poetry. They believed that the way forward was not through some far distant proletarian revolution but in trying to creatively merge art and everyday life in all its immediacy and devising situations where this could happen – hence 'Situationism'. In terms of sociology, the work of Henri Lefebvre (1991) was influential in applying Marxist ideas to everyday life, but more important still was the concept of society as a 'spectacle' as developed by Debord (1976). The idea that modern society is 'spectacular', in being based on the consumption of dazzling commodities, is reminiscent of first generation Critical Theory; both believed it involved the pacification of the masses. However, while Horkheimer et al. were always sceptical of romantic revolutionaries, Debord and the Situationists believed that direct intervention could dispel this illusion.

Early Baudrillard drew on Debord's neo-Marxist ideas but, during the 1970s, gradually came to believe that the era, to which Marxist concepts such as 'alienation' and 'commodity fetishism' applied, had passed. We were now thoroughly immersed in a postmodern world where the 'spectacle' was no longer the illusion but the real thing. He takes Marx to task for his metaphysical belief that an essential unalienated worker-subject exists behind the scenes of capitalism, waiting to come into existence at some point in the future when capitalism has been superseded (Baudrillard 1983). Marx, in his early philosophical work discussed the nature of human 'species-being', the natural creative characteristics of human beings. He talked of human creativity being expressed in our capacity to work cooperatively and how this was distorted under the conditions of capitalism. Under capitalism, by virtue of its exploitative character, we were alienated from others and ourselves and prevented from realising our true creative potential in having to work to produce goods for the benefit of the owners of the means of production. However, for Baudrillard, the human subject has no frustrated inner nature that is trying to get out from under the stone of capitalism.

Baudrillard expresses his opposition to Marx in terms of the latter's distinction between the use-value of a commodity and its exchange-value. The use-value of a commodity is its usefulness to anyone who buys it, while its exchange-value is what people are prepared to pay to acquire it in a world determined by capitalist economic relations, including profits, wages and advertising. However, for Baudrillard, to set use-value in opposition to exchange-value and present the former as something naturally good, as though it were the authentic expression of real human need, in contrast to the distorted world of capitalist exchange, is misleading. What people find useful is always determined within an overall system of meaning, such that there is no 'outside' to the system where the *real* needs of *un*alienated people could exist independent of distortion; what we 'need' is what we buy *within* an overall system of meaning (or signification). The human subject, like the commodities it consumes, exists internally to, and is part of, a system of meaning. In effect, Baudrillard is saying that the idea of the human subject as a creature that could exist *un*alienated, free of distorting conditions, is an illusion because the subject is as much an expression of a system of meaning as its commodities. There is thus no ultimate way to criticise the reality of life in capitalist society because its conditions can only be described relative to those in other societies, not as better or worse.

In many ways Baudrillard presents us with a just-so-story; there is no hidden potential, no naturally unalienated subject lying behind appearances trying to get out. The postmodern world is a 'depthless' world, and that is just the way things are. He describes the world without reference to why it is like that and then (in my view) uncritically reads off what the modern subject is supposedly like from that description. For Baudrillard, the postmodern world involves a breaking down of the punitive constraints of tradition, which if anything should be seen as a liberation from the modernist demand for progress and conformity to the ideals that support it; so what we need now is to be liberated from the liberators.

For Baudrillard, the rapid growth of mass communications, in the form of 24-hour, multi-channel worldwide television, of information technology, the Internet, and cybernetic systems of control, has produced information overload. The effect of this is to destabilise meaning in a radical way. So much information is foisted on us that we (subjects) have merged into the information (objects). So many images of the truth are available that the very idea of there being a real world about which we can know the truth, has become problematic. In the language of Saussure's linguistics, the stable if arbitrary relationship between signifier and signified has broken down. We now live in a world where signifiers are so plentiful that they have become 'free-floating'; a signifier is able to take up in an almost ad hoc way a variety of cross-boundary relationships with other signifiers. The result is that meaning is permanently up for grabs and concepts such as social class may be seen as ephemeral as any other.

In Saussurean terms, the 'signifier' refers to the actual material word as spoken or written, or by extension the image that appears on the screen, whereas the 'signified', refers to the concept or idea it represents. What Baudrillard means by the increasing prevalence of free-floating signifiers can be illustrated by an example. John Storey (1993) recounts going into an Italian restaurant in the north of England and finding a large picture of the American film actor, Marlon Brando, on the wall. He knew straightway that the image signified, 'Italian-ness', via the actor's starring role in the *Godfather* (1972), yet was puzzled at how easy it had become to grasp the dislocated connection between an American cinema icon and Italian-ness. On Baudrillard's account, images are no longer tied to anything specific in the real world, but now move fluidly around, leaping across traditional 'reality' boundaries in almost any way imaginable.

In the 1980s, Baudrillard developed three notions to describe what is going on: simulation, implosion and hyperreality. For Baudrillard, we now live in an era where the mass media simulate reality to the point where reality, including ourselves, has to be understood as a media product. There is no 'real', independent of what is constructed by the media. He does not identify any political or economic forces, which might be behind this change, but regards simulation as the overwhelming factor in defining the era, whatever forces produced it. In the process of simulation, the image or representation of the 'object' collides with the 'real object' and the two implode, or collapse into one another, destabilising any fixed notion of the real. Gradually, a state of hyperreality has come into existence, where what has been simulated, namely the model or representation, replaces any residual element of the real, and *becomes the real* in its place.

British TV viewers may remember the 'Spitting Image' series, which satirised different aspects of public life using grotesque rubber puppets to represent politicians. One particular sketch involved the then Prime Minister, John Major, who was represented by a grey puppet trying to spear a single pea on a plate, declaring to his wife that peas were a 'very interesting vegetable'. I once asked a group of students, quite independently of any reference to the programme, if they were to colour-code politicians, what colour John Major would be? Everyone laughingly agreed he would be grey. The example does not prove Baudrillard's case, but does illustrate the force with which media images become 'realer' than the real, in effect, defining what the real is.

Another example of how we have come to accept the simulation of the 'real' can be found in a British TV show, 'Stars in Their Eyes'. In this, unknown singers sing well-known 'hits' from the past, dressing up like the original singer and imitating his or her voice. The TV audience is then asked to phone in votes for their favourite. After about ten weeks previous winners are brought together in a grand final. The singers are presented as though they were the original artists. It is unclear whether we are being asked to judge how much we like the original singer and song, or the quality of the imitation. The two merge, drowned in a glut of enthusiasm triggered by the first few seconds of the upcoming 'spectacle'. As Baudrillard would suggest, it is futile to ask whether we are watching the 'real' thing or a simulation of it, the two have imploded and we are left only with the image or 'spectacle'.

One of Baudrillard's most (in)famous publications is entitled *The Gulf War Did Not Take Place* (1995). It consists of three essays written at the time of the Gulf war: 'The Gulf war will not take place', 'The Gulf war: is it really taking place?' and, 'The Gulf war did not take place'. His argument, essentially, is that our only access to the truth of the war is through the media, and as a result our feelings and pontifications about the war have no greater basis in reality than any other aspect of life. Like everything else, the war was a piece of media rhetoric with which our daily lives were saturated. He is not suggesting that the media distort the truth, for there is no truth lying behind appearances, rather they reproduce a hyperreality in which questions of truth are merely the outcome of rhetoric. Anyone who hankers after the 'real' truth, he accuses of being nostalgically tied to an obsolete world-view where truth mattered. Truth, for Baudrillard (1994: 81–2), is now a slender thing: those that win 'truth' games have the best rhetoric, but their victories are hollow, and will not hold fast, because:

> the media are producers not of socialization, but of exactly the opposite, the implosion of the social in the masses. And this is only the macroscopic extension of the *implosion of meaning* at the microscopic level of the sign . . . This means that all contents of meaning are absorbed in the only dominant form of the medium. Only the medium can make an event – whatever the contents, whether they are conformist or subversive.

For Baudrillard the contents of the medium (I presume TV) are 'neutralised', the messages of the 'conformists' can be no more successful than that of the 'subversives' but even more:

> there is also the implosion of the medium itself in the real, the implosion of the medium and of the real in a sort of hyperreal nebula, in which even the definition and distinct action of the medium can no longer be determined.

Given that the message, the medium and the real have all collapsed into one another, one suspects, as Norris (1992: 14) points out, that even if one claimed that the Gulf war *did* take place, Baudrillard would argue that any evidence put forward was inevitably pseudo-knowledge, no more or less true than any other nebulous media-inflected claim.

Postmodernist thought tends to insulate itself from challenge by declaring that its critics are nostalgically tied to an archaic world-view where the truth of the alienation of the subject, mattered. This makes a critical comparison with Adorno et al., difficult. The idea of the 'death of the subject', or that the subject has been subsumed by the object, which postmodernists regard as a key insight, is the very thing that Critical Theory feared most. They were under no illusions about the fragility of the subject, but nevertheless insisted that the subject was more than just the product of society or of a 'signifying system', and this needed to be reflected in theory. The idea that the hard-won individualism, however limited, which emerged with capitalism in its competitive stage, should be lost to the consumer society filled them with horror.

Evaluating the postmodernist view against that of Critical Theory is also difficult because neither side accept the criteria the other uses to judge things. For postmodernists the world is a contingent place for which there is no general explanation. It is made up of a multiplicity of free-floating signs of which the sign of the 'subject' is but one and one that is no more real than any other. For Critical Theory, on the other hand, theories, which accept things 'as they are', are regarded as an expression of a society's ideology. This judgement was originally directed against positivism, but applies equally well to postmodernism. Theories, which take the surface 'facts' of the status quo to be the whole of the story, are unable to recognise the potentiality for, or desirability of, things being other than they are. For Critical Theory, postmodernist theory is thus a distinctly *un*critical theory.

The Death of the Subject and Human Needs

The general idea of de-centring the subject, or removing it from being the main explanatory category in social science, has a fairly long history starting in the mid 1970s. Even before this in sociology, Marxist and functionalist explanations always cast doubt on the usefulness of taking the subject's view of things as being the most truthful, regarding the context in which subjects act as a more reliable guide to things. For them, explanation really begins where the subject's self-understanding ends. However, in the 1970s, under the influence of structuralist and poststructuralist styles of thought, particularly as they appeared in psychoanalysis, this de-centring took on a more radical hue. No longer was it thought feasible to conceive of the subject as a unified entity, albeit one produced by the exigencies of the social system. The subject from the outset was not naturally a unit with a single identity, but an effect of language and the inter-play of multiple discourses, of styles of thought, ways of talking, and forms of symbolic representation. In fact, the very idea of a unified subject was thought to be the outcome of modernity's need to produce such a creature. Of course Critical Theorists were already aware that the modern 'individual' existed as a corollary of capitalism's need for 'bourgeois individualism', but poststructuralism pressed the issue further, insisting that the subject's identity was made and remade according to the contingencies of discourse. This malleability is possible because the subject 'does not coincide with itself'. This meant that individuals are never fixed entities but always self-divided, they need to meet the needs of others to be themselves, but equally have an inner life, which pulls them away from being the stable product of socialisation via others.

Increasingly the phrase, 'de-centring the subject', was replaced by the 'death of the subject'. Not only was the interactionist emphasis on motives and intentions to be avoided, but also the whole subject, including both its consciousness and unconsciousness, was seen to be an effect of the power relations existing within and between discourses. Hence, for example, the power a doctor has in defining the state of a patient's health, fitness for work and worthiness of treatment depends on the fact that the doctor is inserted into a discourse of knowledge (medical science) in a particular way. The relative power between doctors and patients derives not from them as subjects with certain intellectual talents, particular educational and socio-economic backgrounds, or their different cultural status, but from the way discourse *produces them* as asymmetrical expressions of discursive power.

I have made a distinction between 'de-centring the subject' and the 'death of the subject', though the two are often taken to refer to the same thing. The former, I think, rightly challenges the idea of subjects being unified self-determining entities, reminding us that we, as individuals, are complex, multifaceted beings, riven with tensions, often willing to act irrationally against our own best interests; something of which Critical Theorists were very much aware. The 'death of the subject', however, is problematic because it denies the existence of subjectivity as such, reducing it to being no more than an effect of language or discourse.

It is the effect of over amplifying the constitutive role of language in constructing reality that has produced this reductive effect. It is not surprising that the 'linguistic turn' in theory has been successful in literary theory, where the object of analysis is the text and the effects it produces. In sociology, however, the object is different. One can certainly consider social reality as having text-like qualities (Ricoeur 1981: ch. 8), being made up of discourses for instance, but it also has an empirical referent, that of actual individuals and the structures they inhabit. Inevitably, in sociology, at some point the idea of a 'subject' implicitly refers to people and what they actually do, think and say at the level of everyday life. Indeed, hermeneutic authors, such as Gadamer and Ricoeur, who also emphasise the importance of language, point out that texts themselves invariably have a referential moment, at some point they refer to a world beyond themselves, they are *about* something, and that something is independent of the text. It is the elimination of the referential moment in postmodernist writing, such as Baudrillard's, which makes dubious its claim to be more radical than Critical Theory.

The distinction between Critical Theory's view of the subject and Baudrillard's can be illustrated by reference to 'human need'. For Baudrillard, a concern with human need is anathema because the subject is wholly the product of a regime of signification, and its needs are no more than a product of the same system that produced it. Thus, it does not matter how poor or rich you are; the system has a place for you and your needs. The mass media have a more than ample supply of images to 'fit' all types of consumer. In his book, *America* (1988: 56), he presents us with a cool, glacial description of his travels in the United States. For example:

> The desert you pass through is like the set of a Western, the city a screen of signs and formulas. . . . The American city seems to have stepped right out of the movies. To grasp its secret, you should not, then, begin with the city and move inwards to the screen; you should begin with the screen and move outwards to the city. It is there that cinema does not assume an exceptional form, but simply invests the streets and the entire town with a mythical atmosphere. That is where it is truly gripping. This is why the cult of the stars is not a secondary phenomenon, but the supreme form of cinema, its mythical transfiguration, the last great myth of modernity.

Film stars, he claims are not so much figures to dream about, rather their representations have become the very fabric of American life, which now exists through images alone. Cinema representations '*embody one single passion only: the passion for images*, and the immanence of desire in the images' (p. 56, original emphasis). In other words, the truth of America is to be found in its complete absorption into cinematic representation.

Leaving aside that for Critical Theory such a state of affairs would be the ultimate in reification, there is no evidence, or indeed possibility, in Baudrillard's account, of a concern with anything that might dent the surface impression he gleans, which might speak of needs un-met, things beyond the surface that might nevertheless relate to the surface, such as poverty, racism, sexism or the conservative Reaganite political hegemony of the 1980s (Best and Kellner 1991: 138). Of course it could be argued that *America* is not a work of sociology or philosophy, it is the personal impression Baudrillard gained from his travels in the United States, and therefore should not be expected to provide any reference to such things as needs. Nevertheless, *America* in style and content is entirely characteristic of his other writings from the 1980s onwards and therefore can be considered as representative of his broader postmodernist outlook.

Marcuse's (1994: 4–8) view of human needs is quite different because he recognises that the subject is not wholly reducible to its circumstances. He acknowledges that needs are socially and historically conditioned, but asks *why* some things appear as needs to us rather than others. What are the structural conditions that produced these particular needs as opposed to others? His answer is that:

> Whether or not the possibility of doing or leaving, enjoying or destroying, possessing or rejecting something is seized as a *need* depends on whether or not it can be seen as desirable and necessary for the prevailing societal institutions and interests (1994: 4).

In other words, if you move beyond the idea that needs are only relative to current 'signifying' conditions and ask what purpose these conditions serve, you are able to do more than describe them; you can explain why they are thus and not otherwise. Even if people identify with the image of the products they purchase, you are still able to open up the question of whether their apparent needs are truly theirs, or whether they have been foisted on them as false needs. Without this conceptual opening up we are left with an uncritical relativism that assumes that people's needs are an exact expression of the images society has on offer.

Of course the business of saying what real human needs are is always going to be difficult given the diversity of societal circumstances that prevail at any time and the effect these have on the constitution of needs. But if we assume that the human subject is not wholly a determination of current 'discursive' conditions, then along with Critical Theory, I believe we can talk meaningfully about society fulfilling or not fulfilling needs, of establishing conditions which either enhance or distort human potential.

Marcuse puts to one side the biological need for food and shelter to solve the problem of the historical and thereby relative nature of other needs He asks us to look at how these are met in our society and what function this serves in the wider scheme of things. In the end, he believes what makes a need 'true' as opposed to 'false' has to be answered by individuals themselves, but only – 'in the end'. At the moment, he insists, the objectivity of needs has to be understood in terms of the way a society manipulates its member's needs according to its own requirements. Hence, in modern (capitalist) society, he claims:

> Most of the prevailing needs to relax, to have fun, to behave and consume in accordance with the advertisements, to love and hate what others love and hate, belong to the category of false needs (1994: 5).

Like Baudrillard, Marcuse resists what might be called the ontologisation of real needs. Critical Theorists have been generally sceptical of 'ontology', which is a concern with the essential nature of things, such as the nature of human being, because this, they believed, leads only to a reification of what currently exists. Our ontological descriptions would inevitably be tied to our present historical assumptions about the authentic subject, which we would mistakenly take to be the whole of the story. In the background to this resistance to ontology is the work of Martin Heidegger, whose *Being and Time* (1962, original 1927) dealt with the question of authenticity. Heidegger's membership of the Nazi party and sometime advocacy of its ideas about the subject, led to considerable scepticism amongst Critical Theorists, including Marcuse, (who was briefly Heidegger's assistant in the late 1920s), towards all ontological claims.

However, *unlike* Baudrillard, Marcuse does not reject the idea of the reality of the subject. In fact, although he does not use the language of ontology, he makes it pretty clear that beyond its physical needs the subject has a need for happiness and self-determination, and a need to seek liberation from conditions that inhibit these needs. Similarly, he believes 'the alleviation of toil and poverty are universally valid standards' even if they vary according to 'area and stage of development' (p. 6).

Adorno, who amongst Critical Theorists believed the process of the reification of consciousness had gone furthest, rejected ontology but also maintained that human needs exist in some degree independent of their context, even if they are inevitably mediated by it. Like Marcuse, he is reluctant to define exactly what needs are because in this peculiarly static (monopoly-capitalist) time, when the possibility of historical change seems slimmest, it is almost impossible to see the wood for the trees:

> When this static situation comes to an end needs will look completely different. If production is redirected towards the unconditional and unlimited satisfaction of needs, including precisely those produced by the hitherto prevailing system, needs themselves will be decisively altered. The indistinguishability of true and false needs is an essential part of the present phase. One day it will be readily apparent that men do not need the trash provided them by the culture industry or the miserable high quality goods proffered them by the more substantial industries (Adorno 1981: 109).

Adorno and Marcuse reject ontology not just because it tends to reify the subject, but also because in the present situation things that *appear* as needs are often no such thing. The idea that in addition to food and lodging, the cinema is a need, is 'true', but only in a world where the interests of that industry have to be serviced. Adorno does not deny that in *some* sense needs are being met in a capitalist society, but they are deflected by a system that mobilises them for its own purposes. It incorporates them and serves them back as what the people really need.

Axel Honneth (1993: 86), for contemporary Critical Theory, argues that Adorno makes the fit between human (instinctual) needs and what consumer

society has on offer too exact, 'leaving no remainder', and thereby no source
of resistance in the human subject, in the effect of producing a Baudrillardrian
view of society as a subject-free zone. But this misses the point that while
Adorno and Marcuse are wary of defining what the subject's needs are in
present circumstances, they do maintain in principle the reality of such things
and the possibility of distinguishing true needs from false ones.

Baudrillard rejects all (ontological) theories of human nature as dubious
because they have a *normalising* effect, they reduce diversity to one significa-
tory code – ours. Yet, Marcuse is fully aware that to impose our 'Reason upon
an entire society is . . . a scandalous idea' (p. 7). He finds paradoxical the right-
eousness of those who ridicule the idea of such an imposition while happily
'making its own population into objects of total administration'. If we are
sensitive to the unfairness of imposing our ways of going on onto others we
cannot happily accept the same dominatory assumptions for ourselves. He
could not have had Baudrillard in mind, given the time at which he was writing
One Dimensional Man, but clearly the point applies to him. For Marcuse, it
is the consciousness of the subject in relation to its own systemic conditions
that is the key to a non-oppressive society. Without this consciousness one
system is merely relative to another. Moreover, to have this consciousness presupposes the existence of a human subject that is more than a creation of a
(signifying) system.

A generation later, Habermas like Marcuse before him also refuses to talk
in ontological terms, but likewise pursues the idea of a universal need in human
beings. He identifies this need in terms of the human subject as a language
user. Because language has the telos or purpose of reaching agreement built
into it, via the necessity of speakers raising validity claims and thence (potentially) arriving at a consensus, there is an implicit need for human beings to
seek out conditions where undistorted communication prevails. Through all
the twists and turns of his theory, Habermas defends a universal potential to
arrive at a genuine consensus as something truly and peculiarly human.

There is also something contradictory in the way Baudrillard and other postmodernist thinkers reject the subject and its needs. Their rejection is based on
the idea that to suggest the subject (and its needs) are in some way universal,
obliterates the importance of cultural difference. In effect, theories of the
subject are culturally imperialistic in that they reduce others to being a version
of ourselves, with the implication that meeting their needs means them rejecting their own cultural uniqueness and adopting our version of progress. Yet
extolling the virtues of cultural diversity itself presupposes a *universal* idea,
that of respect for the 'otherness' of other subjects and the cultural forms
of life they inhabit. It also presupposes that a *universal* moral equality does,
or should, exist between different forms of life (Doyal and Gough 1991).
However, it seems to me that one of the problems of postmodernism's radical
pluralism is that it runs counter to our intuition that some forms of life are
distinctly better or worse than others, regardless of the uniqueness of their

cultural context. Repressive political regimes should not warrant equal favour with those that are not, and while postmodernists have no criteria by which they could evaluate such things, the virtue of Critical Theory is that in spite of all the attendant difficulty, it does have such criteria. If, like Critical Theory we accept the reality of the human subject, the partial autonomy it has from its social environment, then the question of whether its needs are being met or not, becomes an issue for social science.

Whether one identifies Marcuse and Habermas's ideas as a kind of ontology of the subject is a moot point, but what matters is that, for Critical Theory, explanation has to be grounded in something real, something that exists in some degree independent of our descriptions of it, be it the subject's potential for greater happiness, or the intersubjective potential for communicative rationality.

Habermas Versus Postmodernism

While first generation Critical Theory's assessment of the contemporary world stands more or less in opposition to that of postmodernists, Habermas's critique is directly pitched against what he sees as their 'neo-conservatism'. In an essay, 'Modernity: An Unfinished Project' (d'Entreves and Benhabib (1996 [1981]), and a book, *The Philosophical Discourse of Modernity* (1987b), he casts his net wide to identify the intellectual fault lines that produced the postmodernist view of things.

Habermas (1996: 39–40) notes that the idea of the 'modern' is not a particularly recent one but has been used in numerous historical situations to mark off an era's claims about itself from what went before; the implication is that one should be suspicious of those who uncritically claim such a title. The current (modernist) desire to slough off the past, 'to explode the continuum of history', has its historical origins specifically in the cultural domain of aesthetic consciousness, rather than any other area. The essence of modern aesthetic consciousness lies in the value it places on 'the ephemeral, the momentary and the transitory', as though it yearned for a lasting 'immaculate present'. The avant-garde in modern art, be it surrealism or dadaism, despises what went before, anarchically rebelling against the norms of tradition, delighting in the offence it can give while fleeing from questions of 'moral goodness or practical utility'. The more it can offend and the more transgressive it is, the more it thinks itself successful.

However, by the 1960s the avant-garde in art had aged, grown weary of its failure to change things such that we now speak of post-avant-garde art. Habermas wonders if this heralds a wider shift to postmodernity. From the angle of social theory, this is how Daniel Bell in his *The Cultural Contradictions of Capitalism* (1979), sees things. Bell identifies a split between the demands of a modern society and the hedonistic possibilities promised by its culture and affluence. Modern economic and administrative systems require a disciplined individual who adheres to the Protestant work ethic and who is thereby aligned with a generally purposive-rational form of life. The effect of avant-garde art, though, is to promote in the lifeworld the principle of 'unrestrained self-realization, the demand for authentic self experience, the subjectivism of an overstimulated sensibility and the release of hedonistic motivations': all of which is incompatible with the moral outlook needed by economic and administrative systems (Habermas 1996: 42). For Bell, as a neoconservative, the fault lies in a now uncreative and adversary avant-garde culture that undermines the norms of everyday life with seductive but spurious promises. His solution is to renew norms that will restrain libertarianism, and promote the value of self-discipline and the work ethic.

For Habermas, Bell's conservative solution is no solution. One cannot turn the clock back and conjure up the norms of traditional authority from nowhere. What Bell and others overlook is the fact that current cultural values are related to what has happened in wider society. Moreover, the cultural sphere is not an undifferentiated one; it has an internal history of its own. Habermas draws on the work of Max Weber to make the point.

While the idea of cultural modernity is often associated with the development of European art, Weber's work shows that it can be characterised more widely in terms of a process of differentiation, such that where once culture had been held together by a religious or metaphysical world view, it has now split off into three relatively unconnected value spheres that have different ways of justifying themselves. The three spheres are science, morality and art. Science produces 'knowledge' which is justified as 'truth', 'morality' is connected to justice and validates itself through ideas of 'normative rightness', while art is realised in terms of 'authenticity' and 'beauty'. Each has developed its own institutionalised protocols for judging the worth of its products; each has become an autonomous cultural system. Readers of the previous chapter will recognise that Habermas is also implicitly drawing on his idea of 'validity claims' to show that each sphere makes its own claim to be rational by emphasising particular kinds of validity claim.

Each of these spheres, through its autonomy and because it has been abstracted from other spheres, has been able to reveal structures intrinsic to its own knowledge-complex. From another angle though, this autonomy has a downside. The cultural knowledge produced by the separate spheres and marshalled by experts, has become detached from the world of everyday life. Where once culture drew on, and reflected the lifeworld, it now threatens to impoverish it because it has only an external relation to it. For the most part, we do, or have to accept what the experts in science, justice and art tell us. The original intent of Enlightenment thinkers was to apply the knowledge gleaned in different spheres to the world of social praxis and produce an altogether more rational world for everyone. However, at the end of the twentieth century, and in light of its history, there is now more than a thread of cynicism over whether the processes of rationalisation have brought us the

progress it promised. The question for Habermas is whether we should jetti-
son the idea of modernity and its Enlightenment hopes, leaving the lifeworld
to continue without disturbance? His answer is that the process of rationalisation that has taken place in the three spheres, for all its detachment from
the lifeworld and failure to fulfill its promise of the 'good life', should not
jettisoned. The seed of progress has been sown, what it needs is cultivation.

He talks of 'false sublation', particularly as postmodernist philosophers have
attempted it in the aesthetic sphere. By 'false sublation' he means the attempt
to burst and transcend the boundaries of the spheres of knowledge that make
up culture, and reunite them with the lifeworld. The possibility of reuniting
dislocated aspects of society into something more historically progressive,
shows the common ground he still shares with first generation Critical Theory.
He is concerned by what (elsewhere) he calls the process of de-differentiation,
or the breaking up of rules that define what counts as knowledge in the different spheres. Postmodernist thinking in the area of art, for example, seeks
to show that no real distinction exists between high and low art: a soap opera
is as worthy an object of poststructuralist attention as a Shakespeare play. On
the postmodernist account, the rules for evaluating art are socially relative and
thus traditional aesthetic boundaries should be thought artificial. Habermas's
point is that while the rules that govern these boundaries grew up in modern
capitalist societies and express their class history that does not make them
worthless. Art is able to disclose aspects of the world in a particular way that
non-art does not. Poststructuralist accounts of art fail to recognise the transcendent qualities of an autonomous (authentic) work of art, its capacity to
exceed the context of its production, because they reduce it to being *only* a
product of that context. To deny this quality, Habermas believes, means
rejecting the *rational* kernel that emerged via the aesthetic sphere for the sake
of an unprogressive and pointless relativism. Art, for Habermas, like Adorno
before him, has a rational component even if it is quite different from that of
other spheres. Surrealism's attempt to break up the rules of traditional art by
juxtaposing strange dream-like images did not bridge the gap between art and
life, but only succeeded in producing *more* great art. Its radical challenge did
not lead to a reunification of art with the lifeworld, but reinforced the very
categories it hoped to transcend – hence, *false* sublation.

Habermas believes that this attempted sublation is premature and involves
a 'double error'. First, if the vessel of autonomous art has been shattered, the
valuable emancipatory contents of the category of art will be lost. Interpreting Habermas we might say that art may no longer claim to be 'high art' and
it may be more fun because of this, more playful, but it is no longer serious,
and thus no longer commands our attention in the same way. Art has come
out of the museum and is more 'democratic' for that, but it pays the price in
becoming another item of mass culture. What Habermas has in mind here is
the idea that authentic art expresses our deepest needs and hopes for a better
life, but once the rules governing this category of experience are dissolved,
art loses its critical point, its potential emancipatory effects are dispersed and

nullified and we no longer see it as a challenge to the status quo. In this, Habermas affirms the older generation's view that genuine art is an enclave that stands in opposition to the corrosive effects of mass culture. He is also, by implication, siding with Adorno against Benjamin in their dispute over the supposedly 'democratic' effects of mass culture (see Chapter 4).

Secondly, to break up the category boundaries of only *one* sphere of cultural life leaves the lifeworld exactly as it is. In the lifeworld, our responses to different aspects of culture intermingle, and to bring a more rational world into being requires the full range of our cultural tradition to be involved. It would require the other spheres to undergo the same transformation. To force open one sphere alone serves to impoverish the lifeworld leaving it prone to the effects of the others without recourse to the emancipatory potential of the one that has been opened. In short, the lifeworld becomes even more lopsided than before.

Habermas does suggest there are alternatives to the false sublation of culture. It would be foolish to dismantle the expert culture that has grown up around art as this would lead to the degeneration of art's significance. However, art does not have to judged solely in terms of expert taste. When it is related to problems of life by the layperson it changes its functional character. When this happens, Habermas (1996: 51) maintains:

> it enters a language game which is no longer that of art criticism proper. In this case aesthetic experience not only revitalises those need interpretations in light of which we perceive our world, but also influences our cognitive interpretations and our normative expectations.

For Habermas, art does not have to remain aloof, nor should it attempt to break itself up in an attempt to reunite with the lifeworld, but can be appropriated by the layperson in such a way as to illuminate the lifeworld. He cites an example taken from Peter Weiss's book *Aesthetics of Resistance*, when a group of politicised workers in 1937 sought, through attending night classes on the history of painting, to understand European history. In the face of the destruction of art by the Nazis, they are able to draw into their own horizon of experience an understanding of their own lives and their position in the current situation.

In this way, he believes something of value from the false sublation can be preserved as well as the integrity of the aesthetic sphere. It is the desire to *realise* the potential for progress which modernity has generated that Habermas wishes to maintain. Differentiating the spheres of knowledge, morality and art, enabled them to develop autonomously and in the remarkable way that they have. Thus, those who oppose modernity are, in effect, throwing the baby out with the bath water and are regressive forces. He identifies three broad philosophical groups who are guilty of this, the young, the new and the old conservatives.

Most important for our purposes are the young conservatives, which for Habermas are the poststructuralists and postmodernists. These authors reveal and celebrate 'in theory' the complete de-centring of the modern subject as though it already had, or could be freed from the constraints of labour and purposive-rational action, when in fact it remains in the grip of societal imperatives that dominate life under capitalism. They oppose instrumental reason with the force of free-floating 'spontaneous subjectivity', and emphasise rhetoric and feeling at the expense of anything else This is a non-progressive, conservative outlook, because it blindly bypasses other spheres of life which make equal if not greater claims on the subject.

The Habermasian Critique

Whether one can regard Habermas's essay, with its isolated example of workers providing an alternative to surrealism's 'false sublation' of art (which anyway is drawn from a novel), as sufficient to make his case against postmodernists, is doubtful. He continued his critique of poststructuralism and postmodernism in much greater and denser detail in *The Philosophical Discourse of Modernity*. Nevertheless, there are important elements in the essay and his insight that postmodernists tend to over-generalise culture as being the whole truth, seems to me to be a significant one, and one that has had an outcome 'predicted' by Habermas.

Contemporary sociology has undergone a 'culturalist turn', emphasising what is happening at the level of cultural consumption at the expense of other areas. However, while society and culture are related, they are not the same thing. Almost twenty years after Habermas's essay, Rojek and Turner (2000), in their article 'Decorative Sociology: Towards a Critique of the Cultural Turn', point out that sociological insight has now largely been replaced by literary-textualist readings of social phenomena. They argue that postmodernist thinking, to the detriment of the wider sociological enterprise, has heavily influenced this 'cultural studies' form of sociology. Sociology now lacks a stable research agenda, responding slavishly and uncritically to social change with more and more paradigm shifts in theory. It has desperately chased after all the transitory changes that society throws up, denying the validity of its own traditions, with the result that it regularly has to reinvent itself around the constant stream of new concepts that emerge in the wake of supposedly revolutionary changes: 'digital technology, globalisation, post-Fordism, post-nation state, hybridity, network-society, web-world', and so on. Rojek and Turner (2000: 639) summarise the point thus:

> By 'reading' social life as a text, decorative sociology equips itself with a payload of endless terminological disputes and esoteric debates about the disappearance of reality. The privileging of the cultural over the social and economic means that social

and economic issues are interpreted as issues of cultural layering and analysis focuses on deconstructing strategies.

Like Habermas, they sense that in spite of the fact that much culturalist sociology appears to be 'politicised' it does not, and cannot, engage with politics as a broader institutional factor, and thus conservatively confirms the status quo. When feminists coined the phrase 'the personal is political', culturalist sociology took it over and treated *everything* as political. If we analyse sport, music, clothes, shopping, tourism and film as 'political', then politics as a specific area of life loses its meaning.

For Habermas there is a lack of reflexivity in postmodernist ideas. By 'reflexivity' I am not referring to the self-conscious awareness of individuals that Giddens frequently talks about, but to the theoretical awareness of why a particular group of ideas become popular at a particular time. This 'reflexivity' is an awareness of the context that gives ideas their resonance, something Alvin Gouldner described in his *The Coming Crisis in Western Sociology* (1973). Habermas's method in his essay is to place outlooks such as postmodernism in an historical context. It involves examining how different theoretical attitudes relate to the 'modernity' of which we are a product, even if we have reason to challenge it. By contrast, most (postmodernist) cultural sociology treat texts as timeless entities, bearing only contingent relations to other texts. The absence of any historical-developmental dimension leaves the discipline prone to the criticism that it has no sense of why its ideas have emerged, other than that something in the world has caught its eye.

Like the first generation of Critical Theorists who sought to relate positivist ideas to the workings of wider society, Habermas does the same with postmodernist ideas. He believes postmodernists have taken up an anti-modern attitude in denying the ideas of reason progress and truth, seeing them as wholly the product of context. He certainly agrees with Foucault that ideas are 'things of this world', part of the order of things, but that is not *all* they are. The embeddedness of the standards we use to judge these things in our various languages, cultures and practices should not blind us to the partially 'transcendent' claims that are contained within them. The modern power of reason enables us to challenge, criticise and revise our judgements on these matters and to move beyond the traditions we inherit.

Truth, for example, he believes is not an arbitrary concept but one that modern social science has shown to be a necessary feature of life for all human beings because they are language users. The purpose of language is to reveal the nature of things in a way that is collectively understandable as true. Of course, we often lie about things, but even then what we say is related to truth in being a deliberate inversion of it. Truth, for Habermas, is something that is always present when we use language, and he frequently notes that postmodernists like everyone else, write expecting to be believed.

System and Lifeworld Again

One should not conclude that Habermas believes everything in the modern world is rational and working well. He certainly believes that a valuable process of rationalisation has gone on in all three spheres of culture, but their development has happened unevenly and had a mixed effect on the lifeworld.

The modern capitalist system has found greatest use for purposive-rational, or instrumental forms of reason, as these enable it to exploit the world most thoroughly. These forms of reason, which have their counterpart in the cultural sphere of science have 'colonized the lifeworld'. In effect, the needs of the system now shape and dominate what happens in the lifeworld at the expense of other kinds of reason.

He contrasts the systemic needs of modern society with those of the lifeworld – the meaning horizon that forms the background to everyday life where the possibility of arriving at a communicative consensus between subjects is to be found. For this reason, he places great value on its legitimacy as the site where subjects can reciprocally raise validity claims, and where these claims can be criticised or confirmed and genuine agreements reached. The site of the lifeworld is a theoretical, or as Habermas sometimes calls it, a transcendental one, meaning that, in theoretical terms, it exists in its own right. However, while it is the site where agents interact, in empirical terms it is shot through with the demands of the system.

While the lifeworld represents the point of view of active subjects, the system is no less real for Habermas. It represents an external force that can be perceived through the objectivising concepts developed by Talcott Parsons. The modern social system has its origins in the lifeworld, but as systemic structures evolve they take on a life of their own, becoming more complex and differentiated over time. Under capitalism these structures refer back less and less to their origins in the lifeworld, while making more and more inroads into it, shaping agents' assumptions and motives and steering them into forms of life that suit its structural requirements.

It is quite possible to see, for example, that the USA has developed very successfully at the level of the system, but at the cost of the social integration that happens at the level of the lifeworld. The steering demands of the capitalist system have been very successfully met in America, making it a society of great affluence, but at the level of the lifeworld rationalisation has been truncated. The social integration proper to the lifeworld, which is based on arriving at a consensus over norms and values, has not been successfully achieved The levels of crime and other forms of social dis-integration may be seen as an expression of this. In short, the system dominates the lifeworld resulting in the impoverishment of the latter. It is the weakness of postmodernist outlooks to have ignored these processes and assumed that subjects live lives untouched by capitalism.

Of course, one might ask what Habermas hopes for in the way of a resolution to these problems: how does he expect the project of modernity to be completed? Does he anticipate, as postmodernists accuse him, some premodern (Hegelian) organic unity, where system and lifeworld are happily reunited? For postmodernists, notably Lyotard (1984: 72–3), such a 'totalising' hope is repressive because it wraps up all differences into an unbreakable rational consensus that would be repressive because anything that stood out against it would automatically be thought irrational. However, given what Habermas has said about 'false sublations', this seems unlikely. His concern is not to unify different societal spheres but to *reconnect* them. His whole point is that the splitting off of the spheres under modernity has been a virtue in allowing them to develop their own rational potential, albeit under the distorting conditions of capitalism. His ambition, as Dews (1984: 25) puts it, is not to achieve 'a meltdown into a new totality, but rather to the setting-in-motion of a mobile that has become obstinately entangled'. He wants to join up the spheres without sacrificing their unique qualities and in such a way that allows for reciprocal influence.

However, Lyotard's work with its emphasis on the rupture between modernity and postmodernity has, along with the work of Baudrillard, been immensely influential in the social sciences in defining how we should think of the new condition and is worth exploring further.

Lyotard versus Habermas

Habermas and Lyotard never directly debated the issues between them. In *The Postmodern Condition: A Report on Knowledge* (1984) Lyotard makes mention of Habermas, but not to any great degree, while Habermas makes no direct reference to Lyotard's work. Nevertheless, their ideas in some respects stand in opposition to one another. Where Habermas is committed to furthering the project of modernity with its promise of 'enlightenment' at the end of the story, Lyotard opposes all such stories of progress as illusory 'metanarratives' created by the West to aggrandise its own view of things. In fact, in our postmodern condition, he argues, we now have an attitude of 'incredulity towards metanarratives'; we no longer really believe in them and regard them as having run out of steam.

Some readers may find an apparent similarity between Lyotard's opposition to 'metanarratives' and Adorno's scepticism towards 'totality', to the point where the latter is seen as a forerunner of postmodernism (Best and Kellner 1991). There is something to be said for this in that Adorno, like postmodernists, finds western reason deeply problematic. However, his objection, indeed his pessimism about the future lies in its failure to live up to its promise of the 'good life', rather than a willing acceptance of its breakdown. He, like

Habermas, was always opposed to the spurious dovetailing between different areas of life, particularly that between mass culture and art at the expense of the latter.

Lyotard's book is subtitled 'a report on knowledge' as it is concerned with epistemological issues over how we should understand what is happening in modern society, rather than with substantive empirical issues. In pre-modern societies, knowledge invariably took a narrative form, it related things together as a story with a beginning, middle and end. Such stories as myths, folk tales and legends served to unify society and give meaning to the lives of its members. In modern societies, however, narratives of this kind have shrunk back in the face of science which does not take a narrative form, but is based on 'denotative' statements, which are logically connected and can be proved true or false.

However, until recently the cultural success of science in society has itself depended on the continuation of certain narrative myths, those of the 'myth of liberation' and the 'myth of total knowledge'. It has gained its cultural status, to say nothing of government funding, from the idea that it will ultimately enable us to control nature, liberating us from its negative effects. It also has held out the promise of finally providing us with full knowledge of everything. In our postmodern society, though, he predicts that even the nature of scientific knowledge is changing. More and more it has to 'perform', to be exploitable in an immediate, commercial way, rather than providing us with a greater general understanding of things.

Indeed our attitude to epic stories of all kinds, Lyotard believes, has become one of scepticism. At the level of everyday life, our sense of history and the place of our nation in it, along with our sense of patriotism, have all become problematic. In sociology too, theoretical metanarratives such as structural-functionalism and Marxism have not fulfilled their promise of providing total schemas of how the world works and in what direction it should go to achieve human happiness. More broadly, apparently uncontentious cultural metanarratives such as the 'March of Progress', of 'Civilisation', or 'Reason', in the light of much twentieth-century history have been found wanting.

Crucial to Lyotard's critique of metanarratives is the idea that each has its own often vast array of *self-referring* rules and regulations, which justify its view of the world to its supporters. Lyotard adopts the idea of the (later) Wittgenstein that knowledge is made up of different 'language-games' with their own internal vocabulary within which participants make 'moves' to secure a victory. The history of Marxism, for example, on this account consists of a long internecine game, if not battle between groups of players jockeying for position in order to score their theoretical goals. The validity of the Marxist language-game is defined and determined *internally* by Marxists themselves as they struggle for victory, not by some external criterion of truth. Truth itself, therefore, has to be seen as a product of the language-game that produced it in the course of being played. There is no metalanguage which embraces all the different language-games and which could be used to adjudicate the validity of the moves being made at a lower level.

The implication of Lyotard's view is that truth is a *plural* affair and that we should dispense with overarching metanarratives that claim to know the one truth of everything. We should accept that language-games are heterogeneous, not homogeneous. Metanarratives are not only intellectually incredible, but at a political and moral level are dangerous because they 'totalise' different kinds of knowledge into one homogenous whole, which means in effect that they are totalitarian, even terroristic. Lyotard's objection to Habermas is that his theory is based on the idea that language is inherently oriented towards consensus and if this were realised it would produce another repressive metanarrative, one of 'common agreement'.

More specifically, Lyotard (1984: 65) argues, the social language of everyday life is too complex an interweave of different kinds of utterance to be brought under the roof of one super-rational language-game. For this to be possible, two (incorrect) assumptions would have to be made:

(1) that it is possible for all speakers to come to an agreement on which rules or meta-prescriptions are universally valid for language games, when it is clear that language games are heteromorphous, subject to heterogeneous sets of pragmatic rules.

(2) that the goal of dialogue is consensus. But as I have shown in the analysis of the pragmatics of science, consensus is only a particular state of discussion, not its end. Its end on the contrary, is paralogy.

From a sociological point of view, it is easy to sympathise with Lyotard in that much sociological work has brought into focus differences that exist between and within the language-games of different societies, differences that might otherwise be obscured by a dominant metanarrative. However, it is not at all clear that this criticism applies accurately to Habermas's claims. As I have already indicated, Habermas does not reject the splitting of modernity into different spheres with different ways of going on. In fact, he sees this as a positive outcome of modernity and wishes the irreducibility of these areas to be respected.

Lyotard (1 above) also challenges Habermas's views on the basis that they imply a universal metalanguage exists above and beyond the particularities of ordinary language-games and that this should determine what happens there; a sort of dictatorship of the consensus. This, I think, is a plain misunderstanding. Habermas marks off his account of 'universal pragmatics' from what happens at the empirical level where the differences between language-games holds sway. When he talks of 'universal pragmatics' he is not referring to a universal prescription for what should be decided over particular issues at the empirical level, but what happens behind the scenes whether we recognise it or not. Habermas's account of 'universal pragmatics' is not one of an external metalanguage that imperiously oversees all the mini-language-games, but of those general properties inherent in all the utterances of our language-games. Every utterance necessarily raises validity claims; it asks to be considered true, appropriate or authentic, or some combination of the three. Thus, even Lyotard's written utterances ask that its readers consider them 'true', even if their author rejects the notion of truth.

Lyotard's claim (2 above) that the goal of dialogue is not consensus but paralogy, is similarly wide of the mark. Paralogy is a term he uses to refer to the fact that many of our utterances (including those of scientists) do not follow in a happy, logical sequence, but are often discontinuous and paradoxical, designed to secure victory more than anything else. Although he uses the term 'language-game' to describe the process of acquiring knowledge, it often sounds more like a battle than a game. He talks (p. 10) of a 'general agonistics' as characterising verbal interaction, an agonised struggle to achieve verbal success, of interlocutors using 'any available ammunition' such that 'questions, requests, assertions, and narratives are (all) launched pell-mell into battle'.

At first sight, Lyotard's privileging of conflict seems as justified as Habermas's privileging of consensus as the telos or goal of language, perhaps more so in that it could be thought more realistic. However, Habermas's emphasis on consensus is not at the expense of dissent. His concept of the ideal speech situation and of discourse generally is a *critical* one, specifically geared to acknowledge that a genuine consensus requires that all dissenting voices be heard and views acknowledged. As Holub (1991: 142) points out, Lyotard might claim that at an empirical level winners of arguments invariably possess more power than those who lose, but this is exactly Habermas's point. At an empirical level most disputes *are* resolved on the basis of background power relations, but this does not constitute a genuine consensus. Genuine consensus requires that structural power, ideology and cultural capital generally be set aside so the force of the better argument alone be heard. It should also be remembered that Habermas's concept of 'ideal speech' refers to something virtual not actual. It exists only in the sense that in all our communications we *want* others to agree with us – even dictators seek to justify themselves to those they oppress.

Moreover, if we were to take Lyotard at face value and assume that dissent is the natural end-state of language, how should we regard his ideas? If he wants us to agree with his ideas we must disagree with them! If we disagree with them then we are in agreement with them! For Habermas, this kind of 'performative contradiction' is at the heart of much postmodernist thought. It fails to recognise that we *always* implicitly invoke the criteria of rational argument and potential agreement in our use of language, even if we choose to deny its validity.

Summary and Conclusion

In this chapter I have compared the outlook of both generations of Critical Theory with that of postmodernists. Like first generation Critical Theorists, Baudrillard dwells on the effects of mass consumer society, but where they challenged both the inevitability and desirability of this condition, he eliminates the possibility of our taking a critical stance towards it. Baudrillard accepts the human subject is thoroughly 'dead', dissolved completely in the machinations of a media-dominated hyperreality. By contrast, while Marcuse and Adorno were certainly fearful that the subject was being helplessly tossed and turned on the sea of consumerism, they always held on to the idea that the future of the subject was of vital importance. The task of Critical Theory for them was to provide conceptual shelter for the subject until conditions for its realisation were more amenable. It seems to me, to follow Baudrillard, involves us in a dubious acceptance of the status quo where questions of human need play no part. The idea of 'human needs' may be difficult to establish in a clear cut way, but to reject them on principle seems to me to be an abnegation of our responsibilities as social scientists, responsibilities which surely include disclosing what is really happening in the world as truthfully as possible.

With regard to Habermas I have described his objection to postmodernist thought. It involves the postmodernist over-inflation of the aesthetic sphere at the expense of other aspects of society, and the idea that this blinds us to the reality of external conditions, which continue to shape our lives. Moreover, Lyotard's objection that Habermas is fruitlessly tied to a metanarrative of human 'progress' leading to consensus, is based on a misunderstanding. Habermas's claims are couched in terms, not of some future state of perfect (empirical) agreement, but of the general conditions that make any rational agreement possible. Whether agreement actually happens in any particular set of circumstances is another matter, but Habermas's work, like that of Marcuse and Adorno, does provide us with ground for a critique of existing conditions and does not give way to the dubious postmodernist idea that one set of conditions is merely relative to another.

Further Reading

There are few books which contrast first generation Critical Theory with post-modernism, but one that draws connections between them in a well informed way is Best and Kellner's *Postmodern Theory: Critical Interrogations* (1991), which also draws out links between Adorno and postmodernism. J. M. Bernstein's introduction to Adorno's *The Culture Industry* (1991) compares the latter's ideas to postmodernist ones, seeing Adorno's overall project as distinct from that of the postmodernists. Lyotard's *The Postmodern Condition*

(1984) remains a key text for an understanding of the philosophical under-pinnings of postmodernism and is fairly accessible. Holub (1991) provides a detailed account of the Lyotard–Habermas debate, as well as the various other debates in which Habermas has been involved. d'Entreves and Benhabib's (1996) reader has a number of insightful essays on Habermas's relation to the idea of modernity, but is quite difficult as a starting point.

Part 4

Conclusion

9

Why Read Critical
Theory Now?

Introduction

In previous chapters I have tried to show the reader different faces of
Critical Theory, indicating along the way its variegated nature, its historical
development, but most of all I hope its continuing relevance. The basis of
this chapter is the belief that the tradition of Critical Theory in the hands of
both earlier and later generations is relevant to an understanding of the
present, and that if we allow it to speak to us it will open up rich avenues of
thought.

The idea of 'relevance' is a tricky one. In education we have been encour-
aged in the last twenty years to make what students learn relevant to the real
world, by which is usually meant giving them knowledge of the world that
they can use to enhance their position in the labour market. One cannot
gainsay the virtue of this, but giving them knowledge of such is a double-
edged sword. The ostensible aim is to socialise students into the workings of
the contemporary world in such a way as to make them amenable to it, to
socialise them into accepting its norms and values. In this, a knowledge of
Critical Theory does not provide much help; but if the aim of education is to
show students something of how the world really works, then its claims are as
relevant as ever.

Another recurrent problem in the academic world, notably in sociology, is
the production and commodification of ever new ideas, concepts and authors
as though the discipline were straining after an ever more elusive target the
better to appear relevant. Society certainly changes and throws up an array of
new phenomena to be examined, but disciplines that merely mimic this tendency through their own self-proliferation weaken themselves by ignoring the
accumulated wisdom of their own hard-won insights.

Adorno May Have Been an Old Sourpuss but That Doesn't Mean He Was Wrong

Of course Critical Theory is still read, but the work of Adorno, Marcuse and Horkheimer tends to appear in the early chapters of Readers on cultural studies where it is positioned as premature work on mass culture that is too negative in light of what we now know, and where what we know now is assumed to be better. It is 'past it' because it is from the past. Miriam Hansen (2002: 57–8) remarks that the current reception of Adorno's writings on film and mass culture are 'little more than a ritualistic gesture, reiterating the familiar charges of elitism, pessimism, and high modernist myopia'. While Adorno is not above criticism, this attitude prevents us from engaging with his work on any serious level. We neutralise the challenge it offers by refusing to see his work as a 'living' resource that would enable us to trace out the tensions in his work against those in our own. Walter Benjamin, in contrast, gets a better reception because he seems to endorse cinema as a democratising medium, which naturally appeals to anyone who is committed to its virtues. We like Benjamin because he tells us it is OK to enjoy cinema. The effect is to nullify Adorno's ideas and position them as limited or inferior. In effect, we read Adorno and Benjamin in terms of our own unreflective contemporary preferences. I have tried to show in my discussion of them in Chapter 5 that both deserve more careful attention.

If, as Jacoby (1977: 1–2) claims, 'society learns less and less faster and faster' and that the process is now intensifying, then the intellectual habit of thought that ignores the past for the sake of the present will fall into the trap of arrogantly imagining that what is new is all that should hold our attention: that the latest is the greatest. This dismissal of the past, including what its writers had to say, drives out not only the sense that we share much with what went before, but also stultifies any idea that the future might be different. It becomes an ideological alibi for deifying the present. It is against this mental stasis that Critical Theory rails and is something that still makes it worth reading.

Such mental stasis or 'social amnesia', as Jacoby calls it, may be an outcome of the very process that Adorno saw as central to modern capitalism, 'reification'. Reification refers to the way that things that are produced by society, including the way it is organised, appear as entirely natural and beyond question. Reification is a kind of forgetting in that we lose track of the origins of our ideas in the process of living them. For Adorno, the chief organising principle of modern society is capitalist economic relations. The intensification of capital accumulation in the guise of 'globalisation', most notably in the 1980s through to the present time, has accelerated the speed at which goods are produced and consumed across the world. If we treat ideas as 'thought goods' then the same process can be seen at work. Ideas become fashionable, get consumed and then die out with great rapidity in order to make way for new ones. The process has implications not only for the past but for the future too. Without a sense of having come from somewhere there is no sense that the world might move on somewhere else. Critical Theory hangs on to the possibility that things could be different.

Adorno is usually described as the most pessimistic of Critical Theorists, the one who failed to find anything of value in the modern world. For Habermas this sprang from Adorno's lack of an adequate account of the subject via communicative action; others seem to regard it as deliberate anti-empirical exaggeration. In a sense, both points of view are right.

On his own account, Adorno exaggerated things to make them clear. Indeed he once declared 'only exaggeration is true'[16] (Adorno and Horkheimer 1972: 118). In a society that is distorted it is only through exaggeration that the spurious empirical 'normality' of the distortion can be made apparent. He does not try to ward off the implications of what he sees as characteristic of our world by a 'just' empirical analysis but seeks to show what lies behind the different appearance of things. In fact, I would want to argue that in light of the last thirty years, if anything, he did not exaggerate enough. What Adorno feared was that the commodity form was coming to dominate life entirely. As he put it with regard to musical fetishism:

> Music, with all the attributes of the ethereal and sublime, which are generously accorded it, serves in America today as an advertisement for commodities, which one must acquire in order to hear music. If the advertising function is carefully dimmed in the case of serious music, it always breaks through in the case of light music . . . Countless hit song texts praise the hit songs themselves, repeating the titles in capital letters . . . [such that] . . . the quantum of possible enjoyment has disappeared. (Adorno 1991: 33–4 or Arato and Gebhardt 1978: 278–9).

For Adorno, when consumers buy tickets for a concert they are really worshipping the money they have paid for the tickets. The consumer has made the concert a success by buying the ticket, not by liking the concert. In Marxist terms, the use value of the commodity is gradually replaced by its exchange value such that the way we might feel about a commodity is determined by the status of its exchange value. The value of the 'thing' to us appears *as* its exchange value, which is really a determination of the capitalist market place. We identify with, and take pleasure in, the stars (commodities) of the culture industry as though they speak to us personally and thus we sacrifice our individuality in making ourselves thoroughly amenable to them. The price of our individualism is the cost of the commodity.

Jack Zipes (1994) describes the process in terms of his own experience of change. When he was a student thirty years ago in Europe it was easy for Europeans to recognize him as an American by the clothes he wore, his gait and his general physical movements. Now everyone dresses like Americans and

Americans dress like everyone else. Adidas, Timberland and Nike labels are on everyone's shoes, sweatshirts carry advertisements for themselves, even umbrellas and coats have a logo of some kind, while the young all wear their baseball caps backwards. People's physical movements, the way they gesticulate, he argues, also seem to imitate actors on popular TV shows and films with an emphasis on the 'sensational'. It is as though there is no gap between the individual and the commodity; the commodity has insinuated itself in the structure of personality and orientates interaction.

In a similar vein, I remember on one occasion my eleven-year-old daughter and I were shopping locally and I wanted to go into a shop that had white-washed brick walls and sold end-of-line paint and wallpaper. She refused because she thought one of her friends might see her. When I asked her why this was a problem she said that she did not want to be associated with a shop like that. I was amazed to realise that not only did it matter that clothes had the right labels, but the young often label the very space they inhabit and feel personally diminished if it is not right.

However, even if we take Adorno's critiques of mass culture to have grasped something important about the commodified nature of modern society, this was no elitist denunciation of mass culture as his detractors maintain. His critiques were written on behalf of the mass of people and in defence of their right to individuality in a world that promised them so much but delivered so little. His aim was to stir his readers into challenging the status quo, not to be compliant with it.

Of course it might be objected that people are not deceived by the culture industry, that in watching the latest Hollywood film or following TV soaps the audiences are quite aware of how contrived they are and take up a critical-reflective attitude towards them. However, Adorno is not patronising the audience, (an audience that includes me), he is claiming that an audience does *not* have to be naïve for the culture industry to succeed. What he wants to know is why consumers of the culture industry 'feel compelled to buy its products even though they see through them'? (Adorno and Horkheimer 1972: 167).

His conclusion is that insofar as individuals naturally seek gratification in their lives, then the reward for work in a capitalist society lies with the blandishments of the culture industry, which promise much but in their way are just as coercive as the 'economic anxiety' that surrounds work. If what it means to be a 'stand-out' individual in our society is to wear certain clothes and buy certain holidays, then to be an individual at all means you have to consume these goods even if you do see through them.

In his analysis of newspaper astrology columns, Adorno (1994) argues that people take note of the advice without any particular knowledge of, or belief in, the basis of the advice. It speaks to them in terms of their ordinary lives, such as it is a good day to bring creative matters to fruition, or bide your time and avoid confrontation with those in authority. This kind of advice is matter of fact and addresses the normal fears and anxieties everyone has. It provides people with some solace in the face of a contingent world. It looks for compliance in a non-authoritarian way and does not ask people to act against their common sense, only to conform to the way things are. My guess is that people who read these columns (including me) treat them as something of a joke, something we 'buy into' even while seeing through it. As with commodities generally, there is ambivalence about them, they answer a need in a way that has no basis in fact. In the same way that the capitalist system is a kind of 'fate' that goes on independent of the actors that make it happen, so by analogy the ineffable position of the stars offers us some imaginary understanding of our personal position in the wider scheme of things. If Adorno's views are critical of mass culture they are nuanced and not bluntly dismissive of it.

By the same token, his advocacy of 'authentic' or 'autonomous' art as a counterweight to mass culture is not presented as a simple alternative. Both forms, he argued, bore the 'stigmata of capitalism'; they carried all the class-laden assumptions of a bourgeois world-view. (Adorno in Bloch et al. 1977: 123). Indeed, he feared that even autonomous art was gradually being drawn into the commodified world of mass culture. To the extent that 'autonomous' art was autonomous, it was because capitalism specifically allowed it the space to be so, with mass culture as its 'social bad conscience', there to provide it with 'the semblance of legitimacy' (Adorno and Horkheimer 1972: 135). For Adorno, 'autonomous' art was the obverse of the culture industry, both elements he described as the 'torn halves' of something better, that something promising freedom even though a 'broken middle' lay between them. We have to accept that the value of autonomous art cannot be married up with the democratic qualities of mass culture, at least not under present conditions.

There is something contradictory, at least in Marxist terms, in Adorno's claim that 'autonomous' art discloses something generally valid about the oppressive conditions under which the mass of people live, and his judgement that the mass culture people actually enjoy, oppresses them. Nevertheless, he keeps his nerve and does not evade the issue but dwells on it. His solution, if one may call it that, is to retain a dialectical tension between the two without the consolation of a resolution. Given what we know about culture in the last fifty years – that things have become more and more commodified – this is not an example of myopia, but of clear long-sightedness.

Marcuse and Utopianism

In spite of its reputation for pessimism, first generation Critical Theory hung on to a 'utopian' hope. It tried not to get bogged down in the immediacy of the current status quo. It held out the utopian hope that things might not only be different but also radically better, to the extent that the future would in some degree transcend the past. Although its pessimism would seem to be at odds with its utopianism, I believe we should see the two as complementary. Its pessimism should be seen as an expression of antipathy towards a world where hopes for an alternative future were diminishing, its utopianism a refusal to resign in the face of this process. Resignation in the face of the world is the kind of thing one finds in more contemporary postmodernist writers. Indeed Marcuse, when accused of 'utopianism', once remarked that he did not think he was utopian enough. He felt he should be *more* utopian precisely because the idea that things might become radically better was being vanquished. For this reason alone first generation Critical Theory should be read.

Utopianism gets a bad press these days. It is frequently taken to be unrealistic or out of touch with what is going on. Its failure lies in its advocates living in the past or having their heads in the clouds; either way their weakness lies in a lack of attachment to the here and now. It is unsurprising in a society that has become committed to the present almost exclusively in utilitarian terms that utopianism should be thought of in this way. Jacoby (1999) draws attention to how much the utopian spirit has vanished from our culture and how anyone who believes in utopias is considered to be manic, terroristic or just plain 'out to lunch'.

The utopian spirit is not just about things being different and better, but raises this possibility in *universal* terms. It seeks to show that human beings in general can lead fuller, more satisfying lives. The idea that there might be universal standards that are worth developing has largely been replaced in current, radical postmodernist circles, by the celebration of 'difference'. By focusing on the plurality of possible ways of looking at things, of different forms of life, 'difference' is thought virtuous because it finds value in the particular and refuses the authority of a mainstream that marginalises 'otherness'.

In Chapter 8, I dealt with Critical Theory's relation to postmodernism. Postmodernists have set their caps against what they see as the 'totalitarian' implications of theories that have 'universal' ambitions, and thereby of Critical Theory's utopianism. Against this, I want to argue that the retention of the 'universal' is an important aspect of any social theory that would hold our attention.

In Lyotard's (1984) language, 'difference' celebrates 'petits recits' against the utopian 'grands recits' (metanarratives) of western reason, which in effect oppress the narratives of minorities. The trouble is that the 'petits recits' of some minorities, it seems to me, *should* be oppressed. Paedophiles, (my example), might well count themselves oppressed and they certainly seek to justify themselves as misunderstood, often invoking the complicity of the children they abuse as a justification for their actions. The 'paedophile' example may seem exaggerated but the logic of the position seems plain and is found in much contemporary radical literature. Jane Flax, a well-known feminist, declares bluntly that 'truth is always contextual' and therefore truth and falsehood should be abandoned (Flax in Butler and Scott 1992: 450ff). In effect, this would mean the paedophile's 'petit recit' is as valid as the victim's 'petit recit'. Yet claims against particular kinds of behaviour, such as paedophilia, invariably raise *universal* pleas. It is only against standards that have some universal reach that anyone, including intellectuals, can challenge such things. It is only by talking of the nature of the individual, his or her need for autonomy, sensuality and happiness, and the conditions that might produce them, that we can influence the cultural-moral climate of the times.

It should be added that Critical Theorists have also been amongst the most vehement critics of western (instrumental) reason precisely because of its emphasis on domination and control, and the way this squeezes other aspects of life to the margins. But equally they have not succumbed to the idea that 'difference' per se is a virtue, demanding instead that reason in its various guises be informed by the (universal) human condition. A flat rejection of the universal, which often lies behind postmodernism's apparently radical cachet, entails an unwitting but essentially conservative stance. If one isolates local or marginalized forms of reason from any wider or potentially universal conception of validity, we have no means of evaluating them. They can only be affirmed in their particularity and thereby assumed to be legitimate.

Marcuse's most utopian work is *Eros and Civilisation* (1955). In this he sought, like Horkheimer and Fromm before him, to bring together Marx and Freud into a social theory. He sets out to show in a purely theoretical way that Freud's ideas about individual development could be mapped onto the possibility of a non-repressive society. He both utilises Freud and critically develops his ideas.

Eros and Civilisation is quite a difficult read, but the basic argument is that where Freud believed social repression was an inevitable feature of civilisation, Marcuse argues that this was only partly true. Freud had claimed that as the individual grows up he or she must increasingly come to terms with the Reality principle and learn to repress instincts and their gratification, which belong to the order of the Pleasure principle. Growing up means learning to forego gratification (instinct) and coming to terms with the necessities of work and wider society generally (reality), under conditions of material scarcity. Marcuse acknowledges that some repression of instinct was a necessary feature of all societies in order for them to come to terms with the reality of material survival. However, capitalism, as it were, 'pretends' that there is material scarcity, when in terms of its productive capacity there is none. It does this in order to control its members and sustain itself.

Marcuse argues that a more liberated condition can be conceived where the Pleasure principle and the Reality principle are reconciled and would fall under the sway of the Nirvana principle, which is a condition of stasis where all tensions are resolved. Marcuse's claim is that 'reality' is historically variable; it is not the one constant thing that Freud had thought, but takes different forms in different societies. In modern industrial societies it is dominated by the imperatives of instrumental reason and takes the form of what he called the 'performance principle'. He admits that while some repression of instinct will always be necessary, in contemporary capitalist societies there is a 'surplus repression'. It is surplus because although we have the material wealth to enable us to reduce the demands 'reality' makes on us, we cannot do so because our embroilment in capitalist economic relations prevents it. Capitalism requires us to carry on 'performing', working and consuming aggressively and indefinitely, thus keeping the potential for the gratification of instincts and of sensual development under wraps. In fact, the energy underlying this possibility turns inwards and produces the destructive behaviour that often characterises modern life.

Marcuse wrote *Eros and Civilisation* in the 1950s when there was no sign of any empirical tendencies that might move in the direction his work suggested and, as Whitebook (1996: 290) puts it, the USA was economically booming but culturally puerile. Thus, Marcuse's book was a highly utopian piece, with its feet planted firmly in the air and quite unable to draw on elements of the status quo. It nevertheless opened up the idea that the future could be radically different. Ironically, by the mid 1960s, the cultural landscape of Europe and North America had changed dramatically and the prescience of Marcuse's ideas become apparent. The almost libidinal explosion of cultural-political change that occurred during this period was remarkable and certainly unpredicted. Yet, it was in Marcuse's book that explanations for the emergence of the '60s utopian movements were discovered.

Eros and Civilisation is not an unproblematic work. As with the earlier work of Horkheimer, which sought to link Marx and Freud, there is a deterministic element in Marcuse's account that reduces the individual to an effect of either instinct or a mode of production; agency plays no part. It also speaks at a high level of generality and 'resolves' things theoretically without reference to the messiness that makes up actual people's lives. It resolves the tensions and disappointments of life in the idea of a wholly harmonious future, when such things may in fact be an essential part of human life. Nevertheless, its utopianism is its strength; from this thread Marcuse is able to weave a coherent view that enables us to 'think' other possibilities. This, in my view, should be a central feature of any social theory, though it is one that I sense is fairly thin on the ground at the moment.

Rescuing Reason: Habermas's Critical Theory

The attitude towards 'reason' in most contemporary social theory is one of scepticism. Most postmodernist writers, such as Lyotard or Baudrillard, reject the idea that 'reason' can be defined outside the context in which it is being used. Reason has no particular depth to it; it is not an intrinsic human skill nor the highest human achievement, but only the expression of how particular societies see themselves: the crystallization and justification of their world-views.

Other authors might reject this relativist view on the grounds that 'reason' is the human skill to control and dominate things, to choose disinterestedly the most effective means to achieve given ends. Max Weber's account of 'rationalisation' and first generation Critical Theory's views on instrumental reason fall into this category. For none of them, though, was this cause for celebration, given the history of the western world.

Against this Habermas has fought a battle on two fronts: to save reason from either wholesale scepticism or mere instrumentalism. His aim has been to uncover the complexity and diversity of reason, but also to hold on to the idea that reason is what enables us to grasp reality and see the truth of things, even if our understanding is always going to be fallible. It is going to be fallible because the concepts we use to understand things necessarily reflect the assumptions of their originating contexts, and of course these differ. But while knowledge is contextual, for Habermas it is *not only* contextual; knowledge can never be entirely reduced to its context. Contexts may play a large part in determining what we count as knowledge at any one time because embedded in them are the languages, social practices and ethical assumptions through which we live. But this does not mean that we can do away with the distinctions between truth and falsity or right and wrong. Without these 'universals' we could not make sense of the world. Moreover, knowledge is not static but open to revision as circumstances change and we bring new reasons to bear on things that confront us. Of course what we arrive at with new knowledge will still be part of another context, but this does not change the fact that we found *good* reasons to alter our views.

Treading such a delicate path, for Habermas, has meant a constant tacking back and forth between positions, which produces a certain amount restlessness in his work. It is also reminiscent of Adorno's idea that the 'broken middle' is not resolvable under present conditions. Nevertheless, although Habermas's work differs markedly in tone and outlook from that of his predecessors, the effort he makes to hold a line between the two opposing poles and search for some resolution shows the same utopian impulse, even if it sometimes feels like an endless abstract exploration.

Habermas also rejects the historical, universalising Hegelian-Marxism of his predecessors. For the reasons I described in Chapters 2, 4 and 7, he no longer finds credible the idea that history is moving in a purposeful way towards communism. Nevertheless, he does have the impulse to find *universal* criteria of rationality that underpin, and are specific to, the human world. His early work in *Knowledge and Human Interests* sought to show that there were knowledge types. Knowledge was not one thing but several, each with its own 'cognitive interest'. The human interest in control, based on our need to survive physically, has led to the emergence of the natural sciences. Humans also have a need to survive collectively and this practical interest is expressed in the reflections of the humanities with their emphasis on the language-based, intersubjective achievements of society: our social practices, ethical beliefs and cultural artefacts. There is a third human interest in emancipation, which is driven by the human need for self-direction in a world that may illegitimately constrain us either internally or externally. This interest produces knowledge that has something in common with both of the others and gives rise to certain critical disciplines, notably psychoanalysis and Critical Theory. I have discussed these ideas in more detail in Chapter 7 and mention them here to highlight the fact that his aim was to avoid the pitfalls of seeing knowledge as only about control, or the context that produced it.

In a similar vein his subsequent work on communicative rationality drives at the same target albeit in a different way. Instead of saying that knowledge is all one thing, he shows the density and complexity and above all the *universal rationality* of social knowledge. He challenges the idea that what happens in the social world is an arbitrary, 'subjective' affair and argues instead that it has its own specific rationale. The importance of his work lies in his insistence that the social world is a rational one and that once we understand the specific nature of this rationality we can evaluate the validity of actual phenomena in it. We don't have to surrender to the idea that social knowledge is merely relative to context, or that it is only about control.

Though he no longer uses the highly utopian concept of the 'ideal speech situation', it lies at the heart of his enterprise. 'Ideal speech' refers to what for Habermas is the central characteristic of human communication through language. While animals certainly communicate information through sounds that could be called a language, humans have the capacity to arrive at a *consensus*. Such an agreement entails two or more people freely exchanging ideas and reciprocally accepting the *validity* of the other's claims in order to reach a rational agreement. Of course we know that in everyday situations people are hemmed in by myriad constraints, such as economic power, ideology and unconscious forces. However, this is Habermas's point; in most situations it is an irrational consensus that is established. It is irrational because it contravenes the central tenet of human communication, which is to arrive at a freely-achieved common agreement.

We might still ask why we should regard this achieving of consensus as central to communication through language? Habermas's reply is almost phenomenological in that he asks us to think what it is we do when we speak. We are invariably trying to convince others of the validity of the situation as we see it and we look to them to confirm or disconfirm it. We may deliberately lie to them or even deceive ourselves about things, but the point of saying them is to convince others that this is how things are.

Needless to say, there has been considerable discussion of this idealistic aspect of his work when Habermas tries to universalise it into being the lynchpin of his 'discourse ethic' (Heller 1984–85, Ingram 1987, 1990: ch. 7). How could actual individuals ever calculate what is reciprocally in everyone's interests in service of a consensus? When faced with the realities of power should those in a subordinate position feel an obligation to accede to some generalised idea of the common good? For example, if one works in an organisation where decisions are taken to further its interests but which negatively affect a number of people, should those people accept the norm of reciprocity for the sake of everyone's general good, or reject it and act instrumentally to try and ensure their own?

It may also be that Habermas has too rationalistic a conception of communication through language in that when we talk we don't always know what we are trying to convince others of. It may be, as Adam Phillips (2000: XVIII) remarks, 'that one doesn't necessarily say or write something because one believes it, but to find out *whether* one believes it'. Such a view does not contradict Habermas's claims about the reciprocal nature of communication, but does suggest that it is more tentative than he supposes. One never knows ahead of time, for example, what will come out in a conversation?

It is the formal and abstract quality of Habermas's ideas that present us with a problem, as much as their utopianism. Though he presents the 'ideal speech situation' as grounded in a fundamental feature of everyday life, he equally insists that it refers to something virtual, not actual. One will not come across 'ideal speech' even in university seminars where only the force of the better argument is supposed to hold sway, and discourse is apparently at its 'purest'. It is, I think, a concept to be used by social scientists who wish to challenge a set of social arrangements that appear to be accepted by all, but in a wider sense should be seen as springing from an irrational consensus. As with his predecessors' work, there is much more to explore and challenge than I am able to recount here. But if his work is worth reading, it is because, like theirs, it opens up vistas of ideas and avenues of thought, which challenge conventional assumptions and widen our understanding of what is going on.

For a potential reader who might feel that Critical Theory is foolishly utopian because it refuses to accept things as they are, I believe on the contrary, it is its utopianism that should hold our attention. Utopianism is not about contriving something out of nothing, but of using one's imagination and a deal of intellect too, to transcend the limits of what is currently 'real'. It involves working through the possibilities latent in 'what is' to glimpse what might be; in effect, to disclose reality more fully, not to play high and wide with it. It does not mean rejecting Lyotard's 'petits recits', the particulars of life, for the sake of some abstract universal, but of sustaining the relationship between the two. At a time when, if Baudrillard is correct, we live in a hyperreal world empty of meaning, then drawing on the utopian spirit of Critical Theory is more important than ever. A world that can anticipate nothing more vital than Giddens's 'third way' will quickly turn cold, grey, and pointless.

Similarly, for a potential reader who might feel that such work is 'past it', awkwardly written, or out of touch and overtaken by more recent work, I would argue that reading Critical Theory can still enlighten us as to what our world is like.

Conclusion

In a discussion of 'classic' texts, Gadamer (1989: 284–90) remarks on the oddness of finding that we often prefer to read a classic book rather a modern one. He is talking about history books, but the same applies to social theory. Modern publications may be better informed empirically and may refer to subsequent developments in the discipline, but we are able to make allowances for this and may still find more insight in the older works. Something similar exists with novels written in previous centuries; in fact Gadamer has literary art in mind, poetry in particular, as the ideal-type for this idea. The fact that the lives of the people written about are quite different from ours, and the style of writing more formal than is current now, does not prevent us from understanding or identifying with what happens, or from finding an intensity of meaning within a more reserved language style. In fact, he talks about all understanding being a 'fusion of horizons' where the presuppositions of the past and the present are dialogically played out against each other. What the classic text is able to do is to portray something in such a way that it shows us more clearly what we are now in relation to the past.

Gadamer believes classic texts disclose reality more clearly than other texts. They resist being read-off flatly as the direct product of their originating context, and in an odd sense they interpret us as much as we interpret them. What he means is that in reading them we do not encounter an object as such, but are drawn into a relation that transforms us. We find ourselves undergoing an experience that befalls us, one that is not of our own making; one where the text interprets our lives whether we like it or not. In reading such a text we find the truth of that ordinary but mysterious idea of being 'moved' by something.

He often uses the German word '*einleuchten*', meaning to 'shine out', when talking about the truth such texts reveal. In English too, we talk unselfconsciously about a text bringing something to light, of being insightful or clarifying things. In each case, it is the idea that something luminous is happening to which attention is being drawn. Such texts are able to show us things about their subject matter that surpasses what other texts can do. They bring together disparate elements, things that we half know, imagine, or momentarily experience, threads that when aligned in a certain way evoke in us the recognition of truth.

The meaning of the classic text is not static for such texts are not 'above' history but embedded in it; their meaning changes in response to new questions being asked of them. They prove themselves 'classic' by providing answers to questions that emerge in our new horizons. Whether we should regard the texts of Critical Theory as 'classic' is an open question; no one can legislate for what value a reader might find in them. I certainly would not wish them to be imposed as part of a canon, only that they be read with intent, and some patience. They are not easy to read, but as a student remarked to me recently in relation to Michel Foucault, a similarly dense writer, 'Foucault's own work is often a deal easier and makes a lot more sense than many of the commentaries'.

Reading history by brushing it against the grain, as Walter Benjamin (1973: 259) recommended, can be disconcerting, as it does not allow us the comfort of forgetting the horrors of the past, nor the consolation of imagining that things are necessarily better now. Nevertheless, returning to these authors can be a dazzling, if sharp, reminder of where we have come from in relation to where we are now. It could also provide us with a prescient understanding of what the future might hold.

Glossary

The glossary is intended to provide a short cut to understanding some of the key concepts used in the book. It offers only preliminary definitions to help the reader grasp some of the more elliptical terms used by Critical Theorists. In their own work such terms are enmeshed within the broader arguments and not always used consistently. Lack of consistency should not automatically be seen as a bad thing as the speculative thrust of their arguments invites the reader to cross-fertilize his or her ideas. Nevertheless, having some working definitions, however perfunctory, can be an aid to understanding.

Appearance/reality: these two terms are usually set in opposition to one another. For Critical Theory, approaches that accept the appearance of things as the whole truth are ideological because they cannot see beyond what is immediately in front of them; they accept too easily what society wants them to believe. Both empiricism, because it ties itself to the facts, and postmodernism, because it ties itself to the appearance of cultural life, fail to get to the reality that lies behind these things.

Auratic art: art that is surrounded by an aura of quasi-sacred importance. Walter Benjamin, who coined the term, partially challenges the status of this kind of 'high' art on the basis that it bolsters a too respectful and 'undemocratic' world-view. Art that is available to a mass audience, on the other hand, offers a much greater potential for human liberation. His friend and colleague, Adorno, acknowledges the class basis of 'high' art, but nevertheless argues that its authentic (autonomous) qualities are far more effective in disclosing reality than mass culture. The terms 'auratic' and 'autonomous' art, in some degree refer to the same thing; art that has risen above the context of its production even if it carries the assumptions of that context. For Adorno, the aura that surrounds such art remains an unfortunate necessity. Benjamin, on the other hand, is prepared to risk the idea that mass culture has some of the qualities of autonomous art, without the undemocratic drawbacks of an aura.

Critique: criticism that does not merely criticise, but justifies its challenge to something using the same terms that the 'object' of the criticism uses to describe itself. Hence, for Critical Theory, critique is immanent (indwelling) and refers to challenging the ostensible claims society makes about itself with the truth of what is actually going on. Such critique is a dialectical process that allows the rational kernel of a phenomenon to emerge.

Cultural narcissism: a cultural outlook that encourages the individual to be excessively self-concerned with his or her own life, attractiveness, popularity, and so on. As a concept, 'narcissism' derives from Freud's work, which recognised that the human infant naturally goes through a stage where it believes itself to be the centre of things. Gradually it comes to recognise itself as but one ego amongst others. However, if the process is not adequately resolved and narcissism continues into adult life it becomes problematic in the establishment of genuine relationships. Christopher Lasch in his *The*

184

Culture of Narcissism (1979) examines the way various social forces have come together to produce a culture that promotes this tendency.

Culture-industry: a term used derogatorily by Adorno and Horkheimer to highlight the way culture has been taken over by commercial interests. They coined the term, notably in *Dialectic of Enlightenment* (1972), to show their dismay at the effect mass culture had had in eroding our perception of what might be culturally valuable.

Commodity fetishism: the over valuing of a commodity to the point where it seems naturally to have enhanced qualities, when in fact it is the carefully contrived product of capitalist economic relations. Marx emphasised that increasingly goods are produced for exchange in the market rather than for their usefulness as such. First generation Critical Theory amplified this idea to show how far the process had gone in contemporary life; the way commodities are now designed with the 'promise' of personal fulfilment built into them, such promises, of course, are illusory.

Communicative action: action orientated towards common agreement or consensus. Habermas contrasts communicative action with purposive-rational (instrumental) action. The latter involves acting on the basis of relatively predictable empirical events be they physical or social, for example, if I drive into town at 5 pm my journey will take a long time because I know it is rush hour. Such action means predicting outcomes from known empirical facts and the predictions will prove to be correct or incorrect. Science represents the most sophisticated development of this kind of action. Communicative action, on the other hand, involves acting on the basis of consensual norms, which shape the expectations of more than one person. The norms are not 'correct' or 'incorrect' in the technical sense, but are the mutually understood basis of communication and have their own intersubjective *validity*. For example, if I break the norm of politeness by being rude, I am not technically 'correct' or 'incorrect', but the action presupposes that I have 'valid' reasons for doing so, reasons that the other party will understand if I am required to explain them. Communicative action sustains the lifeworld and marks off its unique qualities from those of the natural world. Habermas introduces the concept of strategic action as a half-way house between the other two forms of action, acknowledging that in everyday life people may act instrumentally even within the framework of agreed norms (see **Instrumental action**).

Dialectical: forms of thought or argument that explore the connections between opposites; it involves thinking back and forth between two opposing ideas in hopes of finding a third position that embraces, but also transcends both. Critical Theorists, following Hegel and Marx, expand this idea to include the way historical oppositions interconnect and move history forward. However, Critical Theorists became increasingly pessimistic about idea that history was going anywhere. Adorno once famously remarked that the moment of the (historical) dialectic had passed, meaning that the point at which capitalism could have changed into a genuine communism, had gone.

Empiricism: a sociological and philosophical outlook that sees knowledge as based exclusively on the observation of facts. Knowledge that fails to meet this criterion cannot be tested and therefore cannot be counted as knowledge. Critical Theory opposed this view on the grounds that in social analysis the facts only make sense when placed within a wider, non-observable context of meaning. As a concept, 'empiricism' is close cousin to 'positivism' (see below).

Historical Materialism: usually a synonym for Marxism. Marx was a materialist in the sense that he saw the way we collectively extract food and shelter from physical, material nature as fundamental to the structuring of society. His 'materialism' was 'historical' because it consisted of an analysis of forms or modes of production that developed historically. 'Materialism', as an outlook is often contrasted with 'idealism', with its emphasis on ideas as the motor of history, something Max Weber put forward in *The Protestant Ethic and the Spirit of Capitalism*. Where 'materialism' has a deterministic ring to it, suggesting that ideas are the product of our relations with the material world rather than something we invented, 'idealism' is more open-ended, suggesting that our relations to the material world are the outcome of our more or less conscious ideas. Marx was unusual in that his 'materialism' included awareness that the consciousness of the human subject played an important part in the development of different modes of production. Weber's 'idealism' was also unusual in that it acknowledged forces, other than ideas, were at work in history.

Idealism: an outlook that emphasises the conscious ideas of people as the main mover of history (see **Historical Materialism** above).

Instrumental action: action that is governed by technical rules, which will produce a predicted result. This instrumental orientation to things, an orientation that underpins science, sees things only as objects that can be manipulated. Thus, if I go for a walk in the woods with this attitude of mind, I see only a space where houses could be built or the possibility of cutting the trees down to make paper, rather than something of natural beauty. First generation Critical Theorists regarded this manipulative outlook in a wholly negative light because it reduces everything to being objects we seek to control. The experience of art was a small enclave that still partly resisted this tendency. For the second generation, Habermas has been more sympathetic to the idea of instrumental action, seeing in it an important orientation for physical and social survival. It is also an orientation that underpins work in everyday life in the form of *purposive-rational* action. Work necessarily involves acting purposively to achieve certain ends in the most efficient way. He further subdivides purposive-rational action to include *strategic action*. Where purposive-rational action involves an impersonal, calculative attitude, strategic action is more personal. It involves people, individuals or groups, acting instrumentally to achieve success using appropriate values. For example, at a personal level, in a romantic situation, I might seek to ingratiate myself with the other person, or use the 'treat them mean keep them keen' approach. Likewise, political parties may act entirely strategically to achieve success, regardless of the consensus they claim to have achieved, which should involve the genuine agreement of the voters. It is the inroads these various forms of instrumental action have made, inappropriately, into everyday life, that Habermas objects to. In everyday life the equally important *communicative action* should hold sway, as each form of action has its own legitimate underlying rationality, even if in actual situations they will be intertwined (see **Communicative action**).

Lifeworld, (Lebenswelt): a German word derived from Husserl's phenomenological philosophy. In sociology it is often used synonymously with 'everyday life'. Where Husserl sought to bracket off the 'natural attitude' of everyday life to get to the essence of a phenomenon, sociologists, such as Alfred Schutz, argued that it was the lived experience of social actors in their lifeworld that should be analysed, as that was the bedrock of what really happened in society. First generation Critical Theorists were very sceptical of taking actors' experience as the bedrock of anything other than their alienation. For the second generation, Habermas has taken a much more conciliatory tone towards the 'lifeworld', finding in it the possibility of a genuine communicative consensus between people.

Metanarratives: the big stories or discourses that underpin the western world's view of itself in terms of 'progress', 'truth' and the 'emancipation of the subject'. Jean-François Lyotard claims that such stories prove themselves only in terms that they have already defined, and anyway are no longer credible even in the West. It is more important now to bring the little stories (petits récits) to the fore and celebrate the variety and complexity of life.

One-dimensional Man: the title of Herbert Marcuse's (1964) book captures the idea that in the modern world sources of critique have diminished to such an extent that the possibility of envisaging a different, better future, has virtually disappeared. Hence, we now live in a society that has only one dimension, that of the status quo.

Ontology: the study of 'being', or of what really exists. Expressed in this way, 'ontology' does not make much sense, but if one asks what the social world really consists of, the question comes into focus. One response might be that it consists of people, but what are 'people'? Given the overwhelming variety of different people that exist and have existed, it is difficult to say exactly what people are. Sociologists invariably make assumptions about what the essential nature of the social world is; Marx assumed it consists of our collective relations to the material world, that is, how the economy is organised, Durkheim, that it consists of collectively imposed 'social facts', 'interactionists' assume it is the outcome of myriad individual social 'negotiations'. Critical Theorists always refused to provide ontological descriptions as they feared that our current accounts would fix human nature in its present form and stultify the idea that human nature was a developing phenomenon. However, that does not mean they did not have a tacit ontology.

Performative contradiction: a contradiction between the claims made in a piece of communication and the way it is communicated. Habermas frequently uses this idea to challenge other authors. A 'performative contradiction' bears some similarity to the more familiar term, 'logical contradiction'; but where the latter refers to the contradiction between the logic of two statements, the former refers to the contradiction between the logic of a statement and its broader *communicative* intent. So, for example, postmodernist authors, who in their writings deny the validity of the concept of truth, still write with the expectation that what they are saying is true. Habermas uses a similar strategy to critique Adorno et al. arguing that their pessimistic tone belies the aims of the Marxian concepts they use.

Philosophy of consciousness: a philosophical outlook based on the idea of a clear split between subject and object. Habermas uses this term to refer to an outlook that sees the world as made up of conscious human subjects facing a separate external world of objects, including other people. This (ontological) assumption leads us to think that reason is ultimately about subjects trying to manipulate their object world – their environment. In contrast to this instrumental view, he affirms the importance of a communicative paradigm, where the subject is seen in an *inter-subjective* light. He justifies this with his emphasis on human identity emerging within the dialogic framework of a language community (see **Communicative action**).

Postmodernism: a notoriously difficult concept to pin down and one that gets defined differently by different disciplines. In sociology it is both a description and a theory of what is happening in the contemporary world. Descriptively, it refers to the break up of many traditional assumptions about social identity. The growth of the mass media, with their kaleidoscope of ever-new images is thought to have radically undermined any stability of meaning, including our social identity. Theoretically, it represents a challenge to modernist theories by denying that there are universal criteria by which we can judge notions such as 'progress', 'freedom' or 'knowledge'. Modernist theories that make 'universal' claims are thought to be 'totalising', with the implication that such outlooks are effectively totalitarian. Instead, postmodernists emphasise the plurality of the social world and the plethora of different views that emerge from it.

Positivism: the doctrine that real knowledge is universally true because it is based on the disinterested observation of facts regardless of their social-historical origin, rather than on speculation. The popularity of the doctrine owes a lot to the success of modern science, as it appears to underpin scientific method with its emphasis on objectivity and value-freedom. In the social sciences, there has been a long-running battle with positivism, in part because in the social world the meaning of facts are not 'given', but invariably contestable, changeable and affected by the actors' own views. For Critical Theory, the objections to positivism were two-fold. 1) Treating facts as 'given' meant abstracting them from the wider historical totality that shaped them, thus producing a distorted picture of what was going on. 2) Positivism was an unreflexive doctrine because it failed to recognise the 'interest' it had in the control of things and that this was built into its own assumptions. It was unreflexive also because it could not allow that other forms of knowledge with different 'interests' were just as valid.

Reason: the ability of humans to make logical connections between phenomena and thereby gain some control over them. Critical Theorists opposed this kind of definition because it had too 'instrumental' a ring to it. If reason was only about controlling things it squeezed out the idea that Art has 'reason' in it too, albeit of a different kind.

Reification: the process whereby socially produced phenomena take on a fixed, thing-like quality as though they were part of nature. The economic laws of 'supply and demand' or 'gender roles' are two examples of things that appear to be immutable facts of life, when in reality they are the outcome of particular forms of economic and social relationships.

Repressive de-sublimation: the apparent releasing of sublimated drives, only for them to work in a repressive fashion. Marcuse argued that the sexualised nature of much modern culture calls out a libidinous response from us, but only for the purpose of selling commodities. Participating in a 'sexy' culture may be exciting but it is not the royal road to happiness, which is something that requires a more profound liberation.

Social integration/system integration: a distinction made originally made by David Lockwood (1964), challenging the assumptions of Parsons' systems theory. System integration refers to the way the parts of society, such as the family, or work, are aligned with each other at a structural level. Social integration refers to the way people at the level of interaction are integrated into, and happy with, the values that should make their lives worthwhile. Systems theory tended to *assume* that the latter automatically flowed from the former, which Lockwood denied, that is, the parts of the system may function harmoniously but this does not mean that people are happy living in them. The importance of the distinction for sociology lies in being able to recognise that society is made up of different levels that relate to each other, but which have their own distinct reality. For Critical Theory, Habermas uses a similar distinction between system and lifeworld. (For discussions of this 'dualism' and others see Archer 1996 and Carter 2000).

Surplus repression: an excess of the necessary repression required to maintain civilisation. Marcuse coined the term to capture the idea that modern capitalist societies had largely overcome material shortages, but still kept people under control through a mixture of economic anxiety about work, and the desire to purchase commodities.

Totality: everything, including ourselves! The concept of totality came to the fore in Georg Lukacs' *History and Class Consciousness* (1971). He wanted to highlight the fact that modern forms of knowledge were invariably fragmented and partial; what was required was a theory that would relate these fragments to the whole. He believed that Marxism could do the trick. It was the one theory that laid claim to have grasped the totality of things as they emerged in history, and that Marxism itself was part of that historical totality. In a more limited and less metaphysical way early Critical Theory believed that most knowledge was partial and fragmented and needed to take a wider view of things. (For a detailed account of the concept of totality in different authors' hands, see Jay 1984).

Notes

1 I discovered only later that Marcuse had written an article published in 1941 called, 'Some Social Implications of Modern Technology', that pointed up the anti-individualist elements in technological rationality, a theme brought to fruition in *One Dimensional Man*.

2 Given that Grunberg had been forced to retire because of a stroke, this was hardly the time or place to proffer anything personally critical, even assuming Horkheimer wanted to. In fact Horkheimer praises Grunberg as a 'great scholar' and notes the 'immeasurable distance' between Grunberg's high reputation and his own lack of one (Horkheimer 1993: 10).

3 'Idea' is another Hegelian concept and like most, difficult to define. Roughly speaking it refers to the ultimate purpose or reason behind reality.

4 A biographical novel that captures well the last desperate years of Walter Benjamin's life is J. Parini's *Benjamin's Crossing* (1998).

5 Martin Jay (1986) in his essay, 'The Frankfurt School's Critique of Marxist Humanism' makes the point that Horkheimer et al. fairly consistently criticised the Lukacsian version of this concept, though Marcuse in conversation with Douglas Kellner in 1978 pointed out that he had a more positive view of Lukacs' work in the 1930s than Horkheimer and the others. See Kellner 1984: 387, note 15.

6 For an excellent discussion of the implications of this idea to the contemporary issue of 'race' see Carter 2000.

7 For the earliest Institute work on mass culture see Adorno's essay 'On the Social Situation of Music' (1978 [1932]).

8 In fact, Adorno went with Marcuse in 1961 to see one of the last people to have known Nietzsche, see Putz (1981: 164).

9 See Foucault on Nietzsche in 'Nietzsche, Genealogy and History' in Bouchard, D. (ed.), (1977).

10 In Germany an *Habilitation* is a higher degree that equips someone to teach in universities.

11 It is not exactly clear to me why Horkheimer kept the early papers locked up, but it seems he wanted to keep the idea of a 'glorious past' safe from too critical an inspection.

12 Habermas sets out in more detail the characteristics of empirical-analytic knowledge and compares it to dialectical knowledge, in his essay, 'The Analytical Theory of Science and Dialectics', in Adorno et al. (1976).

13 I will not attempt to find a way through the complex issue of whether Marx embraced the subject in his later work, or increasingly dispensed with such romantic, humanistic ideas. In Chapter 1 of *Capital*, the discussion is fairly much geared to the objective characteristics of capitalist economic relations, but the negative implications, presumably for a human subject, are also there.

14 See Gillian Rose's *The Broken Middle* (1992). Rose's book is more wide-ranging

and difficult than is suggested here. Nevertheless, this work is concerned with the suppression of a potential in our tradition.

15 For a view that challenges Bauman on this issue see Stones (1996: 119–29).

16 Adorno is referring to the 'black' writers of the bourgeoisie such as de Sade who expose the gross villainy that lies behind the rationality of the bourgeois world.

Bibliography

To help place the historical origin of texts where there is a long gap between first publication and its subsequent availability in English, I have put the original date of publication in square brackets.

Adorno, T. W. (1941) 'On Popular Music', with the assistance of George Simpson, *Studies in Philosophy and Social Research*, **IX** (1), 17–48.

Adorno, T. W. (1945) 'A Social Critique of Radio Music', *Keynon Review*, **VII** (2), 208–17.

Adorno, T. et al. (1950) *The Authoritarian Personality*, New York: Harper Row.

Adorno, T. (1967/68) 'Sociology and Psychology', Part 1 translated by Irving N. Wohlfarth, *New Left Review* **46**, 67–80, Part 2 translated by Irving N. Wohlfarth, *New Left Review* **47**, 79–97.

Adorno, T. (1973a) *The Jargon of Authenticity*, translated by Knut Tarnowski and Frederic Will, London: Routledge and Kegan Paul.

Adorno, T. (1973b) *Negative Dialectics*, translated by E. B. Ashton, London: Routledge and Kegan Paul.

Adorno, T. (1974 [1951]) *Minima Moralia: Reflections from Damaged Life*, London: New Left Books.

Adorno, T. et al. (1976) *The Positivist Dispute in German Sociology*, London: Heinemann Educational Books.

Adorno, T. (1977) 'The Actuality of Philosophy', Telos, **31**, 120–33.

Adorno, T. (1978 [1932]) 'On the Social Situation of Music', translated by Wes Blomster, *Telos* **35**, 128–64.

Adorno, T. (1981) *Prisms*, translated from the German by Samuel and Shierry Weber, Cambridge, Mass.: MIT Press.

Adorno, T. (1984) *Aesthetic Theory*, translated by C. Lenhardt, eds, Gretel Adorno and Ralph Tiedmann, London: Routledge and Kegan Paul. (see also Adorno 1997)

Adorno, T. (1989) 'Lyric Poetry and Society', in Bronner, S. E and Kellner, D. M., eds, *Critical Theory and Society: A Reader*, London: Routledge.

Adorno, T. (1991) *The Culture Industry: Selected Essays on Mass Culture*, edited with an Introduction by J. M. Bernstein, London: Routledge.

Adorno, T. (1993) 'Theory of Pseudo-Culture', Telos, **95**, 15–38.

Adorno, T. (1994) *The Stars Down to Earth and Other Essays on the Irrational in Culture*, ed. Stephen Crook, London: Routledge.

Adorno, T. (1997) *Aesthetic Theory*, translated by Robert Hullot-Kentor, Minneapolis: University of Minnesota Press.

Adorno, T. and Horkheimer, M. (1972 [1947]) *Dialectic of Enlightenment*, New York: Herder and Herder Inc.

Anderson, P. (1976) *Considerations on Western Marxism*, London: New Left Books.

Arato, A. and Gebhardt, E. eds. (1978) *The Essential Frankfurt School Reader*, New York: Urizon.

Archer, M. (1996) 'Social Integration and System Integration', Sociology **30** (4), 679–99.

Barrett, M. and McIntosh, M. (1991) *The Anti-Social Family*, London: Verso Books.

Baudrillard, J. (1983) *In the Shadow of the Silent Majorities*, New York: Semiotext(e).

Baudrillard, J. (1988) *America,* London: Verso.

Baudrillard, J (1994) *Simulacra and Simulation*, translated by Sheila Faria Glaser, Ann Arbor: Michigan University Press.

Baudrillard, J. (1995) *The Gulf War Did Not Take Place*, translated and introduced by Paul Patton, Sydney: Power Publications.

Bauman, Z. (1989) *Modernity and the Holocaust*, Cambridge: Polity Press.

Bell, D (1979) *The Cultural Contradictions of Capitalism*, London: Heinemann.

Benhabib, S. (1986) *Critique, Norm and Utopia: A Study of the Foundations of Critical Theory*, New York: Columbia University Press.

Benhabib, S. (1992) *Situating the Self: Gender, Community, and Postmodernism in Contemporary Ethics*, Cambridge: Polity Press.

Benjamin, J. (1977) 'The End of Internalization: Adorno's Social Psychology', *Telos* **32**, 42–64.

Benjamin, J. (1978) 'Authority and the Family Revisited: Or a World Without Fathers', *New German Critique*, **5**, 35–57.

Benjamin, W. (1973) *Illuminations*, translated by Harry Zohn, edited with an Introduction by Hannah Arendt, London: Collins/Fontana.

Bernstein, J. (1994) 'Critical Theory – The Very Idea (Reflections on Nihilism and Domination)', introductory essay in J. Bernstein, ed., *The Frankfurt School: Critical Assessments*, London: Routledge.

Bernstein, R., ed., (1985) *Habermas and Modernity*, Oxford: Polity Press with Basil Blackwell.

Best, S. and Kellner, D. (1991) *Postmodern Theory: Critical Interrogations*, New York: The Guildford Press.

Bleicher, J. (1980) *Contemporary Hermeneutics: Hermeneutics as Method, Philosophy and Critique*, London: Routledge and Kegan Paul.

Bloch, E. et al. (1977) *Aesthetics and Politics*, translated and edited by Ronald Taylor, Afterword by Frederic Jameson, London: New Left Books.

Bottomore, T. (1984) *The Frankfurt School*, Chichester: Ellis Horwood Ltd. and London: Tavistock Publications.

Bouchard, D. (ed.) (1977) *Language, Counter-Memory and Practice: Selected Essays and Interviews by Michel Foucault*, Ithaca: Cornell University Press.

Brand, A. (1990) *The Force of Reason: An Introduction to Habermas' Theory of Communication Action*, Sydney: Allen and Unwin.

Braverman, H. (1974) *Labour and Monopoly Capitalism; The Degradation of Work in the 20th Century*, New York: Monthly Review Press.

Bronner, S. and Kellner, D., eds. (1989) *Critical Theory and Society: A Reader*, London: Routledge.

Butler, J and Scott, J. W., eds. (1992) *Feminists Theorize the Political*, New York: Routledge.

Calhoun, C. (ed.) (1992) *Habermas and the Public Sphere*, Cambridge Mass.: MIT.

Carter, B. (2000) *Realism and Racism: Concepts of Race in Sociological Research*, London: Routledge.

Castoriadis, C. (1997) *The Castoriadis Reader*, translated and edited by David Ames Curtis, Oxford: Blackwell Publishers Limited.

Cook, D. (1996) *The Culture Industry Revisited: Theodor Adorno on Mass Culture*, Lanham, Maryland: Rowman and Littlefield Publishers Inc.

Cook, D. (1998) 'Adorno on Late Capitalism: Totalitarianism and the Welfare State, *Radical Philosophy* **89**, May/June, 16–26.

Cook, M. (1994) *Language and Reason: A Study of Habermas's Pragmatics*, Cambridge, Mass.: MIT Press.

Craib, I. (1992) *Anthony Giddens*, London: Routledge, an imprint of Taylor and Francis Books Ltd.

Craib, I. (1989) *Psychoanalysis and Social Theory: The Limits of Sociology*, Hemel Hempstead: Harvester Wheatsheaf.

Craib, I. (1994) *The Importance of Disappointment*, London: Routledge.

Craib, I. (1997) 'Social Constructionism as Social Psychosis', *Sociology*, **31** (1), 1–15.

Craib, I. (1998) *Experiencing Identity*, London: Sage Publications.

Dallmayr, F. (1972) 'Critical Theory Criticized: Habermas's Knowledge and Human Interests and its Aftermath, *Philosophy of the Social Sciences* (2).

Debord, G. (1976) *The Society of the Spectacle*, Detroit: Black and Red.

d'Entreves, M. P. and Benhabib, S. (1996 [1981]) *Habermas and the Unfinished Project of Modernity: Critical Essays on the Unfinished Project of Modernity*, Oxford: Polity Press in association with Basil Blackwell Publishers Limited.

Dews, P. (1986) (ed.) *Habermas, Autonomy and Solidarity: Interviews with Jürgen Habermas*, London: Verso, New Left Books.

Doane, J. and Hodges, D. (1987) *Nostalgia and Sexual Difference: The Resistance to Contemporary Feminism*, London: Methuen and Company Ltd.

Doyal, L. and Gough, I. (1991) *A Theory of Human Need*, London: Macmillan – now Palgrave Macmillan.

Dubiel, H. (1985) *Theory and Politics: Studies in the Development of Critical Theory*, Cambridge, Mass.: MIT Press.

Dubiel, H. (1992) 'Domination or Emancipation: The Debate over the Heritage of Critical Theory', in *Cultural-Political Interventions in the Unfinished Project of Enlightenment*, eds, Axel Honneth et al., Cambridge Mass: MIT Press.

Eder, K. (1998) 'Societies Learn and Yet the World is Hard to Change' *European Journal of Social Theory*, **2**, 195–215.

Foucault, M. (1979) *Discipline and Punish*, Harmondsworth: Penguin Books.

Frisby, D. (1972) 'The Popper-Adorno Controversy: The Methodological Dispute in German Sociology' *Philosophy of the Social Sciences*, **1** (2), 105–19.

Frisby, D. (1974) 'The Frankfurt School: Critical Theory and Positivism', in J. Rex ed., *Approaches to Sociology*, Routledge and Kegan Paul.

Fromm, E, (1942) *The Fear of Freedom*, London: Routledge and Kegan Paul.

Fromm, E. (1956) *The Sane Society*, London: Routledge.

Fromm, E. (1978 [1932]) 'The Method and Function of an Analytic Social Psychology: Notes on Psychoanalysis and Historical Materialism' in Arato, A. and Gebhardt, E. eds, *The Essential Frankfurt School Reader*, New York: Urizon.

Fromm, E. (1989a [1929]) 'Psychoanalysis and Sociology' in Bronner, S. E. and Kellner, D., eds, *Critical Theory and Society: A Reader*, London: Routledge.

Fromm, E. (1989b [1931]) 'Politics and Psychoanalysis' in Bronner, S. E. and Kellner, D., eds, *Critical Theory and Society: A Reader*, London: Routledge.

Gadamer, H-G. (1977) *Philosophical Hermeneutics*, Berkeley: University of California Press.

Gadamer, H-G. (1989) [1960] *Truth and Method*, 2nd revised edn, translated and revised by Joel Weinsheimer and Donald G. Marshall, London: Sheed and Ward.

Gadamer, H-G. (1996) *The Enigma of Health: The Art of Healing in a Scientific Age*, Oxford: Polity Press.

Giddens, A. (1987) *Social Theory and Modern Sociology*, Oxford: Polity Press.

Giddens, A. (1991) *Modernity and Self-Identity*, Cambridge: Polity Press in association Blackwell Publishers Limited.

Goffman, E. (1971) *The Presentation of the Self in Everyday Life*, London: Penguin Books.

Gouldner, A. (1971) *The Coming Crisis of Western Sociology*, London: Heinemann Educational Books.

Habermas, J. (1970) 'Towards a Theory of Communicative Competence', *Inquiry* 13, 360–75.

Habermas, J. (1971a) *Towards a Rational Society: Student Protest, Science and Politics*, London: Heinemann Educational Books.

Habermas, J. (1971b) *Knowledge and Human Interests*, Boston: Beacon Press.

Habermas, J. (1974) *Theory and Practice*, London: Heinemann Educational Books.

Habermas, J. (1976) *Legitimation Crisis*, London: Heinemann Educational Books.

Habermas, J. (1979) *Communication and the Evolution of Society*, translated and with an Introduction by Thomas McCarthy, London: Heinemann Educational Books.

Habermas, J. (1983) 'Interpretive Social Science vs. Hermeneuticism', in *Social Science as Moral Inquiry*, eds, Norma Haan et al., New York: Columbia University Press.

Habermas, J. (1984) *The Theory of Communicative Action, Volume One: Reason and the Rationalization of Society*, London: Heinemann Educational Books.

Habermas, J. (1986) 'On Hermeneutics' Claim to Universality' in *The Hermeneutics Reader: Texts of the German Tradition from the Enlightenment to the Present*, ed., Kurt Mueller-Vollmer, Oxford: Basil Blackwell. Another translation of this essay appears in Bleicher (1980).

Habermas, J. (1987a) *The Theory of Communicative Action, Volume Two: The Critique of Functionalist Reason*, Cambridge: Polity Press in association with Basil Blackwell.

Habermas, J. (1987b) *The Philosophical Discourse of Modernity: Twelve Lectures*, Oxford: Polity Press in association with Basil Blackwell Publishers Limited.

Habermas, J. (1988 [1971]) *On the Logic of the Social Sciences*, translated by Shierry Weber Nicholson and Jerry A. Stark, Oxford: Polity Press with Basil Blackwell Ltd.

Habermas, J. (1989 [1962]) *The Structural Transformation of the Public Sphere: An Inquiry into a Category of Bourgeois Society*, translated by Thomas Burger with the assistance of Frederick Lawrence, Oxford: Polity Press.

Habermas, J. (1992) *Between Facts and Norms: Contributions to a Discourse Theory of Law and Democracy*, translated by William Rehg, Oxford: Polity Press.

Habermas, J. (1993a) 'Notes on the Development of Horkheimer's Work', *Theory, Culture and Society*, **10**, 61–77.

Habermas, J. (1993b) *Justification and Application: Remarks on Discourse Ethics*, Oxford: Polity Press.

Habermas, J. (1996) 'Modernity an Unfinished Project' in d'Entreves, M. P. and Benhabib, S. (eds) *Habermas and the Unfinished Project of Modernity: Critical Essays on the Philosophical Discourse of Modernity*, Cambridge: Polity Press with Blackwell.

Hansen, M. (2002) 'Mass Culture as Hieroglyphic Writing: Adorno, Derrida, Kracauer', in *Adorno: A Critical Reader*, eds, Nigel Gibson and Andrew Rubin, Oxford: Basil Blackwell.

Harding, S. ed. (1987) *Feminism and Methodology*, Bloomington and Indiana: Indiana University Press with Milton Keynes: Open University Press.

Heidegger, M. (1962 [1927]) *Being and Time*, translated by John Macquarrie and Edward Robinson: Oxford: Basil Blackwell.

Held, D. (1980) *Introduction to Critical Theory: Horkheimer to Habermas*, London: Hutchinson & Co Ltd.

Heller, A. (1984–85) 'The Discourse Ethics of Habermas: Critique and Appraisal', *Thesis Eleven*, X–XI.

Holub, R. C. (1991) *Jürgen Habermas: Critic in the Public Sphere*, London: Routledge.

Honneth, A. (1979) 'Communication and Reconciliation: Habermas's Critique of Adorno', *Telos* **29**, Spring, 45–61.

Honneth, A. (1987) 'Critical Theory' in *Social Theory Today*, eds, A. Giddens & J Turner, Cambridge: Polity Press.

Honneth, A. (1993) *The Critique of Power: Reflective Stages in a Critical Social Theory*, translated by Kenneth Baynes, Cambridge, Mass.: MIT Press.

Honneth, A. (1995) *The Struggle for Recognition: The Moral Grammar of Social Recognition*, translated by Joel Anderson, Oxford: Polity Press.

Honneth. A. (1999) 'The Social Dynamics of Disrespect: Situating Critical Theory Today' in *Habermas: A Critical Reader* ed., Peter Dews, Oxford: Blackwell Publishers Limited.

Horkheimer, M. (1947) *Eclipse of Reason*, New York: Oxford University Press.

Horkheimer, M. (1949) 'Authoritarianism and the Family Today' in *The Family: Its Function and Destiny*, ed., R. N. Anshen, New York: Harper Row.

Horkheimer, M. (1972) *Critical Theory: Selected Essays*, New York: Continuum Publishing Company, Herder and Herder.

Horkheimer, M. (1993) *Between Philosophy and Social Science: Selected Early Writings*, Cambridge, Mass: MIT Press.

Horkheimer, M. and Adorno, T. (1973) *Aspects of Sociology by the Institute for Social Research*, translated by John Viertal, London: Heinemann Educational Books.

How, A. (1995) *The Habermas–Gadamer Debate and the Nature of the Social*, Aldershot: Avebury Ashgate.

How, A. (1998) 'That's Classic! A Gadamerian Defence of the Classic Text in Sociology', *The Sociological Review*, **46** (4), 828–48.

How, A. (2001) 'Habermas, History and Social Evolution: Moral Learning and the Trial of Louis XVI', *Sociology*, **35**:1.

Hoy, D. C. and McCarthy, T. (1994) *Critical Theory*, Oxford: Blackwell Publishers.

Ingram, D. (1982) 'Habermas, Gadamer and Bourdieu on Discourse: A Communication Ethic Reconsidered', *Man and World*, **15**, 149–61.

Ingram, D. (1987) *Habermas and the Dialectic of Reason*, New Haven, Connecticut: Yale University Press.

Ingram, D. (1990) *Critical Theory and Philosophy*, Paragon Issues in Philosophy, Paragon House: New York.

Ingram, D. and Simon-Ingram, J., eds. (1992) *Critical Theory: The Essential Readings*, Paragon Issues in Philosophy Series, St Paul Minnesota: Paragon House.

Jacoby, R. (1977) *Social Amnesia: A Critique of Conformist Psychology from Adler to Laing*, Sussex: Harvester Press.

Jacoby, R. (1999) *The End of Utopia: Politics and Culture in an Age of Apathy*, New York: Basic Books.

James, O. (1998) *Britain on the Couch: Treating a Low Serotonin Society*, London: Arrow Books.

James, O. (2000) 'Why Don't We Feel Happier?' The Ecologist, May.

Jarvis, S. (1998) *Adorno: A Critical Introduction*, Oxford: Polity Press.

Jay, M. (1973) *The Dialectical Imagination: A History of the Frankfurt School and the Institute for Social Research 1925–50*, London: Heinemann Educational Books Ltd.

Jay, M. (1984) *Marxism and Totality: The Adventures of a Concept: From Lukacs to Habermas*, Berkeley: University of California Press.

Jay, M. (1985) *Permanent Exiles: Essays on the Intellectual Migration from Germany to America*, New York: Columbia University Press.

Jay, M. (1993) *Force Fields: Between Intellectual History and Cultural Critique*, London: Routledge.

Jay, M. (1996) 'Urban Flights: The Institute of Social Research between Frankfurt and New York', in D. Rasmussen, ed., *The Handbook of Critical Theory*, Oxford: Blackwell Publishers Ltd. This essay is also to be found in Jay (1993).

Katz, B. (1982) *Herbert Marcuse and the Art of Liberation*, London: Verso.

Kellner, D. (1973) 'The Frankfurt School Revisited: A Critique of Martin Jay's "Dialectical Imagination"', *New German Critique*, **4**, 131–52.

Kellner, D. (1984) *Herbert Marcuse and the Crisis of Marxism*, London: Macmillan Press – now Palgrave Macmillan.

Kellner, D. (1989) *Critical Theory, Marxism and Modernity*, Cambridge: Polity Press.

Kellner, D. (1995) *Media Culture: Cultural Studies, Identity and Politics between the Modern and the Postmodern*, London: Routledge.

Kellner, D. and Ryan, M. (1988) *Camera Politica*, Bloomington Indiana: Indiana University Press.

Kohlberg, L. (1971) 'From Is to Ought: How to Commit the Naturalistic Fallacy and Get Away with it in the Study of Moral Development', in T. Mischel, ed., *Cognitive Development and Epistemology*, New York: Academic Press.

Kraus, K. (1986) *Half Truths and One and a Half Truths: Selected Aphorisms*, Manchester: Carcanet Press.

Laing, R. D. and Esterson, A. (1968) *Sanity, Madness and the Family*, Harmondsworth: Penguin Books.

Lasch, C. (1977) *Haven in a Heartless World: The Family Besieged*, New York: Basic Books.

Lasch, C. (1979) *The Culture of Narcissism*, London: Abacus Sphere Books.

Layder, D. (1990) *The Realist Image in Social Science*, London: Macmillan – now Palgrave Macmillan.

Layder, D. (1997) *Modern Social Theory: Key Debates and New Directions*, London: UCL Press.

Lee, D. and Newby, H. (1983) *The Problem of Sociology*, London: Hutchinson.

Lefebvre, H. (1991*) Critique of Everyday Life*, Volume 1, translated by John Moore with a Preface by Michael Trebitsch, London: Verso.

Leledakis, K. (1995) *Society and Psyche: Social Theory and the Unconscious Dimension of the Social*, Oxford: Berg Publishers Limited.

Lockwood, D. (1964) 'Social Integration and System Integration', in *Explanations in Social Change*, eds, G. K Zollschan and W. Hirsch, London: Routledge and Kegan Paul.

Loewald, H. W. (1980) *Papers on Psychoanalysis*, New Haven: Yale University Press.

Lukacs, G. (1971 [1922]), *History and Class Consciousness: Studies in Marxist Dialectics*, London: The Merlin Press.

Lyotard, J-F. (1984) *The Postmodern Condition: A Report on Knowledge*, Manchester: Manchester University Press.

MacPherson, C. B. (1962) *The Political Theory of Possessive Individualism*, Oxford: Oxford University Press.

Marcuse, H. (1941) 'Some Social Implications of Modern Technology', *Studies in Philosophy and Social Science*, **IX**, 414–39.

Marcuse, H. (1955) *Eros and Civilisation: A Philosophical Inquiry into Freud*, Boston: Beacon Press.

Marcuse, H. (1968 [1934]) *Negations: Essays in Critical Theory*, translated from the German by Jeremy J. Shapiro, Harmondsworth: Allen Lane The Penguin Press.

Marcuse, H. (1970) *Counterrevolution and Revolt*, Boston: Beacon Press.

Marcuse, H. (1972 [1948]) 'Sartre's Existentialism' in *Studies in Critical Philosophy*, translated by Joris De Bres, London: New Left Books.

Marcuse, H. (1973 [1941]) *Reason and Revolution: Hegel and the Rise of Social Theory*, London: Routledge and Kegan Paul.

Marcuse, H. 1978/79 'Theory and Politics: A Discussion between H. Marcuse, J. Habermas, H. Lubasz and T. Spengler', *Telos* **38**, 124–53.

Marcuse, H. (1979) *The Aesthetic Dimension: Towards a Critique of Marxist Aesthetics*, London: Macmillan – now Palgrave Macmillan.

Marcuse, H. (1994 [1964]) *One Dimensional Man: Studies in the Ideology of Advanced Industrial Society*, with a new Introduction by Douglas Kellner, London: Routledge.

Martin, S. (1998) 'Renewing Aesthetic Theory' *Radical Philosophy* **89**, 46–47.

Marx, K. (1961) *Capital: A Critical Analysis of Capitalist Production*, Volume 1, London: Lawrence and Wishart.

McCarthy, T. (1979) *The Critical Theory of Jurgen Habermas*, London: Hutchinson and Company Limited.

McCarthy, T. (1982) 'Rationality and Relativism: Habermas' Overcoming of Hermeneutics' in J. B. Thompson and D. Held, eds, *Habermas: Critical Debates*, London: Macmillan Press – now Palgrave Macmillan.

Mouzelis, N. (1992) 'Social and System Integration: Habermas's View', *British Journal of Sociology* **43**, 267–88.

Miller, D. (1987) *Material Culture and Mass Consumption*, Oxford: Blackwell.

Mitchell, J. (1987) 'Working for Progress', in *New Introductory Reader in Sociology*, 2nd edn, (ed.) Mike O'Donnell, Walton on Thames: Nelson.

Mueller-Vollmer, K. ed. (1986) *The Hermeneutics Reader: Texts of the German Tradition from the Enlightenment to the Present*, Oxford: Basil Blackwell.

Nesbitt, N. (1999) 'Sounding Autonomy: Adorno, Coltrane and Jazz', *Telos*, **116**, 81–98.

Neumann, F. (1963 [1944]) *Behemoth: The Structure and Practice of National Socialism, 1933–44*, 2nd revised edn, Toronto: Oxford University Press.

Norris, C. (1992) *Uncritical Theory: Postmodernism, Intellectuals and the Gulf War*, London: Lawrence and Wishart.

Ormiston, G. and Schrift, A. (1990) *The Hermeneutic Tradition: From Ast to Ricoeur*, Albany: The State University of New York.

Outhwaite, W. (1987) *New Philosophies of Social Science: Realism, Hermeneutics and Critical Theory*, London: Macmillan Education Ltd – now Palgrave Macmillan.

Outhwaite, W. (1994) *Habermas: A Critical Introduction*, Oxford: Polity Press in Association with Blackwell Publishers.

Parini, J. (1998) *Benjamin's Crossing*, London: Anchor Transworld Publishing Ltd.

Phillips, A. (2000) *Promises, Promises: Essays on Literature and Psychoanalysis*, London: Faber and Faber.

Piccone, P. (1978) 'General Introduction', to Arato, A. and Gebhardt, E. (1978).

Pollock, F. (1941) 'State Capitalism: Its Possibilities and Limitations', *Studies in Philosophy and Social Science*, Vol. IX, reprinted in Arato and Gebhardt (eds) (1978), and in Bronner, S. and Kellner, D., eds (1989).

Pusey, M. (1987) *Jürgen Habermas*, London: Routledge.

Putz, P. (1981) 'Nietzsche and Critical Theory', *Telos* **50**, 103–11.

Rasmussen, D. M. (1990) *Reading Habermas*, Oxford: Blackwell.

Rasmussen, D., ed. (1996) *The Handbook of Critical Theory*, Oxford: Blackwell Publishers Ltd.

Rex, J. (1971) *Approaches to Sociology: An Introduction to Major Trends in British Sociology*, London: Routledge and Kegan Paul.

Ricoeur, P. (1981) *Hermeneutics and the Human Sciences*, edited and translated by John B. Thompson, Cambridge: Cambridge University Press.

Rockmore, T. (1989) *Habermas on Historical Materialism*: Bloomington and Indiana: Indiana University Press.

Rojek, C. and Turner, B. (2000) 'Decorative Sociology: Towards a Critique of the Cultural Turn' *The Sociological Review*, **48**, 4, 629–48.

Rose, G. (1978) *The Melancholy Science: An Introduction to the Thought of Theodor W. Adorno*, London: Macmillan Press – now Palgrave Macmillan.

Rose, G. (1992) *The Broken Middle: Out of Our Ancient Society*, Oxford: Blackwell.

Sennett, R. (1998) *The Corrosion of Character: The Personal Consequences of Working in the New Capitalism*, New York: W. W. Norton & Company.

Skinner, Q. (1969) 'Meaning and Understanding in the History of Ideas', *History and Theory*, **8**, 1, 3–52.

Skinner, Q. (1970) 'Conventions and the Understanding of Speech Acts', *Philosophy* **20**, 120–38.

Skinner, Q. (1974) 'Some Problems in the Analysis of Political Thought and Action', *Political Theory* **2**, 3, 277–303.

Slater, P. (1977) *Origin and Significance of the Frankfurt School: A Marxist Perspective*, London: Routledge and Kegan Paul.

Smail, D. (1993) *The Origins of Unhappiness*, London: Harper Collins.

Smith, D. (1987) *The Everyday World as Problematic: A Feminist Sociology*, Milton. Keynes: Open University Press.

Stacey, J. (1990) *Brave New Families*, New York: Basic Books.

Stanley, L. and Wise, A. (1993) *Breaking Out Again: Feminist Ontology and Epistemology*, London: Routledge, an imprint of Taylor and Francis Books Ltd.

Stones, R. (1996*) Sociological Reasoning: Towards a Post-modern Sociology*, London: Macmillan – now Palgrave Macmillan.

Storey, J. (1993) *An Introductory Guide to Cultural Theory and Popular Culture*, London: Harvester Wheatsheaf.

Strinati, D. (1995) *An Introduction to Theories of Popular Culture*, London: Routledge.

Strydom, P. (1992) 'The Ontogenetic Fallacy: The Immanent Critique of Habermas' Developmental Logical Theory of Evolution', *Theory, Culture and Society*, **9**, 65–93.

Tilman, R. (1999) 'The Frankfurt School and the Problem of Social Rationality in Thorstein Veblen', *History of the Social Sciences*, **12**, 1, 91–109.

Turner, B. and Elliot, A. (2001) *Profiles in Contemporary Social Theory*, London: Sage Publications.

Veblen, T. (1994 [1899]) *The Theory of the Leisure Class*, New York: Dover Publications Inc.

Weber, M. (1978 [1922]) *Economy and Society: An Outline of Interpretive Sociology*, eds, G. Roth and C. Wittich, translated by E. Fischoff et al., Berkeley and Los Angeles: University of California Press.

Wellmer, A. (1991) *The Persistence of Modernity: Essays on Aesthetics, Ethics and Post-modernism*, translated by David Midgley, Oxford: Polity Press.

White, S. (1988) *The Recent work of Jürgen Habermas: Reason, Justice and Modernity*, Cambridge: Cambridge University Press.

Whitebook, J. (1995) *Perversion and Utopia: A Study in Psychoanalysis and Critical Theory*, Cambridge, Mass.: MIT Press.

Whitebook, J. (1996) 'Fantasy and Critique: Some Thoughts on Freud and the Frankfurt School, in Rasmussen (ed.), *The Handbook of Critical Theory*, Oxford: Blackwell Publishers Ltd, 1996.

Wiggerhaus, R. (1994) *The Frankfurt School: Its History, Theories and Political Significance*, translated by Michael Robertson, Cambridge: Polity Press in association with Basil Blackwell.

Williams, C. (2002) 'A Critical Evaluation of the Commodification Thesis', *The Sociological Review*, Volume 51.

Wilson, H. T. (1977) 'Science, Critique and Criticism' in O'Neill, J., ed., *On Critical Theory*, London: Heinemann Educational Books.

Wolin, R. (1994) *Walter Benjamin: An Aesthetic of Redemption*, Berkeley: University of California Press.

Womack, P. (1999) 'Ac-cen-tchuate the Positive', *The Council for College & University English News*, Issue 10.

Wolff, J. (1975a) *Hermeneutic Philosophy and the Sociology of Art*, London: Routledge and Kegan Paul.

Wolff, J. (1975b) 'Hermeneutics and the Critique of Ideology', *The Sociological Review*, 811–29.

Zipes, J. (1994) 'Adorno May Still Be Right' *Telos* **101**, 157–67.

Index

Readers who wish to pursue some of the ideas mentioned in the index will find words with an asterisk next to them given fuller treatment in the Glossary on page 184ff.